"Every aspect of The Art of Coaching Workbook *demonstrates meticulous attention to the goal of yielding quantifiable results; Elena Aguilar has truly found a way to decode the often elusive process of becoming an effective, inspiring coach."*

CHIARA KUPIEC, INSTRUCTIONAL COACH, BERNARDS TOWNSHIP PUBLIC SCHOOL DISTRICT, BASKING RIDGE, NJ

"This companion to The Art of Coaching *is the book coaches have been clamoring for! Elena skillfully translates complex coaching skills into bite-sized exercises that make it possible for coaches to hone their craft."*

RAIZA CRUZ LISBOA, TRAINER OF COACHES, WASHINGTON, D.C.

"Elena has done it again! This workbook is an amazing addition to The Art of Coaching *and will deepen coaching relationships, strengthen coaching conversations, and make some serious changes in education."*

LIZZIE FORTIN, INSTRUCTIONAL COACH AND VISUAL ART EDUCATOR, WORCESTER, MA, PUBLIC SCHOOLS

"The Art of Coaching Workbook *will be an essential resource for anyone in coaching or leadership in schools who wants to refine their coaching skills. It provides real-life examples of coaching conversations and explicit guidance on how to be a transformational coach—it's going to support my coaching on a whole new level!*"

JILL AYABEI, COACH, NAMPA, ID

"*A coach's dream come true! Wherever you may be on the continuum of your coaching journey,* The Art of Coaching Workbook *serves as the premium Swiss Army knife providing all the tools necessary to help prepare, navigate, and troubleshoot any coaching session with purpose and success!*"

KATHRINA MENDEZ, CALIFORNIA READING & LITERATURE PROJECT

"*This workbook is for anyone who wants to move transformational coaching from 'theory on the page' to 'practical daily application.' I highly recommend this workbook for any coach's toolkit.*"

NICHOLAS CAINS, INSTRUCTIONAL LEADERSHIP COACH, TULSA, OK

"The Art of Coach of Coaching Workbook *is an exceptional coaching toolset to ensure competence and confidence as a coach! This is a must-have accompaniment to* The Art of Coaching. *I am eager to share this workbook with colleagues across the country!*"

TONIA HOLMES-SUTTON, EDD, NBCT, EXECUTIVE DIRECTOR, NATIONAL BOARD NETWORK OF ACCOMPLISHED MINORITIZED EDUCATORS

The Art of Coaching Workbook

The Art of Coaching Workbook

Tools to Make Every Conversation Count

Elena Aguilar

JB JOSSEY-BASS™

A Wiley Brand

Jossey-Bass
A Wiley Imprint
111 River St, Hoboken, NJ 07030
www.josseybass.com

Library of Congress Cataloging-in-Publication Data is Available:

ISBN 9781119758990 (paperback)
ISBN 9781119759003 (ePDF)
ISBN 9781119759027 (epub)

Cover Design: Wiley
Cover Images: Red lotus flower © Jeja/Getty Images

Printed in the United States of America

FIRST EDITION SKY10021330_092120

CONTENTS

INTRODUCTION

This introduction and the activities in this chapter can be read before, during, or after reading the introduction to *The Art of Coaching*.

Welcome

We're so glad you're here. We know that you are a committed educator, and we're excited that you've taken the leap into a coaching role—or perhaps you've been thrown into one! Well, here you are: eager to coach and wondering what exactly you are supposed to do.

We want to help you feel confident in this wonderful world of coaching—and help you build your skills as a coach. We wish that all coaches had coaches, so imagine us as your coaches, sitting by your side as you embark on, or continue, this journey. We'll provide maps and a compass, we'll share tips for getting through rough waters, we'll offer exercises that'll build your coaching muscles quickly, and we'll encourage you. In addition, we'll help you figure out who you want to be as a coach and how you can find joy and fulfillment in this work.

We hope that some of you who have picked up this workbook have been a coach for a minute. Maybe you read *The Art of Coaching* a few years ago; maybe you've even attended an in-person or virtual workshop with Elena. You've got the basics down, and you're ready to take your coaching to the next level. If so—we've got you. This workbook contains resources, tools, and exercises that Elena has never published and that are designed to advance a coach's skills beyond what's in *The Art of Coaching*.

We assume, of course, that you know this workbook is a companion to Elena's *The Art of Coaching*. Though it provides a robust introduction to Transformational Coaching, we know that coaches need a whole lot more than one book to master it—including guidance to internalize the ideas and activities to practice applying the concepts. If you haven't read *The Art of Coaching* yet, you'll definitely need to read it alongside this workbook. You're in for a rich learning experience.

The Art of Coaching was published in 2013, and since then Elena has trained thousands of coaches around the world in the Transformational Coaching model that's described in it. Through this process, and her continued learning about coaching (she still coaches educators today), she's deepened her understanding of how to teach others about this model and has created additional content. About a third of this workbook covers content that's not in *The Art of Coaching*—it's new material and additional strategies. As such, we anticipate that those of you who are very familiar with *The Art of Coaching* (and perhaps have attended one of Elena's workshops) will find a good amount of new learning to integrate with what you've already acquired.

As we created this workbook, we realized that there is so much to learn to be an exceptional coach. Our initial outline contained enough content for three books, so we imagine this will be the first in a series. We also surveyed hundreds of coaches and asked what they'd want included. We are grateful for their input.

Note on Pronouns

In this book, we use the traditional pronouns *he* and *she*, and in recognition of nonbinary gender identification, we also use *they*. Additionally, we use *Latinx* as a gender-neutral or nonbinary alternative to Latino or Latina.

Who This Book Is For

First and foremost, this book is for the new and novice coach who senses the potential of coaching and is overwhelmed by the magnitude of skills to acquire. We vividly remember being in your shoes, and we're sure that we can guide you to a place of confidence and competence.

For those who have read *The Art of Coaching* and perhaps have been a coach for a few years, we know this workbook will help you refine your coaching skills. In it, many exercises ask you to draw on your own experiences; doing so through the lens of some new reflective prompts or activities will help you improve your skills.

This workbook is also for those of you who lead, manage, or coach coaches. We know it can be hard to make choices about how to guide a new coach's development. We'll help you figure that out.

Finally, this workbook is for teacher leaders, department heads, school and organizational leaders, and anyone who wants to effectively use coaching strategies to guide an educator's growth and development.

At their essence, *coaching strategies* are exceptionally refined *communication skills*. Coaching is all about listening and speaking—and everyone can benefit from further developing their communication. When our communication skills are refined, we can make every conversation count toward creating a more just and equitable world.

Who We Are

Elena is the author of five books about coaching, team development, resilience, and equity and the founder and president of Bright Morning Consulting. She worked in the Oakland public schools, in Oakland, California, for 19 years, and she writes about these experiences in all of her books. In her journeys sharing her work, Elena met Lori and Laurelin, who became friends and colleagues and contributors to this workbook. Lori and Laurelin bring unique perspectives and insights into how Transformational Coaching can be learned and applied. Also, Elena is a coffee-drinking, cat-loving introverted Sagittarius who loves to read and travel.

Lori is an education consultant and senior associate at Bright Morning Consulting. She has worked in public and independent schools since 1999 and has served in a range of capacities, including classroom teacher, instructional coach, and site-level leader overseeing teaching and learning. *The Art of Coaching* has shaped Lori's work as a coach, teacher, school leader, and team member at Bright Morning—from the way she approaches coaching to how she designs adult learning experiences. Also, Lori is a cheese-loving Capricorn who wears socks that reflect her values.

Laurelin is a coach and educator who has spent the last 2 decades working for educational equity in the United States and abroad. After 10 years as a classroom teacher, Laurelin dove headfirst into Transformational Coaching and hasn't looked back. Elena was a key mentor in those early days and remains a cherished collaborator and friend. Also, Laurelin is a globe-trotting Sagittarius who is learning how to put down roots.

How to Make the Most of This Workbook

This workbook is a both a companion to *The Art of Coaching* and an extension of it. Each chapter contains exercises that allow you to dig deeper into the content in the corresponding chapter of *The Art of Coaching*. We encourage you to first read the chapter in *The Art of Coaching* and then do the exercises in this workbook for that chapter. That'll allow you to fully integrate the new content.

At the beginning of each activity, we've included a brief statement about what you'll get from doing it so that if your time is limited you can make a decision about what to prioritize. In each chapter, we've also identified the activities that we feel are super, super important for you to do—and we've indicated that with the stars symbol next to the title.

In this workbook, you'll find a lot of activities that ask you to read and write. You'll also find a handful that invite you to draw or sketch. We're big fans of stick people and simple drawings, and you'll find some of those in here. We know that if we create visual images from content we're learning, we're far more likely to internalize the ideas and remember them. We encourage you to manage any art phobia you might have developed and draw as much as possible. We've included some places for you to do that but also encourage you to tape, glue, or staple pages in where you create visual representations of your learning.

Create a Coaching Portfolio

As you work through this workbook you might consider putting together a coaching portfolio. This is a place where you can organize your coaching artifacts and resources so that you can see your own growth. This could be a digital folder, a paper folder, large notebook, or even a box. As you build your coaching skill set, you'll likely collect artifacts like transcripts of coaching conversations or the audio or video files themselves. The thinking you do in this workbook will also be a part of your portfolio, but you'll likely need more space to keep your writing and longer reflection activities. The purpose of creating a portfolio is to see your own learning. Set yourself up now to see the growth you'll make as you work through the exercises.

Find Learning Partners

Although everyone has different learning styles, we all benefit from learning with others at some point. We hope that you have colleagues with whom you can discuss the activities in this book, share how you're applying the ideas, and practice the skills. If you lead a team of coaches or facilitate learning for coaches, you'll find the content in Chapter 15 especially useful. But if you don't, we urge you to find some folks with whom you can practice. We offer virtual workshops every month at Bright Morning for this purpose—to provide a learning space for coaches and leaders to practice. In these workshops, Elena (or a Bright Morning presenter) models Transformational Coaching, and then participants practice the skills. Reading about coaching and engaging in the exercises in this workbook will set you on the path to becoming a phenomenal coach, but if you don't actually practice getting feedback and see what exceptional coaching looks and sounds like you'll be limited in how far you can go. It would be like if you wanted to be painter but all you did was read about painting and reflect on previous paintings you'd created. To grow, find people with whom to practice.

Seek Out Additional Resources

On our website, http://www.brightmorningteam.com, you'll find downloadable free resources, online classes, and more support to guide you in your journey as a coach and leader. In addition, on *The Bright Morning Podcast* (available where all podcasts are offered) you can hear Elena engaging in real coaching conversations and sharing her reflections on the conversation. And of course, if you haven't yet read Elena's other books, those are a great resource, too.

We're excited to help you make every conversation count!

Eavesdropping on a Transformational Coaching Conversation

Do this activity to get excited about what you'll learn to do by engaging in the activities in this book!

We're guessing you might not have ever observed or been a part of a Transformational Coaching conversation, and you might be wondering what one sounds like. We always start our coaching workshops by demonstrating one, and if you participate in any of our virtual, in-person, or online classes you'll see Elena coaching at the start of the event. But here we are, in a book. And we want you to get a sense right away of what this model is all about so that you'll be so excited to get started developing your skills.

In this exercise, imagine that you are wearing an invisibility cloak and sitting in a classroom where a teacher meets with her coach. Carmen is a first-year teacher, teaching third grade, and it's mid-September. Her coach has been practicing Transformational Coaching for some time. As you read this conversation, do the following:

- Circle phrases that the coach says that surprise you.
- Underline phrases that you'd like to incorporate into your coaching.

CARMEN: I am so exhausted. I have no idea how teachers do this year after year. I just want to go home and get in bed and sleep for a month, but I have piles of grading to do and my principal asked me to stop by his office today. I have calls to make to parents, and if I don't clean up the science experiment we did last week my classroom will become a health hazard. Do you mind if I clean up as we talk? I can multitask. I mean, how am I supposed to do all of this? I still have to finish my plans for tomorrow—can we work on those together? I need to cut out 100 triangles from construction paper.

COACH: Oh, Carmen. [Coach exhales audibly] I'm glad we're meeting. How can I help you today?

CARMEN: I thought about canceling our session, but I don't think I have a choice about meeting with you if I want to clear my credential, so here I am.

COACH: I'm glad you're here. What would be most useful for us to talk about?

CARMEN: You tell me what we should talk about. I don't know. I'm overwhelmed, I feel like I'm doing everything poorly, and like I said, I have so much more to do this evening. And then, when I do get in bed, I can't sleep. I can't even

	remember why I wanted to be a teacher. I'd appreciate it if you would just tell me what to do. I can't think clearly.
COACH:	Okay, I hear that you're open to help. Can I make a suggestion? [Carmen nods]. Let's stand up for a moment. [They stand] Now reach your arms out and open your chest and take five deep breaths. [Carmen looks dubious but does this. Two minutes later they sit down]. How do you feel?
CARMEN:	A little tiny bit better. But I realized how achy my body feels. I haven't been to the gym in months. I used to go almost every day. Exercise really helps with my anxiety, and I miss it.
COACH:	It's good that you recognize that ache and that you feel a tiny bit better. Carmen, I am wondering if you've ever felt this overwhelmed in your life. Was there a time in college, high school, or another time in your life when you felt anything like what you're feeling now?
CARMEN:	[Thinks for about 10 seconds] I had some rough semesters in college. There was 1 year when my dad was sick and I had to go home a lot to take care of him. That was hard.
COACH:	Do you see any more similarities between that time and this one? Either in terms of what was hard or how you coped?
CARMEN:	Caring for someone you love who is sick is horrible. I couldn't sleep then either. I don't know how I coped—I just got through it. I did what I had to do every day, and my dad got better. My grades weren't the best that year, but I passed each class.
COACH:	What did you learn about yourself from that experience?
CARMEN:	I guess that I'm stronger than I think I am. I remember crying a lot that year and saying I didn't think I could "do this."
COACH:	Um. [Pause] What else?
CARMEN:	I learned that I didn't need to get As in every class. I'd always been an A or B+ student, so getting Bs and Cs was hard—but it wasn't the end of the world.
COACH:	[Nodding] What else? What else did you learn about how you cope with hard situations?
CARMEN:	I had to just put one foot in front of the next and do what had to be done.
COACH:	When you recall that year and how you got through it, do you see any lessons that you can apply to this hard time? To help you get through this time?
CARMEN:	I guess the reminder that I don't need to always be perfect. The reminder that I do persevere during hard times. The reminder that hard times pass.

	[Pause] But that was different—I was only responsible for me and my dad then. Now I am responsible for 30 people. And they're children!
COACH:	Ah. That must feel like a tremendous responsibility.
CARMEN:	It is! I know what the implications are for my kids if they don't learn to read well this year. I know how that will affect them going forward. It'll affect them for the rest of their lives!
COACH:	Oh, Carmen. That must feel overwhelming.
CARMEN:	It *is* overwhelming, and it's also terrifying. I didn't become a teacher so that I could fail kids. But that is what I'm doing.
COACH:	I'm hearing two things right now, Carmen. First, I hear that *you do* remember why you became a teacher, you know why you made this choice; and second, I hear that the hardest thing about this moment right now is that you feel like you're failing children and not feeling like you're being who you want to be—an effective teacher.
CARMEN:	[Nodding and eyes welling with tears] It's just so hard. Is it always going to be this hard?
COACH:	What do you think? Given how you've experienced challenges before, given what you know about teachers and teaching, do you think it'll always be this hard?
CARMEN:	No, I guess not.
COACH:	Say more about that.
CARMEN:	I mean, if it was always this hard, there wouldn't be any teachers. So it must get easier. And yes, I know I've dealt with challenges before.
COACH:	What else?
CARMEN:	I guess I need to lower my expectations for myself. [Pause] But I believe in high expectations! If I lower my expectations for myself it's like I'm saying it's okay if my kids don't learn to read.
COACH:	Are those the only two options? You lower your expectations for yourself and your kids don't learn to read?
CARMEN:	[Shaking her head] I hear what you're saying. Maybe it's not all or nothing.
COACH:	What else?
CARMEN:	I guess I could tell myself that this year it's okay if I get a B as a teacher. I don't need to get an A my first year.
COACH:	I'm also hearing—correct me if I'm wrong—that it's really important to you that your kids learn to read this year. Is that right?
CARMEN:	Yes, it is. Of course.

COACH:	So, let's see if we can figure this out together. This year, you want to be a "B teacher," meaning a good teacher, right? Maybe not an exemplary teacher, which I think is realistic given it's your first year and it's inevitable that you'll make some mistakes. But you want to be a really good teacher. [Carmen nods] And you want your kids to learn to read, right? [Carmen nods] And I'm going to assume you'll measure their reading skills with a set of assessments, and you'll measure their growth, and that'll be a key indicator of their success and yours too. Right? [Carmen nods] So teaching reading is your top priority.
CARMEN:	Well, I guess so, but what about math? They also need to learn math. And I want them to learn science. And I also want them to have art because we can't take that out of the curriculum—that does them a disservice.
COACH:	Prioritizing something doesn't mean you cut other things out.
CARMEN:	[Nodding] Okay. I'm just so anxious.
COACH:	I hear that. And we'll continue to explore your fears because they deserve attention. And I think if we explore them, you'll sleep better. And we'll also focus on how to teach reading really well. Okay? How does that sound?
CARMEN:	I guess that sounds good. I didn't expect you to talk to me about anxiety. Do you think I'm overly anxious?
COACH:	You're experiencing a great deal of the emotions that first-year teachers experience. What you're feeling is completely normal. I encourage you to talk to some of your colleagues here about their first year. Ask them about how they got through their first year.
CARMEN:	I've wanted to do that, but I'm afraid of hearing horror stories.
COACH:	Ask them what helped, what they learned about themselves, what they'd do differently if they could go back and do it over. Carmen, what have you learned about yourself in our conversation today?
CARMEN:	I guess I remembered that I'm stronger than I think I am. I don't like to think about that year in college because it was so hard. But remembering it made me realize that I have been through hard times.
COACH:	What else?
CARMEN:	I know why I became a teacher. I do want to be here. I want to teach.
COACH:	What else?
CARMEN:	I love my kids. I'm afraid of letting them down.
COACH:	What else?
CARMEN:	I need to go to the gym tomorrow. I want to go.
COACH:	Ok, let's talk about our next steps now.

Reflect

What did the coach say or do that was unexpected?

How did this conversation differ from ones you've had with new teachers or from conversations you had with others when you were a new teacher?

Based on what you know about Transformational Coaching, what makes this conversation potentially transformational?

In the spaces that follow, draw two images that reflect your big takeaways from this conversation. These could be insights you had, something that surprised you, or something that you want to incorporate into your own coaching.

BIG TAKEAWAY #1

BIG TAKEAWAY #2

Introducing the Three Bs

Do this activity to get clear on one of the most important concepts in Transformational Coaching.

We want to introduce you to, or remind you of, a key concept in Transformational Coaching. It'll help you understand the conversation you just eavesdropped on between Carmen and her coach, and it'll help you begin to see how Transformational Coaching can change our schools. It's such a foundational concept that we've included it here in the introduction because it'll help you understand everything else in this book. We'll return to this concept in Chapter 2.

Here's the big idea: A Transformational Coach guides someone in building awareness of their *behaviors*, *beliefs*, and ways of *being*—the three Bs. When we work with someone and when we think about how to foster their growth and development, we always think about their behaviors, their beliefs, and their ways of being. Transformational Coaching is a holistic method because it attends to these three domains of who we are. In this workbook, when we're focusing on strategies for coaching one of the three Bs we'll use the symbols that you'll see in Table I.1 to indicate as such.

Table I.1: The Three Bs

	What it is	**How we see it**
BEHAVIOR	What we do. Includes the ability to design lessons, deliver instruction, create a productive learning environment, select curriculum, and analyze data.	Behavior is evident in a skill set. It's what can be captured on video.
BELIEFS	What we think and believe. Comes from our knowledge, values, and experiences. Many beliefs can be subconscious.	Beliefs are reflected in decision-making, assumptions, interpretation, and conclusions. Behaviors emerge from beliefs.
WAYS OF BEING	Who we are. How we show up and how we are experienced. A blend of values, attitudes, dispositions, will, and sense of identity.	A way of being manifests in the expression of emotions, verbal and nonverbal communication, and levels of resilience.

Figure I.1 shows a pyramid representing the idea that behaviors emerge from beliefs and beliefs emerge from ways of being. However, the boundaries between beliefs and ways of being and between beliefs and behaviors are porous. Addressing only behaviors without surfacing, evaluating, and shifting the underlying beliefs and ways of being will not result in transformation or even in sustained change.

Figure I.1: The Three Bs

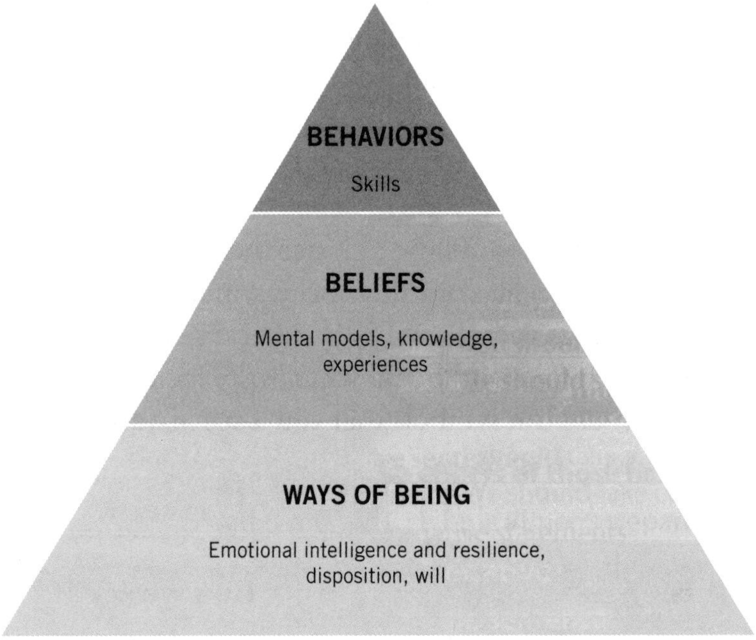

Your Turn

Recall your experience as a teacher and identify the connection between your behaviors, beliefs, and ways of being. When reflecting on your three Bs, you can begin anywhere—you can start with the behavior, the belief, or the way of being. Do this reflection a few times so that you really get a feel for the relationships between the three Bs. You'll see an example to get you started.

Elena Reflects

As a teacher, I . . . (**behavior**)

Solicited anonymous feedback from students every semester.

Because I **believed**. . .

That their opinions and experiences mattered, that they deserved to be heard, and also that I could be a better teacher if I listened to them.

Because I am. . . (**way of being**)

Committed to justice and equity and to mitigating power dynamics whenever possible.

Here are some behaviors that might get you started in thinking about your beliefs and ways of being:

- greeting students at the door by name
- taking time to review completed exams as a class
- addressing behavior issues one on one
- making positive phone calls home
- starting the day with a community circle

One

As a teacher, I . . . (**behavior**)

Because I **believed**. . .

Because I am. . . (**way of being**)

Two

As a teacher, I. . . (**behavior**)

Because I **believed**. . .

Because I am. . . (**way of being**)

Three

As a teacher, I. . . (**behavior**)

Because I **believed**. . .

Because I am. . . (**way of being**)

Reflect

Look back at the conversation between Carmen and her coach. Where do you see the coach focusing on Carmen's ways of being and beliefs? Go through the text again and mark where you see that the coach addressed beliefs and ways of being using the symbols of a spiral for beliefs, and a heart for ways of being. The reason we're not asking you to look for places where behavior was addressed is that for most of us it's pretty obvious when a coach is focused on behaviors. It's also the dominant kind of coaching that happens in schools—what we think of as *instructional coaching*. We want you to learn about Transformational Coaching, which is characterized by an inclusion of beliefs and ways of being.

How does this understanding of coaching around beliefs and ways of being help you understand this conversation between Carmen and her coach?

What is the potential you see in using Transformational Coaching? What impact do you think it could have on teachers and indirectly on students?

Presenting the Three Buckets

Read this section to understand how we organize coaching skills and how the activities in this book are categorized.

Elena Reflects

Some years ago, I realized that I could group the things I did in a coaching conversation into three buckets. First, I listened. There are many ways to listen, and all of them require that I am aware of my beliefs and ways of being. I can listen with an open heart and mind, or I can listen with judgment. I can listen with a desire to fix my client's problem, or I can listen with a commitment to hold space for them to find their own way forward. I can listen and be distracted or worried about whether I'm being a good coach, or I can listen with full presence. I can also listen to the words my client uses, and to their nonverbal communication. I call this the *listening part* of coaching.

Second, as I took in what my client said, I processed. I thought about what I heard. Sometimes I drew on my knowledge about instruction or leadership and that helped me understand what they shared. Sometimes I drew on my understanding of working with adult learners, or facilitating a process of change, or equity and that helped me process what I heard. Sometimes I filtered everything I heard through a commitment to surfacing someone's strengths. Other times I found myself applying insights from my learning about emotional resilience. I call this the *thinking part* of coaching.

Then, third, there came a time in a conversation when I said something—I asked a question or responded. I saw that when my thinking was thorough, and when I considered a number of different theories and frameworks, I asked better questions. And as I paid attention to the kinds of responses I offered, I realized that I asked a wider variety of questions. I call this the *responding part* of coaching.

Although it can be tempting to think of these three parts as steps, it's not accurate to think about them sequentially. It's more useful to think about them as components of a coach's skillset, or as the buckets into which coaching skills can be organized. Table I.2 describes these three buckets.

The majority of the activities in this workbook will help you build your skills in these three areas. These are the essential skills for any coach given that we're in conversations so often. It'll be easy to know when you're working on a listening activity in this

Table I.2: The Three Buckets of Transformational Coaching Skills

	Listen When we talk about listening, we're going to include how we listen through our identity markers—how the way that we listen is influenced by our gender, age, race, socioeconomic status, and so on. This is one way Transformational Coaching is different from other coaching models. We'll also talk about how we listen to our client's body language, how we listen for hope and possibility, and how we listen with full awareness.
	**Think** We all have default ways of thinking, and sometimes these create blind spots. In fact, it's almost inevitable that we'll have blind spots. Transformational *thinking tools* can help reduce our blind spots. Transformational Coaching offers a robust set of what we call *thinking tools*. This is what makes this model unique among coaching approaches used in schools (and outside of schools where coaching is used).
	Respond We categorize the responses we make in a Transformational Coaching conversation. We can paraphrase or reflect what we hear, we can ask clarifying questions, or we can use facilitative or directive approaches. You'll learn about all of these and more in this workbook (and in *The Art of Coaching*).

workbook, and also the responding activities are obvious. However, to be sure that you know when you're learning about a thinking tool, we've coded those activities with the thought bubble symbol.

Finally, you might want to take a peek at Appendix A. It's massive and can feel overwhelming, but it can also help you see a map for how Elena organizes coaching skills. And now that you know about these three buckets, you'll understand it better.

By the way, be warned: We like metaphors a whole lot, and we're going to use a whole bunch of them. We encourage you to decide which ones really work for you and to adopt those—because we might mix our metaphors and you'll be like, Wait! Now we're talking tools, and I thought we were talking buckets? Use the metaphors that work for you, or make up your own!

Pause. Breathe. Reflect.

Do this activity to synthesize your learning from this introduction and to acknowledge the skills you already have as a coach.

Whew! There was a lot in this introduction! We want you to pause for a moment. Take a deep breath. Now give yourself a little time to reflect and synthesize your learning.

Reflect on the behaviors, beliefs, and ways of being that you already have as an educator and human being. Which ones do you think will help you to be an extraordinary Transformational Coaching? In the graphic or around the edges of it, jot down the words and phrases that reflect the behaviors, beliefs, and ways of being that you already bring as a coach. For example, you might know that you can ask thoughtful questions or design a great lesson—those are behaviors that you'll use as a coach. You might believe that all children can learn—which will definitely help you as a coach. You might know that you're empathetic and enjoy helping people—those are ways of being that will serve you as a coach.

Reflect: My Three Bs

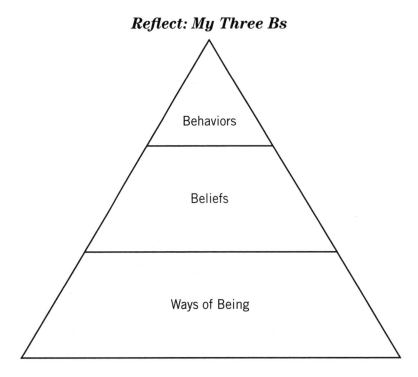

Synthesize: Big Takeaways

What are your three biggest takeaways from this introduction?

1.

2.

3.

The Art of Coaching Workbook

CHAPTER 1

Figuring Out Who You Want to Be

Who Am I As a Coach?

This activity will introduce you to the content of this chapter and will help you begin to articulate a vision for yourself as a coach.

The activist Grace Lee Boggs once said that if you want to transform the world, you have to transform yourself. If you aspire to be a Transformational Coach, we echo this need for personal transformation. We also guarantee you'll find this a worthwhile journey—that your transformation will have ripples of positive influence in all aspects of your life. You'll first embark on this journey by getting to know yourself better. As you come to understand how your values influence how you show up in the world, you'll find yourself feeling more empowered and confident. As you understand your personality type, you'll find ways to be more effective. As you recognize the role your identity markers play in how you coach, you'll learn new ways to connect with others. This chapter will set you on the part of this learning journey which is about who you are. We think you'll enjoy this learning—it feels affirming and energizing.

Before you get started, storyboard your journey using some imagination and visualization. This workbook serves as a guide in becoming the coach you *want* to be, and a good place to start that journey is creating a vision of who you are as that coach. This activity will also help you reflect at a later time (when you reach the end of this workbook) on how much you've grown.

In the first box, draw the way you perceive yourself now. Stick figures are fine. Thought or speech bubbles are also great. The point is to create a simple visual that reflects how you feel about yourself as a coach now. In the second box, do the same—but imagine yourself a year from now, after learning about coaching and practicing

Transformational Coaching. Feel free to use a separate sheet of paper if you find you need more than the provided boxes to capture this visualization.

Me (as a coach) now

Me (as a coach) in a year

Identifying Core Values

This activity will help you identify your core values. This is also an activity that we highly recommend when you begin working with a new coachee. You can download this activity from our website, https://brightmorningteam.com

We all have what are considered core values, but often we're not aware of what those are. Core values are foundational pillars that form our ways of being, our beliefs, and our behaviors. By identifying those values, we form a much deeper understanding of how they show up in the three Bs and beyond. We recommend revisiting this exercise at least once per year and using that opportunity to reflect on how these values grow and change (or stay the same) over time.

Process

1. Read through the following list of values. Circle 10 that you feel are most important to you.
2. Narrow those ten values down to a list of five that you feel are most important.
3. Now, from your list of five values, cross off two, leaving you with the *three* values that are most important to you. These are your core values.

Values

The following values apply to both work and personal life. It's important to select these based on you overall as a person, not just what you value at work or at home exclusively. This is not an exhaustive list—you're welcome to add your own.

Acceptance	Appreciation	Belonging
Achievement	Arts	Caring
Advancement	Authenticity	Celebration
Adventure	Authority	Challenge
Affection	Autonomy	Choice
Altruism	Balance	Collaboration
Ambition	Beauty	Commitment

Communication	Harmony	Power
Community	Health	Pride
Compassion	Helping others	Privacy
Competition	High expectations	Productivity
Connection	Honesty	Recognition
Contribution	Hope	Reflection
Cooperation	Humor	Reputation
Creativity	Imagination	Respect
Democracy	Independence	Responsibility
Effectiveness	Influence	Results
Efficiency	Initiative	Risk-taking
Empathy	Integrity	Romance
Equality	Interdependence	Routine
Equity	Intuition	Self-expression
Excellence	Justice	Self-respect
Excitement	Kindness	Service
Expertise	Knowledge	Sharing
Fairness	Leadership	Solitude
Faith	Loyalty	Spirituality
Fame	Making a difference	Success
Family	Meaningful work	Support
Flexibility	Mindfulness	Teamwork
Focus	Nature	Time
Forgiveness	Nurturing	Togetherness
Freedom	Order	Tolerance
Friendship	Passion	Tradition
Fun	Peace	Travel
Generosity	Perseverance	Trust
Goals	Personal development	Truth
Gratitude	Personal growth	Unity
Growth	Pleasure	Variety
Happiness	Positive attitude	Zest

Reflect

- What came up for you when completing this activity?

- One year ago, what do you suspect your core values might have been? Ten years ago, what do you think they might have been?

- Consider how your actions reflect your core values. Which values show up more often in your actions at work? At home? In social circles? With family?

- What are some ways your actions reflect your core values? Think of one example of how actions you take reflect your core values.

- Can you think of a time—or two—when your actions conflicted with a core value? How does it feel to remember those moments when there was a discrepancy between a value and your actions?

- Write your three core values on a piece of paper and post them somewhere prominent. Reflect on them for a few months. See if they still feel like "core" values. If they don't feel like they represent your deepest beliefs and commitments, do this activity again.

Suggestions for Sharing Your Core Values

This activity is first in this book for a couple of reasons. First, you need to know your own core values because they are central to knowing yourself. We also want you to think about your client's core values in a parallel way, and we offer this activity to clients early in the coaching relationship. We think of core values as our internal compass. As a coach, your job is to guide someone back to their core values, to remind them of what their values are and to help them recognize when they are not acting from their core values.

When using the core values activity to get to know a client, these are some initial questions to ask:

- What do your core values mean to you?
- Describe the elimination process you went through to arrive at your three core values. How are the ones that you crossed off reflected in your top three?
- Share a time when you acted on your core values.
- Which of your core values feels easiest to uphold? Which feels hardest?

The Things That Get Under My Skin

This activity will help you identify and reflect on your triggers, or the things that get under your skin as a coach.

Let's be clear on something: Coaches are human beings. As much as we can try to be neutral and objective, compassionate and curious, we also have our histories, experiences, beliefs, pain, and passions. It's likely that we'll have strong emotional responses, and—while there is nothing wrong with strong emotions (in fact, they can be very helpful)—we need to be aware of when we experience them and how we respond to them. Some of the things that get under our skin are

- a teacher who says, "These kids can't. . ."
- a teacher who begs for appreciation and recognition—especially when she's really only doing the basics
- an administrator who calls a lot of "emergency meetings" after school—and they really aren't emergencies at all
- a teacher who sends students to a "time-out chair" that faces the corner of the room
- an administrator who seems to have a favorite staff member

What do you have a strong emotional response to when it comes to things you see, hear, or experience in schools? What comes to mind when you think about what triggers you?

Do you see any connection between your triggers and your core values? Often there's a tight correlation because when something we really value is not honored by someone else, it can feel like our values have been trampled on. If responsibility is one of your core values, and you see someone else shirking their responsibility or blaming others, you might have a strong reaction. If you value authenticity, and you perceive someone as being inauthentic, you might feel triggered.

Write down your three core values and any connections you can make with things that other people do that really bother you.

1. I value:
   My value feels like it's being trampled on when other people. . .

2. I value:
   My value feels like it's being trampled on when other people. . .

3. I value:
   My value feels like it's being trampled on when other people. . .

Extend Your Learning

Over the next week, see if you can stay alert to any and all triggers when you're working. Write them down—there's power in capturing them in writing. At the end of the week, reflect on what you've noticed in yourself. Do you see any trends or patterns in what triggers you?

Understanding Personality Types

This activity will help you understand aspects of your personality. It's also one to invite clients to do since it's helpful to have an understanding of their personality, too.

There are many ways to understand your personality. We have found the Myers-Briggs Type Indicator (MBTI) to be invaluable in understanding ourselves and our clients. A good MBTI assessment shows your results on a continuum. Most people have shades of all of these aspects but have a dominance in one tendency. Here's a quick overview of the four personality elements according to the MBTI and an opportunity for you to predict what you are before taking the full test, which is a part of the following exercise.

1. Energy: whether you draw energy from the outer or inner world	
Extroversion (E)	Extroverts • Enjoy being in large groups of people and meeting lots of new people; they walk away from a daylong conference feeling energized and ready to socialize in the evening • Have a strong desire to form teams and can work well in teams • Appreciate a lot of time to talk and work through their thoughts using verbal processing • Tend to have many friends and associates
Introversion (I)	Introverts • Are drained by large groups of people and prefer interacting with one other person or a small group; they walk away from a daylong conference feeling exhausted and wanting to be alone or perhaps with one other person in the evening • Need planning time and thrive when they have it • Need quiet processing time before being asked to speak about something • Tend to have a small group of close friends or a best friend • Enjoy being alone

Place an X where you believe you fall:

←——→

Introversion   **Extroversion**

I think I fall here because. . .

How do you feel about where you are on this continuum? Do you feel accepting of who you are, or do you wish you were different?

Important to Know
Our tendency toward introversion or extroversion has nothing to do with shyness, social awkwardness, fear of public speaking, or ability to make friends. This is the element of your personality that is most likely to change as you get older. Most people become more introverted as they age, so if you were an extrovert in high school, it's possible that by your 40s you might be an introvert. It's also likely, psychologists say, that these results may change as you get older because when you were a young adult, if you took a personality test, you may have answered the questions according to what you *thought* you should say—for example, when asked what you prefer to do on a Saturday night: go to a party or stay at home and watch a movie, you may have felt socially compelled to say party.

2. Perception of information: your tendency to focus on factual information or to interpret and add meaning to information	
Sensing (S)	Sensors • Rely mainly on concrete, actual information • Value data (and might be driven by data) • Focus on what is realistic in relation to current constraints • Can struggle to step back and determine a path to success, especially when resources are scarce and tasks are overwhelming • Can be overwhelmed by details and may have a hard time seeing possibilities for new approaches

Intuition (N)	Intuitives
	• Rely on their conception about things based on their understanding of the world
	• Are always looking at the big picture and prefer to backward plan
	• Before moving ahead, want to know why something isn't working when there are problems
	• Plan for long-term success and aren't tempted by short-term tasks
	• Delegate responsibility for implementing big projects

Place an X where you believe you fall:

$\longleftarrow$ $\longrightarrow$

Sensing   **Intuition**

I think I fall here because. . .

How do you feel about where you are on this continuum? Do you feel accepting of who you are, or do you wish you were different?

3. Decision-making (how you process information): whether you first look at logic and consistency or at people and circumstances	
Thinking (T)	Thinkers
	• Make decisions based on logical reasoning and are less affected by feelings and emotions
	• Can be objective in the face of emotionally charged issues
	• Are able to look at and analyze data and enjoy it
	• Are less concerned with wanting to be liked and more focused on enduring results
	• Can be insensitive to others and can create conflict

Feeling (F)	Feelers • Base decisions in emotions • Are relationship oriented • Cultivate a positive climate in the classroom or school • Can struggle to hold people accountable because they worry about damaging relationships

Important to Know

Thinkers do have emotions, and feelers do use their cognitive capacities as well.

Place an X where you believe you fall:

$\longleftarrow$ ———————————————————————— $\longrightarrow$

Thinking   **Feeling**

I think I fall here because. . .

How do you feel about where you are on this continuum? Do you feel accepting of who you are, or do you wish you were different?

---

4. External structure (how you like to live your outer life): whether you prefer things to be decided or to stay open and flexible

Judging (J)	Judgers • Are outcome oriented and decisive • Choose a plan of action and stay focused • Like to develop and execute plans • Are deadline oriented • Find changes to plans disruptive
Perceiving (P)	Perceivers • Are creative problem solvers always looking for new ideas and innovations • Like to keep options open • Often have new ideas and get overwhelmed with the number of things that could be tried • Can find change exciting

Place an X where you believe you fall:

$\longleftarrow \hspace{5cm} \longrightarrow$

Judging   **Perceiving**

I think I fall here because. . .

How do you feel about where you are on this continuum? Do you feel accepting of who you are, or do you wish you were different?

Extend Your Learning

Take the free, online test at http://www.16personalities.com or http://www.humanmetrics.com (or you can take both and compare your results).

Write your four-letter personality type here:

Respond to the following questions:

Given your personality type, what really resonated? Were there any descriptions that felt particularly "like you"?

What were you surprised by in your results?

Were there any results that didn't feel accurate?

What are the implications of knowing these personality tendencies? Are there implications for what kind of work you do, where you work, whom you work with, and what you might be able to do?

Who are a few famous people who have shared your personality type? How does sharing this type with them make you feel?

Read about other types. Which types do you suspect are hardest for you to work with?

Exploring Identity Markers

This activity will help you understand your sociopolitical identities and how those influence you as you move through your life.

Our sociopolitical identity is a central part of who we are and greatly influences how we move through the world. A Transformational Coach needs to understand their own identity markers and experiences and needs skills to understand both their own and their clients' identity markers.

We all have intersecting social identities. Our inner sense of racial, cultural, or ethnic identity is one aspect; how we're perceived racially or culturally is another aspect; our gender is another social identity; our age is another; our class background is another. Each identity is more or less salient depending on the context. Racial identity markers often take on particularly outsized roles. Although the concept of race as a biological classification system is absurd (it has no basis in biology), we live in a cultural world in which race is very, very real.

The way that we understand ourselves has a big impact on who we are and how we show up in the world. To understand your own and others' experience in the world, it's useful to understand the difference between an *internal identity* and an *external experience*. Your internal identity is how you see yourself and feel inside. Your external identity is how the majority of other people see you. Racial identity markers are a part of both these identities.

Use the following activity to explore your concept of your identity. This can be downloaded from our website and can also be offered to your clients (we'll cover how to do that in Chapter 5).

Reflecting on Identity Markers

	Which of these were you aware of as a child?	Which ones feel important to you now?	Which three are the most important to you?	Which ones do you prioritize sharing about yourself?	Which ones do you think others typically notice about you?	Which ones do you tend not to think about?
Age						
Education						
Ethnicity						
Family status						
Gender						
Geographical location						
Immigrant status						
Language						
Marital status						

	Which of these were you aware of as a child?	Which ones feel important to you now?	Which three are the most important to you?	Which ones do you prioritize sharing about yourself?	Which ones do you think others typically notice about you?	Which ones do you tend not to think about?
Nationality						
Physical appearance						
Physical ability (able-bodiedness)						
Race						
Religion						
Sexual orientation						
Socioeconomic status						
Other						

Reflect

- When you look at your three most important identity markers, which specific life experiences made those so prominent?

- What impact have your top three identity markers had on your life?

- Have any of your identity markers felt more salient or relevant during other periods of your life? How so?

- Do your closest friends share aspects of your identity? How so?

- What thoughts and feelings arose in you in doing this reflection?

Do this activity so that you can appreciate yourself and gain insight into how to play to your strengths as a coach.

An educator's strengths could be categorized into three areas: head based, heart based, and hand based. Most of us have strengths in all of these areas, although we can also have one area in which we're stronger than the others. The ability to see someone's strengths is key when coaching—your clients will trust you and be more receptive to your coaching if they know that you see their potential and strengths (Table 1.1).

Table 1.1: Strengths-Based Coaching: Head, Heart, Hands

Area	Description and examples	People I know who have these strengths
Head-based strengths	Knowledge of content, curriculum, instruction; analytical abilities and verbal skills; research oriented, intellectually curious. This person is great at unit design, budgeting, or creating a master schedule.	
Heart-based strengths	Strong self-awareness and emotional intelligence; ability to form trusting relationships; passion, will, and commitment to a mission. This person remembers the names of students' parents, boosts morale during hard times, or speaks up when there's tension in a team.	
Hands-based strengths	The ability to get stuff done, take care of business, develop systems and structures; creative capabilities. This person organizes Back-to-School Night, creates beautiful displays of student work, or has a very organized classroom.	

Think about yourself as a coach, teacher, and educator. What are your strengths? Jot them down in Figure 1.1. Decorate the human to look like you if you want.

Figure 1.1: Heads, Hearts, Hands

How Do I Learn?

This activity will help you understand yourself as a learner so that you can understand other people as learners.

There are many ways to understand yourself as a learner, including multiple intelligence analyses and learning style inventories. As a quick entry into self-reflection on your learning preferences, consider where you fall on the following lines.

If you find yourself tempted to put your X in the middle of more than one line, consider a few learning experiences that you found particularly powerful or off-putting. Did these experiences tend more toward one end of the spectrum than the other? And, of course, know that these are not true dichotomies. Strong learning experiences will often have elements of both. Forcing a choice is just a shortcut to illuminate your preferences.

When I am learning, I tend to prefer. . .
Seeing a model - Experimenting myself
Reading and writing - Listening and speaking
Theory then practice - Practice then theory
Facilitator-guided - Self-guided
Learning alone - Learning with others
Concrete thinking - Abstract thinking
Logic - Creativity
Practice -Reflection

Reflect

Look back over the preferences you just identified, and then consider the following questions.

How much does this self-image align with or challenge the kind of learner that was affirmed in your own schooling experience?

How do these preferences show up when you are in a learning space with others?

How do you tend to respond when asked to learn in ways that differ from your preferences?

How do these preferences show up when you are designing or facilitating learning spaces for others?

Consider that our schools tend to be designed to favor the preferences on the left side of these spectra. What were the implications of this for you as a learner? What might be the implications for your clients?

How might your learning preferences manifest when you're coaching?

What do you know about the learning preferences of the people you coach? How could you find out more?

CHAPTER 2

Defining Coaching

What's been true for you as a coach? Check all that apply:

☐ No one at my school seems to know what a coach does.
☐ I also have no idea what a coach does.
☐ My principal has ideas about what I should do, but I am not sure I agree.
☐ I know what I want to do as a coach, but teachers think I'm a spy for admin.
☐ My assistant principal thinks a coach is a glorified admin assistant.
☐ Everyone at my school is clear and on the same page about what a coach does. I'm on board too, and everything is awesome!

Most coaches we know go through an identity crisis when they become a coach, asking themselves over and over, *Who am I? What am I supposed to do?* And *I miss teaching. I wonder if this was a mistake?* Part of the reason for this identity crisis is that there isn't a clear agreement or understanding about what coaching is or what a coach does. This chapter will help you work through this. More than anything, this chapter will help you take control of defining this field—because a coach is a leader and a leader determines for themselves who they are and what their role entails and communicates that to others. Get ready to take back the reins, understand what a coach does, and determine the coach you aspire to be.

Analogies for Coaching

Do this activity to surface and explore your own thinking about coaching.

As you hone your own definition of coaching, consider how the following analogies illuminate different aspects of the coach role. Jot down your own thoughts first. Then turn the page to read how we relate each analogy to coaching—but we want to beg you not to skip ahead yet. You'll gain so much from this exercise if you explore your own thinking first.

HOW IS A COACH LIKE. . .

A FARMER	A CHIROPRACTOR

A TOUR GUIDE	YEAST

AN ATHLETIC COACH	A MIRROR

Now that you've considered these analogies for yourself, read some of our thoughts. There are no right answers here. Consider underlining the elements that feel truest to your own developing vision of coaching and adding your own ideas in the margins.

Farmers are the original systems thinkers. Like coaches, they must be closely attuned to the optimal conditions for growth. A farmer knows that many factors impact growth and so considers soil quality, water, sunlight, and wind. A coach also considers a client's "climate"—their working conditions, identity, capacity, demands, and the like. Farmers operate with patience and optimism, knowing that the seed planted today might not bear fruit for months or even years.

Chiropractors likewise think in systems—internal systems. They understand that adjustments in one part of the system can have ripple effects throughout, much like the coach who helps the new teacher clean up their classroom routines in the fall, knowing this will create the space for more student-led learning later on. The chiropractor also highlights the client's responsibility in the adjustment process—offering at-home exercises, knowing they both have a role in making the change stick.

Tour guides are adept at leading and supporting others on their journey. They can offer reassurance and guidance along the way. The best tour guides, like the best coaches, understand that the journey is mutual. Clients will see things they've missed and through new eyes, and learning is enhanced by exchanging these perspectives. They will say both, "Yes, you can make it up this mountain!" and "Hey, it's time to stop and rest."

Yeast is the ultimate catalyst. Just a little yeast transforms the potential of flour and water. Coaches use their words like yeast, sharing a question here or a reflection there to help clients grow into their full potential. Yet yeast requires certain conditions to thrive: moisture, a little heat, food. Likewise, coaches build the trust and credibility needed for their words to nurture, not bruise.

Athletic coaches are masters at helping others improve their physical performance. They break skills down into discrete parts and offer modeling and bite-size feedback to fuel incremental progress ("Move your elbow a centimeter to the right"). In doing so, they help athletes build the muscle memory needed for top performance come game time. Many of the best professional sports coaches were not themselves star players. Like skilled leadership coaches, they have a respect for and deep understanding of the underlying *science* of their field and use that to guide others to excellence.

Mirrors offer a nonjudgmental reflection of what is. So it is with coaches, who reflect what clients may not yet see in themselves: word choices, nonverbal cues, posture, patterns. While the one looking in the mirror may distort what they see to fit their mental image, the mirror remains impartial. Over time, through reflection without judgment, a coach can support clients to shift their self-image and build the ability to critically examine their own mental models.

Reflect

At its core, coaching is a way to help all of us get better and better, to grow into our most expansive and capable selves. Consider:

Which analogy do you most relate to? Why?

What other analogies can you think of? How do they add to your definition?

How do these analogies lend nuance to your definition of coaching?

What Is Transformational Coaching?

Transformational Coaching is a holistic approach to guiding adults in a learning journey. If you've read from *Coaching for Equity* this might be review, but we find it's a great analogy to help you understand Transformational Coaching more deeply. As you read the following description of Transformational Coaching, annotate the text using these two symbols:

★ This resonates.

✚ This is a new idea.

The Bridge of Transformational Coaching

Imagine that we are standing on one side of a chasm with the current ways of doing school. This is the side where Black and Brown kids are suspended for rolling their eyes, where security guards patrol the halls, where teachers say, "These kids can't. . ." On this side, schools serve to reproduce the status quo, which grants access and privilege to some groups (White, middle and upper class, English speaking) and further marginalizes other groups.

Perhaps your own children attend schools on this side. Some children from dominant cultures are more or less served on this side—meaning they have decent experiences in school and graduate ready for college or career. But be honest: The quality of education on this side of the chasm has much to be desired. There's still too much bullying; kids and adults are far too stressed; and lectures, textbooks, and testing consume much of everyone's time. We can try to reform bits and pieces or grit our teeth and make the best of it, or we can look across the chasm where a different reality can exist.

On the other side of this chasm, schools can be places of healing and liberation. They can be a microcosm for a more just and equitable society, a place where adults and children learn to be together in a healthy community, a place where we learn about ourselves and others. On that side, children are in classes where they engage in critical thinking about complex ideas, where they have access to means of creative expression, and where they collaborate to generate novel approaches to addressing the social, economic, political, and environmental challenges that our planet faces. On that side, children encounter kindness and understanding from adults; it is a place where every child thrives. It is a place that children love to be, where their full humanity is embraced.

There are two reasons more schools like this don't exist. First, they are hard to imagine—or we are afraid to imagine them—and then even when we do hold this vision we don't know how

---

From *The Art of Coaching Workbook: Tools to Make Every Conversation Count* by Elena Aguilar. Copyright © 2021 by Elena Aguilar. Reproduced by permission.

to get there. I believe in the power of our imagination, and I know that in the company of others, with commitment it can grow. We humans are brilliantly creative, imaginative creatures.

I believe that you want to cross this chasm between where we are now and a place characterized by kindness, justice, freedom, and learning. I believe you want this for yourself, for the young people you love, and for the students you serve. Look across this divide, and you will see a bridge. This bridge is Transformational Coaching. This is a model for change—a model that can be used by teachers, coaches, principals, and superintendents and by any team or organizational leader. Transformational Coaching can take us from where we are now to where we want to be.

Let me be your guide right now to show you the key features of this bridge. First, you'll see multiple lanes on the deck of the bridge—these will take us from our current reality to our ideal reality. One lane is all about emotional resilience. When you walk or drive along that lane, you coach for emotional resilience. In another lane, you coach teams, creating healthy and productive groups of people. And in another lane, you coach for equity. You interrupt the practices, beliefs, and systems that are inequitable. Another lane focuses on leaders, and when you're in that lane you coach toward leadership development. There's also a lane for traditional coaching of instructional practices, for example, designing lessons or assessments.

We'll travel in each of these lanes as we create a new reality—sometimes spending more time in one lane than another, sometimes crossing back and forth within one conversation. Maybe while analyzing student work and discussing how to support English language learners the teacher you're coaching will express emotional exhaustion and you'll shift into coaching for resilience. Or perhaps as you coach for equity, it becomes apparent that decisions made in the grade-level team make it difficult to implement equitable practices—perhaps curriculum or scheduling decisions—and then you shift to developing leadership skills and to coaching teams.

Reflect

Look at the places that resonated. Which of your own values, experiences, or beliefs were reflected in those sections?

Look at one of the places where you found a new idea. What were the feelings that that new idea activated in you?

The Essential Components of Transformational Coaching

What makes Transformational Coaching *transformational* is that a coach attends to three areas—to themselves, their client, and systems. This means that they think about these three areas when they are making decisions about coaching, it means that they give time to reflection and action in each of these areas, it means that they value each of these areas. Here's an overview of this concept.

As *coaches,* we value and prioritize our own learning. We examine our beliefs. We reflect on who we are being and how our actions align with our commitments. A Transformational Coach attends to their own behaviors, beliefs, and ways of being.

We also pay attention to our *clients'* actions and coach them on their instructional practices, and we engage our clients in deep exploration of the beliefs from which they operate, and we guide them to surface and explore beliefs that are limiting for themselves and for their students and those they serve. Perhaps most importantly, we pay close attention to and coach around ways of being—how someone shows up, how they express their thoughts and feelings. Transformational Coaching takes a holistic approach, addressing a client's behaviors, beliefs, and ways of being.

And with *systems,* while we work with individuals, we surface the often invisible, often problematic, and inequitable structures and policies in which our clients work. These structures and policies, such as a school's discipline system, hiring decisions, and curriculum choices, reflect larger inequitable systems. A Transformational Coach recognizes, identifies, and understands the larger systems in which we live and work and takes action to transform them.

A Quick Self-Assessment

As you read the statements that follow, put an X in as many boxes that apply to you in each line.

Component of Transformational Coaching	I know what this means.	I do this.	I value this.	I do this well.
In general, I attend to my own behaviors, beliefs, and ways of being.				
I prioritize my own learning.				
I reflect on my own beliefs.				

Component of Transformational Coaching	I know what this means.	I do this.	I value this.	I do this well.
I reflect on my own ways of being.				
I coach my client's behaviors.				
I coach my client's beliefs.				
I coach my client's ways of being.				
I can identify the larger systems in which we live and work.				
I understand the larger systems in which we live and work.				
I understand how to coach to change the larger systems in which we live and work.				

Reflect

What insights did you gain about yourself from this reflection?

What implications are there for yourself based on this reflection? What does it tell you about what you might focus on as you develop your coaching skills?

What surprised you from doing this reflection?

Coaching Behaviors, Beliefs, and Ways of Being

Do this activity to understand and practice how to coach the three Bs.

We introduced this concept in the introduction and asked you to reflect on your own behaviors, beliefs, and ways of being. Now we'll explore this as it relates to coaching. In case you skipped that section in the intro, go back to it first.

In Table 2.1, you'll see some examples of what it sounds like to coach in these three domains. As you read these, use the following codes to engage with the text:

✓ = I have said this when I've coached someone.

! = This would be hard for me to say. It would feel awkward.

* = I'd like to incorporate this into coaching conversations. I want to say this.

→ = I wish someone would ask me this question. I want to think about this for myself.

Table 2.1: What Does It Sound Like to Coach the Three Bs?

Behavior	• How will you introduce this lesson? • What vocabulary will students need to understand to access this text? • How will you check for understanding before students move into independent practice? • What was your thinking about putting students into small groups for that activity? • Why do you think students struggled with that part of the lesson? • How can you communicate this decision to parents in a way that they'll respond positively?
Beliefs	• How did you interpret that student behavior? • What assumptions were you operating under when you decided to change that part of the lesson? • How do you think you arrived at that belief? • Where do you think those beliefs came from? • When you were a student, what was it like to. . .? • What conclusions did you come to about yourself when your principal said. . .?

(Continued)

Ways of Being	<ul><li>Which emotions came up for you in that experience? How does it feel to remember it?</li><li>How are you feeling? Where do you sense those feelings in your body?</li><li>Which of your core values were you acting on?</li><li>What made it hard for you to speak in alignment with your core values in this situation?</li><li>What really matters to you? What's most important right now?</li><li>How do you want to be remembered by your students?</li><li>How do you want to remember this experience?</li><li>How do you think this experience impacted you because of the identity markers you hold?</li><li>What did this experience mean about who you are?</li><li>What are you learning about yourself?</li><li>Who do you want to be?</li></ul>

Now read some excerpts from a coaching conversation. As you read, identify the places where the coach is addressing behaviors, beliefs, and ways of being. You're welcome to use our symbols to annotate or devise your own.

COACH: Hi Marco. I'm so glad we're able to meet today. I'm really excited to hear about how the unit launch went. I know you spent so much time planning it.

MARCO: Oh, it went so well! I was worried that I was introducing too much new content at the same time as asking them to engage in new routines. The learning centers were a hit and they loved having the freedom to decide what order to go in.

COACH: What kind of exit ticket did you end up doing? I know you were thinking about how you'd assess what they learned and how they felt at the end of the day.

MARCO: I'll show you. After we met last time, I went and talked to Ms. Owala like you'd suggested, and she had just done these. . .

COACH: This is incredible data! How are you feeling about it?

MARCO: I'm so proud of them. Every week I just feel amazed by them. I had no idea that third graders were capable of this kind of scientific inquiry. It's incredible.

COACH: So how would you say that your beliefs about your students are changing?

MARCO: I guess they're able to take in a lot more than I assumed. But also they're able to self-regulate and manage their behavior in ways that I didn't think eight-year-olds could.

COACH: Where do you think those inaccurate assumptions about what they were capable of came from?

MARCO: Honestly, I think it's just because I haven't taught third grade before. I taught fifth grade for 6 years, and so I was used to older kids. But I mean, I don't think I've underestimated them. I grew up in this community. I know what they're capable of. I guess it was just the age thing.

COACH: That's very likely. It takes a bit to understand different age groups. Given what you learned about them during the launch, how will you adjust your plans for the unit?

MARCO: Good question. I want to spend some time going back through it. I can definitely up the rigor and create a lot more opportunities for them to be self-directed. I'd love your thought partnership on that.

COACH: We can do that today if you'd like. I'm curious, what are you learning about yourself as a teacher from this experience?

MARCO: Well, one thing is that I'm reminded of how much I love teaching. For all the hard moments, there's nothing like seeing kids deeply engaged in learning activities that feel really relevant to them and to me. And then at the end of the day, seeing them go home with big smiles and Ricardo, who often has a hard time in school, was happy today. Those days make it all worth it. So I guess I'm learning that I'm glad that I followed this path!

COACH: It sounds like you feel affirmed in your decisions?

MARCO: Yeah, definitely.

COACH: And like you can trust yourself to take risks?

MARCO: That too. I mean, you know that I didn't want to teach third grade this year—that I had to because of enrollment numbers. So I don't really feel like this was a risk I wanted to take. But I guess I'm learning that I can adapt, and things I think will be difficult have silver linings. And it's been fun to try something new, teaching these little ones.

COACH: Has this experience made you think about any other risks you want to take, or paths you'd want to explore within education?

MARCO: I'm really enjoying teaching third grade now—and I have so many things I want to try this year. Someday I might think about becoming a coach

	or something, but I also love teaching. I don't want to be thinking about what's next or how to move up some ladder.
COACH:	I'm so glad that you're happy. I'm excited to keep working with you this year to help you fulfill the vision you have for yourself as a teacher. What would be most useful for us to talk about now?
MARCO:	I'd like to go through my unit plan and look for places where I can add more opportunity for students to direct their own learning. I am also rethinking the rubric I created for the final project and wondering whether students could be brought in to define excellence and create that rubric.
COACH:	That sounds great. Where do you want to start?

Toward a Coaching Mission and Vision

Do this activity so you can articulate why you coach. This will make you feel more grounded and empowered.

In this chapter, we offer a variety of entry points to get clear on who you are as a coach, what you stand for, and why. It is possible that some of this has been defined for you in your workplace. Perhaps you are lucky enough to work in a setting with a clear mission statement and vision for coaching. (In our experience, this is rare). Even so, it can help to get clear on your personal vision and to articulate that mission statement in a form that can serve as a north star by which to guide your work.

First, some definitions:

A **vision** describes a compelling future. It is a basis for assessing the current reality and it provides a sense of direction. In the context of coaching, it describes what a coach hopes will be true as a result of their coaching.

A **mission** helps establish priorities and guides decisions. Our mission is our fundamental purpose. It explains how we intend to realize our vision. In the context of coaching, it describes a coach's contribution.

Reflect

1. My core values are. . .

2. My definition of coaching is. . .

3. I coach because. . .

4. I know I am an effective coach when. . .

5. I hope that, as a result of my coaching, . . .

Now look across your responses. What themes do you notice? How do these themes help you clarify your vision and mission?

Here are some examples of a vision and mission statement for coaching:

- I coach to heal and transform the world. I coach teachers and leaders to discover ways of working and being that are joyful and rewarding, that bring communities together, and that result in positive outcomes for children. I coach people to find their own power and to empower others so that we can transform our education system, our society, and our world. (From *The Art of Coaching*)
- I coach so that students in marginalized communities get the quality education that the world needs them to have to create a more just and equitable society.
- I coach to validate the work that our leaders do so that they can positively impact our students. As a coach I am supportive but will push for learning and growth. I believe in the integrity that our leaders have to advocate for the fulfillment of all students' inherent potential. As a result, schools will become a refuge for learning.
- I am dedicated to finding multiple pathways for teachers to feel successful. Our teachers need to be reminded of success, no matter how small, and reminded of the variations on and adaptations to each lesson that will make it more successful for students. I want to make success visible, tangible, frequent, and visceral.

Notice some of the ways these statements link the mission and vision of coaching:

I coach so that. . . [Vision]
I coach to. . . [Mission]
[Mission] so that. . . [Vision]
[Mission]. As a result, [Vision].

Create

Now it's your turn to write your mission. It might be easiest to simply complete the following sentence stems several times, and then combine your responses:

I coach so that. . .

And I coach to. . .

I coach so that. . .

And I coach to. . .

Once you've got a draft that you like, write it up or type it, and put it in the front of your coaching notebook or tape it onto your office wall. If you're inclined, spend some time playing with fonts and colors and layout so that it looks and feels inspiring. Below in Figure 2.1 you'll see Lori's Coaching Mission.

Figure 2.1: Lori's

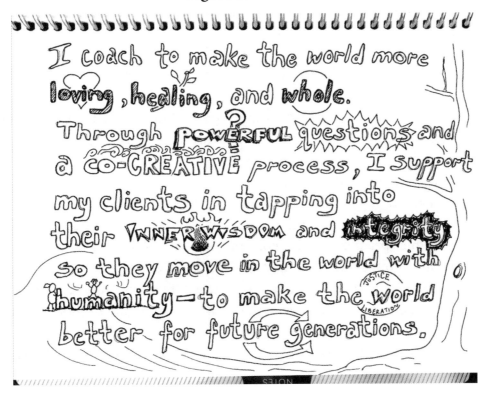

From *The Art of Coaching Workbook: Tools to Make Every Conversation Count* by Elena Aguilar. Copyright © 2021 by Elena Aguilar. Reproduced by permission.

How to Get Clarity from Your Boss About What You're Supposed to Do

Do this activity to prepare for a conversation with your supervisor about what your role entails.

There have been enough coaches passing through schools in recent decades that most educators have some idea about what a coach might do. But what a coach *might do* is not the same as a clear, shared articulation of what their work entails. Because the broad definition of *coach* leaves so much unsaid, it is important to clarify your roles and responsibilities with supervisors before the school year begins. This conversation is crucial to setting yourself up for success in the multiple roles you may play as a coach.

What follows is a conversation between a coach, Jorge, and his new supervisor, the assistant principal, Wanda, to gain role clarity. Jorge is entering his first year as a coach at John Lewis Elementary; he coached for 3 years in another school. Jorge will work with Grades K–2, alongside Serena, the school's third–fifth-grade instructional coach. As you read this transcript, put a star in the margin by the questions that you might want to ask your supervisor or the things you might want to say to them.

JORGE:	Thank you for setting up this meeting with me, Wanda. I'm excited by this role, but to be honest I think I need more information to be successful in this role here.
WANDA:	Yes, Jorge, I can understand that. Coaching is still relatively new at our school, and I imagine you'll help design the role.
JORGE:	That's exciting to hear. I have a lot of ideas about how I'd like to support teachers. The description says I'll be working with K–2 teachers on lesson design and instructional practice, and that can mean a lot of things. What do you envision that looks like?
WANDA:	I envision that you're in classes at least three times a week, observing teachers at each grade level and having a follow-up conversation with them about their practice. I know coaching is confidential so I won't ask what you talk about or who you have visited. I also am hoping you can run a professional learning community for teachers in the culturally responsive teaching group. That will be about 1 hour a month after school on Tuesdays. And I'm hoping you and Serena will meet to talk about your coaching together, too. I would like to check in with you once a quarter to see

how it is going, too, and we can talk about trends in the feedback you're receiving. But I also have to be honest and say that I learned last year that I asked Serena to do too much, so I am still shaping this vision.

JORGE: It sounds like you have an expansive vision for what it looks like to support teachers to improve their teaching. This is exciting. Of these areas, what is the greatest priority for the school right now? And I'm also curious how that priority was determined?

WANDA: Good questions. You can design a schedule that works best, but the PLC and the meetings with Serena need to happen once a month. The greatest priority for the school is for teachers to differentiate their instructional practice and create more dynamic experiences that engage all students. I see connections between lesson design and pedagogy there. I notice that second graders in particular have a lot of seat time. I also notice that our Black and Brown students, especially our boys in kindergarten and first grade, are not thriving. Too many of them are being sent out of class for "acting out," and they don't have the opportunity to learn. That's why we have a priority on differentiating and creating engaging lessons.

JORGE: I appreciate your commitment to equity, and to be honest, one of the reasons I wanted to work here is because of this school's commitment to equity. Are teachers aware that these are priorities?

WANDA: Yes, I've talked about this at staff meetings and have shared reports with the school as well that note these trends at our site and at the district. But I think some teachers don't see how they contribute to inequities.

JORGE: That's definitely the case in many places. Since coaching is relatively new to this site, how has it been communicated to teachers? How have they responded to it?

WANDA: Teachers often are wary when they hear something from an administrator, so when I first talked about coaching a year ago people thought it was another layer of admin to "spy" on teachers. And a handful of teachers don't think they need coaching. We've only had coaching here for a short time, and not all teachers are on board; we say our culture is about growth, but I am not sure we are there yet. It is going to take some time. I did share that coaching is confidential, and I don't know what Serena talks about with those she is coaching. The feedback so far is mixed. In an anonymous survey Serena shared with Grade 3–5 teachers, the majority of teachers have appreciated the coaching, but some haven't worked with her at all.

JORGE:	I can talk more with Serena about this, but it sounds like I'll have to spend time building trust with teachers.
WANDA:	Yes, that's correct.
JORGE:	Building trust is critical everywhere, with everyone. I'll start with a conversation with Serena then. I'm curious: what indicates to you that coaching is working so far?
WANDA:	Last year the fourth-grade team did a lot more collaboration so students were having a more common class experience. Students completed an end-of-year STEM [science, technology, engineering, and math] project, and I saw high levels of engagement during my learning walks. I know Serena had been spending time in fourth-grade classrooms, and there were fewer incidences of discipline overall in that grade level. It may be too early to tell, but that gives me hope.
JORGE:	That sounds really promising. I'm excited to get started. Can we discuss how often you and I will meet? And perhaps it would be good to have times when you and I and Serena can meet. What do you think?
WANDA:	Yes, that sounds great. I'm glad you're here, Jorge.

Reflect

How did this conversation help you think about how to get clarity about your role?

Here are some more questions you can ask to get clarity on your role. Check the ones that might be useful for you to ask.

- ☐ How is coaching defined here? How has this definition been communicated to teachers?
- ☐ Who has explained what coaching is to teachers? When was the last time that happened?
- ☐ How has the rationale for coaching been explained to teachers? What's their understanding of who gets coaching and why?
- ☐ What do you see as the goal for coaching? How do you determine whether coaching has been successful?

- ☐ How are teachers invited to give feedback on coaching and on coaches? How frequently is their feedback solicited?
- ☐ How are you determining who engages in coaching? Is your vision that all teachers will work with me at some point over the year?
- ☐ How would you like me to share my schedule with you? How would you like me to let you know if my schedule changes?
- ☐ Do you expect me to be present at events like Back-to-School Night and student performances?
- ☐ How often would you like to meet? Will you have agendas for those meetings, or would you like to co-create the agendas?
- ☐ Do you have a preference for how I communicate with you? My preference is [fill in the blank]. How do you feel about that?
- ☐ What does professional development for coaches look like here? Is there a budget for my professional development?
- ☐ How will you give me feedback? How will I be evaluated? How will I know if you have concerns about my performance or if you're feeling good about it?
- ☐ What's the best way for me to give you feedback? How do you prefer to get feedback?

Is there anything else you want to ask your supervisor about to get clarity on your role? Jot down those questions here:

Creating Coaching Mantras

This activity will help you prepare the deepest parts of yourself to coach—and it'll help you create a constellation of guiding stars when you have challenging coaching moments.

In every conversation, we have a choice about where our words come from. They can come from the part of us that is frustrated, or they can come from a part of us that is hopeful. When we practice Transformational Coaching, we speak from the hopeful part of us, from potential and possibility. We speak from the part of us that lives in the world we'd like to live in. We create the future by behaving as if we were in that future now. Read on to understand what this means and how you can ask questions from the future.

Elena Reflects

Sometimes when I'm coaching, I get stumped. My mind goes blank, and I can't think of what to ask next. In those moments, I listen to an inner voice that guides me back to my vision for the world I'd like to live in.

The world I'd like to live in is far more humane than this one we're in now. It's a world of kindness and compassion, where we respect the truth of our biological, social, and emotional interconnectedness, where we honor that your well-being, health, safety, and freedom is intrinsically intertwined with my well-being, health, safety, and freedom and that of all our young people.

The world I'd like to live in is also slower than this one we're in now. It's a world in which we have time for meaningful conversation, time to listen to each other without feeling like we're going to be late for the next thing. It's a world where we can pause in our conversations and let what we're hearing and feeling sink deep into who we are.

The world I'd like to live in is a brave and bold world, where we've developed the skills to say what needs to be said in a way that someone else can hear it. It's a world where I speak my truths and you speak your truths. Where I listen to your truths and you listen to my truths. It's a world of open-hearted courage.

In those moments in a coaching conversation when I run up against a wall of some kind, when I'm at a loss for words, I know I need to return to my vision of the world I hope for. A handful of mantras guide me to pivot toward this potential and possibility:

- Do the human thing.
- Slow down.
- Trust the process.
- Be brave.

When I tell myself to *do the human thing*, I think about how I'd like to be treated. I anchor in compassion and interconnectedness. I think, *If I was sitting in front of me right now, what would I want someone to say to me?*

When I tell myself to *slow down,* I give myself permission to take a deep breath and allow for silence in the conversation. I might also tell my client, "I'm taking in what you said. I just need a moment to think."

When I tell myself to *trust the process*, I'm remembering that there are many factors at play in transformation and that just because I'm not seeing evidence of change in that moment doesn't mean that change can't happen.

When I tell myself to *be brave*, I remember that I have developed the communication skills to say what needs to be said, even if it feels uncomfortable. I remind myself that I can manage discomfort and that I have a responsibility to children and to the greater good.

Reflect

In the clouds, describe the world you'd like to live in. Jot down phrases, short descriptions, and anything that comes to mind. Start by simply completing the phrase, "In the world I'd like to live in. . ."

From *The Art of Coaching Workbook: Tools to Make Every Conversation Count* by Elena Aguilar. Copyright © 2021 by Elena Aguilar. Reproduced by permission.

Now, write down some short sayings or mantras that reflect your vision for the world you'd like to live in. You might find inspiration for these mantras in poems, contemplative or spiritual texts, song lyrics, or proverbs. Imagine these as lights that guide you, so write each inspiration in a star here.

During the next week, continue to think about sayings that help you anchor in your vision. Sometimes phrases float through our minds when we least expect it—when we're taking a shower or a walk or when we're just waking up. Stay open and receptive to those thoughts and phrases that remind you of the world you want to live in and add them on this page. You might also want to put a sticky note on this page and come back here as you work through the rest of this book so that you can add to your coaching mantras. Remember: the most powerful mantras reflect the world you want to live in.

Toward a Definition of Coaching

This activity will guide you to craft a cohesive, succinct, and personal definition of coaching.

Now that you've considered your mission and vision as a coach, now that you're clearer on the roles you'll be playing, and now that you've crafted some mantras to guide you through storms, it's time to bring all of these newfound understandings together. To do this, start by considering the context in which you coach. See how many of these questions you can answer:

- How is coaching defined in your school, district, or organization?
- Do teachers, coaches, administrators, and district personnel use the same definition?
- Where is this definition communicated? How is it communicated? (Can you find a written definition of coaching anywhere?)

We've found that it's common for coaches to work in organizations that don't have articulated, shared definitions of coaching. We encourage you to advocate for a process that results in clear, shared definitions, but we also encourage you to create your own definitions.

In Chapter 2 of *The Art of Coaching*, Elena lays out why we need a definition of coaching, outlines the two main approaches to coaching, and defines her model, Transformational Coaching (see pp. 18–29). We recommend you reread these pages before completing the following exercises.

Create

Draft your own elevator pitch for coaching. Imagine you were responding to a colleague who asked, "So what exactly do you do as a coach?" (If you're feeling stuck on this, reread *The Art of Coaching*, pp. 19, 24–25.)

Read your script aloud a few times until it feels natural. Try it in front of the mirror. When you feel ready, say it aloud to a trusted partner. How did it feel? Revise your pitch until it feels clear and compelling.

As a fun extension activity, see if you can craft a pitch to share with folks you meet at a cocktail party who have never heard about instructional coaching—those people who give you a very confused look when you say you're a coach because the only reference they have for coaches in schools are athletic coaches and you don't look like a volleyball or football coach. What can you concisely say to them about what you do?

Reflect

One reason to articulate your own definition of coaching is that it can help you in sticky situations when people ask you to do things outside the scope of your role as a coach. In the speech bubble on the left, you'll read a statement that you might hear from a teacher or staff member at a school. In the speech bubble on the right, write down what you could say in response that would help them understand your role. To extend this activity, practice your responses with a partner and practice responding to any others you may have heard. This can turn into a meaningful role-play practice.

From *The Art of Coaching Workbook: Tools to Make Every Conversation Count* by Elena Aguilar. Copyright © 2021 by Elena Aguilar. Reproduced by permission.

Creating a Coaching Manifesto

Do this activity to wrap up your understanding of who you want to be as a coach.

In the same way that schools and organizations have norms or community agreements that guide the behavior of their members, you need your own guidelines as a coach. These guidelines will remind you of how to behave and who to be. They will also reflect your beliefs. We like to think of the statement that encapsulates all of these ideas as a *manifesto*. A coaching manifesto emerges from your core values and your mission and vision. A manifesto articulates your intention for a way of being that emerges from your beliefs. It's the final activity for this chapter because it'll push you to synthesize your insights.

Because we change, our beliefs change over time. Consider this manifesto to be a *living document* that deserves annual revisiting and revision.

Here's a process to develop your coaching manifesto.

1. **Return to the core values exercise you completed in Chapter 1.** List those values here:

2. **Translate your core values into belief statements.**
   Your core values reflect beliefs, but they can also be the starting point for you to articulate other beliefs. For example, if one of your core values is appreciation, then a corresponding belief statement might be, "Always acknowledge the positive," which could guide your actions in a coaching conversation. Several beliefs can emerge from each core value. If your core value is kindness, then your beliefs could include, "There's no good reason to shout at anyone. Always put yourself in someone else's shoes when you feel judgmental of them. If someone doesn't act kind, that's because they've been hurt. Being unkind will not make them be kind." Generate at least five belief statements from your core values.

3. **Try on your beliefs.**
   This might sound strange, but imagine each belief statement as an outfit. Put it on and see how it feels. Say your belief statement aloud. As you try on each belief statement, see which ones give you the most energy and clarity. Use these questions to reflect on your belief statements:

   - Does the belief bring you a sense of relief?
   - Do you feel more empowered when you're wearing the belief?
   - Does the belief statement open more paths for action? Does it point to new directions?
   - Does your belief align with your core values?
   - Does it allow you to fulfill your vision for coaching?

4. **Put it all together.**
   Identify the 5–10 belief statements that feel most empowering. Then write a short paragraph to accompany each belief statement and explain what it means to you. You might want to reread Elena's coaching manifesto in *The Art of Coaching* (pp. 40–43).

   Draft your coaching manifesto. Include symbols or drawings if you'd like. Of course, you may need a lot more space, so perhaps you can write it in a computer document and then paste it in here.

From *The Art of Coaching Workbook: Tools to Make Every Conversation Count* by Elena Aguilar. Copyright © 2021 by Elena Aguilar. Reproduced by permission.

Depicting Your Role

We hope that by the end of this chapter you feel clearer on what your role is as a coach. We encourage you to draw or sketch an image that reflects this understanding.

CHAPTER 3

Understanding How to Coach Beliefs

It's likely that you've quickly discovered that one of the hardest things about coaching is confronting unconstructive beliefs your clients hold. Maybe you've heard teachers say things like, "That class is impossible! Nothing I do works with them," or "No one ever appreciates me!" You may have recognized that those are *beliefs*—and you weren't sure how to respond.

As you thought about how beliefs are hard to coach, did you reflect on your own beliefs? Perhaps you wondered why, as a teacher, you could always figure out how to engage a group of students or why you had affirming beliefs about your own abilities. Or maybe you frequently say things like, "I know we can figure this out!"

Transformational Coaches work to surface and explore beliefs and to shift those that don't serve the emotional and academic well-being of every child every day. If we don't do what we do with this intention, our work isn't likely to be transformational.

Transformational Coaches are acutely aware of our own beliefs—this is what makes us effective. We know what we believe about ourselves, about coaching, and about schools and the purpose of education.

This chapter will guide you to deeper understanding of beliefs and how to coach someone around their beliefs. There are also activities to help you dig deeper into your beliefs and to speak about them with others.

The National Public Radio show "This I Believe," inspired by radio pioneer Edward R. Murrow, invited folks from all walks of life to share their most closely held beliefs. Now it's your turn: What do you believe? Write as much as you want. Perhaps write about your beliefs about schools and kids and learning. Or write about your beliefs about everything in the world. It's your choice.

This I believe. . .

The Iceberg Principle: Examining Beliefs That Lurk Below the Surface

Here's why it's imperative that we coach beliefs: Everything we do, everything we say, emerges from a belief. Figure 3.1 depicts a concept that comes from organizational development and reminds us that some 90% of an iceberg lies below the surface of the water. Just as the ice that lurks beneath the water poses a danger to ships, beliefs that lie below the level of our awareness can sink our best efforts. However, when we consciously act from beliefs, they can serve and support us. Beliefs aren't necessarily good or bad, but they can be dangerous or underappreciated if they lie outside of our awareness.

Practice

Sometimes when we start exploring the beliefs that we're aware of, we become more aware of the beliefs that lie just below our consciousness. By articulating beliefs, you are paying attention to them in a way that pushes you be more conscious of them and to determine whether they are helping you (and other people) or hurting you (and other people).

Identify two beliefs that serve you and two beliefs that don't serve you (or haven't in the past). Then identify the actions that emerge from your beliefs. These could be beliefs related to your professional or personal life.

Figure 3.1: The Iceberg Principle

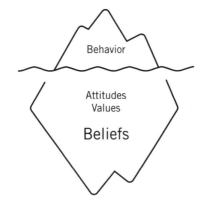

> **_Example of Elena's Beliefs_**
>
> ### A Belief That Serves Me
>
> *I believe* that I have important ideas and messages to share with others and that I have a right to speak my truths.
>
> *The actions that emerge from this belief* include that I write blogs and books and host a podcast in which I say what I want to say.
>
> ### A Belief That Doesn't Serve Me
>
> *I believe* that I am not taken as seriously as others (as men, as white people, as professors) because I don't have the status symbols that are most respected in this society.
>
> *The actions that emerge from this belief* include I'm afraid to submit articles for publication to big outlets and I can be deferential to the books and ideas of others when I'm asked to speak.

Beliefs That Serve Me

I believe. . .

The actions that emerge from this belief. . .

I believe. . .

The actions that emerge from this belief. . .

Beliefs That Don't Serve Me

I believe. . .

The actions that emerge from this belief. . .

I believe. . .

The actions that emerge from this belief. . .

Which Comes First—Beliefs Change or Behavior Change?

This activity will help you identify a path to coaching around beliefs.

Many new coaches become aware of the role that beliefs play when they hear their clients express one of two kinds of beliefs: beliefs about *themselves*, which might be limited beliefs; or beliefs about *students*, which might also be limited or inaccurate. The following statements that we've heard from teachers reflect beliefs:

- I'm so overwhelmed. I can't do this for another year.
- Nothing I try works with that student. I don't think anyone can get through to them.
- This district is hopeless. It'll never get things together.
- These kids are already so behind, so we've stopped using the textbook. I just want them to be happy when they're in my class.

Now, here's the first challenge for you to dive into. Can you identify the beliefs that are lurking below these statements? Imagine a teacher you've known saying one of these statements. What do you think they believe about themselves or their students that they're expressing in these words? Give it a try.

Statement	Underlying belief
I'm so overwhelmed. I can't do this for another year.	
Nothing I try works with that student. I don't think anyone can get through to them.	
This district is hopeless. It'll never get things together.	
These kids are already so behind, so we've stopped using the textbook. I just want them to be happy when they're in my class.	

Now it's your turn to think of some beliefs you've actually heard said by teachers in the recent or distant past. Can you come up with four things you've heard, and then can you identify what the underlying beliefs they are expressing might be?

Statement	Underlying belief

The first step in working with beliefs is to recognize when you hear one. Here's a key idea to remember:

A belief is a strongly held opinion.
A belief is not the truth—even if it feels like it is.

When we think about coaching beliefs in this way, it feels like a relief. A belief is not the truth. We know that opinions change (that's happened to us plenty of times), so thinking about beliefs as strongly held opinions makes us feel hopeful that we can effect meaningful change in schools.

Now the question for us to contemplate is this one: Where do we start? Do we change behaviors by coaching clients around their beliefs? It makes sense that if all of our actions emerge from beliefs, then to create sustainable, transformational change that gets at the root cause of problems we should start by coaching those beliefs. And then after we've coached to surface, explore, and shift underlying problematic beliefs, then we can coach behaviors, right?

What at first might seem a straightforward situation soon becomes a chicken-and-egg scenario. Consider that behaviors create beliefs, which in turn create behaviors, which then create more beliefs. Stepping outside schools to think about this cycle of behaviors and beliefs can be helpful to understanding how it shapes all we do. Imagine you decide you want to run a 10K, even though you can't run a mile. Every day you run a little bit more. After 3 months, you run a 10K. You now believe you can run. Now you decide you want to run a marathon, and you believe you can. Eventually, training hard, you do run that marathon. And now you firmly believe you can run a marathon and pursue another physically challenging goal.

Think about your own life and experiences. Can you recall a behavior that led to a belief?

So where do we start coaching—behaviors or beliefs? The answer: Coach behaviors and beliefs at the same time.

Practice

Scenario 1

You've just observed Mr. Jimenez introduce a new novel to his ninth graders. He says things like, "We'll take this book slowly since I know it'll be tough. There's a lot of language that you won't know." And, "I'll be reading big portions of this aloud, so you'll mostly be listening." You know you need to surface his underlying beliefs about his students' reading abilities and about how to teach reading. You also want to share some reading strategies that he could implement with students tomorrow. Consider the following responses.

- I'm curious about your thoughts on reading aloud. What do you hope students will learn through that activity?

- What do you know about your students' reading abilities? What data do you have? What specifically in this novel do you anticipate will be challenging for students to understand?
- What are your beliefs about how students improve their reading skills?
- It sounds like you have concerns about your students' ability to understand the vocabulary in this novel. If that's the case, I'd love to share some vocabulary front-loading strategies with you that could be helpful.
- I'm hearing that you're aware that this book could be challenging for your students. There are different ways we can scaffold texts. Which strategies have you tried before?
- It sounds like you have reliable data about your students' reading skills, and I'm assuming that among your students there's a range of ability. How about if we look at that data in more detail and figure out who needs differentiated instruction with this novel?

You could use all of these responses with Mr. Jimenez—they all explore behaviors and beliefs. What order would you go in? Where would you start? Number the bullet points, and then explain your rationale.

Scenario 2

Ms. Applegate is a new first-grade teacher. She is distressed by what she says is her students' inability to behave like they're in school. "I can't believe how many of them think it's okay to jump on furniture or run around the class. It's like they think they're still on the yard. When I ask them kindly to take their seats, they laugh at me. I tell them I'll just wait until they've settled down and are ready to learn, but yesterday I waited for 15 minutes and they just ignored me. I don't know what to do."

What are the beliefs you hear Ms. Applegate expressing?

What are a couple of questions you could ask Ms. Applegate to explore her beliefs?

What are a couple of questions you could ask Ms. Applegate (or suggestions you could make) to coach her on her behaviors?

Where would you start in the cycle of coaching behaviors and beliefs? With questions about beliefs? Or suggestions for behavior? Why?

The Ladder of Inference in Action

This activity will demonstrate how to use the Ladder of Inference in a coaching conversation.

The Ladder of Inference, originally developed by Chris Argyris, is an invaluable tool for helping us see how our beliefs are formed and why we do what we do (Figure 3.2). The model describes how we unconsciously climb up a mental pathway of increasing abstraction that can reinforce existing assumptions and result in misguided actions.

Figure 3.2: The Ladder of Inference

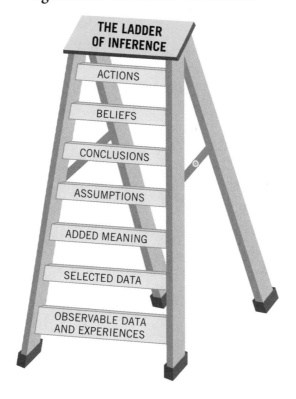

In *The Art of Coaching*, Elena describes a conversation in which she uses the Ladder to coach a principal after observing a classroom together (pp. 36–38). The conversation between them is not included in *The Art of Coaching*, so we've provided it here.

Round 1

We recommend you read through this transcript a few times. On your first read you'll get familiar with the situation and how the conversation unfolds. Use these codes to engage with the text:

✓ = I have said this when I've coached someone.

! = This would be hard for me to say. It would feel awkward.

☆ = I'd like to incorporate this into coaching conversations. I want to say this.

→ = I wish someone would ask me this question. I want to think about this for myself.

COACH:	Would you be willing to explore how you arrived at the decision to have Ms. Smith implement a behavior management program immediately?
PRINCIPAL:	[Sighs] Sure, but I have a feeling I'm not gonna like this.
COACH:	[Smiles] Let's just see. If nothing else, this could be a helpful exercise to better understand the beliefs you bring with you into a classroom observation.
PRINCIPAL:	Okay.
COACH:	Let's start by revisiting what you observed in Ms. Smith's room.
PRINCIPAL:	It was a disaster! The kids were totally out of control, and she was wholly unequipped to keep the class in line.
COACH:	[Gently interrupting] Those sound like *interpretations*, and we'll definitely get to those. For the moment, let's try to stick with observable facts. What would a video of Ms. Smith's classroom this morning show?
PRINCIPAL:	Well, it would show the teacher asking questions and a boy shouting out the answer. It would show the teacher ignoring that boy and calling on a girl with her hand raised. It would show that boy accusing her of ignoring him and other boys agreeing loudly.
COACH:	"Accuse" is an interpretation. I know, it's hard to stick to facts. A good rule of thumb is that adjectives, adverbs, and emotionally charged words are usually interpretation. The fact is that a boy said, "How come you don't call on me?" made a sound, and put his head on the desk. The fact is that a boy said, "She always calls on girls."
PRINCIPAL:	Someone said that? I must have missed it. I was so focused on the boy in the back with his head down and the fact that Ms. Smith didn't reprimand him.

COACH: I get it. It's really hard for us humans to see the world impassively. I'd love to share a graphic with you of a concept that's really helpful. [Opens to a graphic of the Ladder of Inference in her coaching binder.] This image of a ladder represents how we move, usually subconsciously, from experience to meaning to reaction. Even in this conversation we're having, we're already on the second rung of the ladder. Each of us is selecting data from all the observable data, from what a video might have captured.

PRINCIPAL: [Studying the graphic] Hmm. . . Kind of makes me wish we did have a video recording. I wonder what else I missed.

COACH: You know, I often use video when coaching teachers for that very reason. [Pauses] So what else stood out to you?

PRINCIPAL: I noticed Ms. Smith speaking very softly. Hmm. . . As I look back, I'm remembering some things that I didn't focus on at the time, but that might be significant. Like, I remember her talking to that boy who put his head down at the start of class. He's one of our star basketball players.

COACH: That's great. Even just acknowledging that there are the facts, and then there are the facts we pay attention to, can help broaden what we notice. Let's pick up one of the data points that has some emotional charge to it for you.

PRINCIPAL: Sure, let's go with the boy speaking out of turn and then checking out.

COACH: So, the boy said, "Why don't you call on me?" and put his head on the desk, and the meaning you made is that he was speaking out of turn and was disengaged. Does that seem accurate?

PRINCIPAL: [Breathes deeply] Yes, though when you put it that way, I can see that I'm already on rung three. That's the meaning I attached to the data, not the data itself.

COACH: Okay. Are there other meanings you could make from this data?

PRINCIPAL: Hmm. . . As I look back over the lesson as a whole, it's possible he had a point. She only called on girls during the 15 minutes we were in there. And it's possible that he was disengaged, but it's also possible that he was frustrated, that he *wanted* to engage and was feeling shut out.

COACH: How do you think your cultural and personal background affected the meaning that you made of what you saw?

PRINCIPAL: Well, when I was going through school it *never* would have been acceptable to speak out like that in class, even if the teacher was favoring girls. Students should show respect to their teachers no matter what.

COACH: That's super helpful to name. And I can see that we're already climbing up to step 4. You assumed from his behaviors that he doesn't respect his teacher.

PRINCIPAL: [Pauses to think] Yes. . . Yes, I do think, well I did assume that.

COACH: [Stays silent, as the principal appears deep in thought]

PRINCIPAL: I'm not quite ready to let go of that idea. But I can see now that it's an assumption, and I can see how I climbed up the ladder to reach it.

COACH: Great. Using the Ladder of Inference isn't necessarily about changing what we think; it's about making this whole process visible to us so we don't go through these loops on autopilot. It's about creating openings to notice more of the observable data, question the meaning we make of it, and maybe follow that through to a different set of conclusions and actions if needed.

PRINCIPAL: Yeah. I definitely assumed from what I saw this morning that the boys in that class don't respect Ms. Smith and that she either doesn't want to confront them or doesn't know how.

COACH: And what conclusion did you draw from that?

PRINCIPAL: That she needs a strict behavior management plan in place immediately.

COACH: Can you identify how your background led you to that conclusion?

PRINCIPAL: Well, like I said, when I was growing up the teacher gave directions, students cooperated, and that was it. I would never have dreamed of acting like the boys in that class! I'd have been sent straight to the principal's office and likely chewed out at home. I've always known how to toe the line. It's part of self-respect, you know? Show respect to others, and they'll respect you back. And look where it's gotten me. I'm a principal myself now. If I'd spoken to my superiors the way that boy spoke to Ms. Smith, I'd never be in this role. They've got to learn that there's a time and a place for speaking your mind.

COACH: I can hear some beliefs surfacing now. Shall we name them?

PRINCIPAL: Hmm. . . Well, yes. I believe you're not going to get far in life being disrespectful. And I believe kids should practice that while they're in school. I believe teachers deserve respect. It's a hard job.

COACH: Are there any other beliefs you might hold based on the meaning you've made and the conclusions you've drawn?

PRINCIPAL: [Sighs] Yeah. I believe strict discipline systems are needed to keep kids in line.

COACH: [Smiles warmly] Do you believe that?

PRINCIPAL: No. No, I don't. [Pauses] I mean, I was taught to believe that. But it's not actually what I think. I know now that it's the culture in the classroom, the relationship between teachers and their students that leads to productive behavior. I mean, I was respectful to my teachers growing up, but I didn't like very many of them. The classes where I learned the most, where I really felt motivated and like I was learning more than just the basics—those were with teachers who really took the time to get to know me, to connect with me. And I can see that same pattern in my work now. I'll give anyone a basic level of respect no matter what, but if someone wants me to go above and beyond, well, I've got to like them first. [Pauses again] I think I was looking for a quick fix. I know those boys. I know their potential. And I know Ms. Smith is struggling. I don't want to walk in there a month from now and see the same kind of scene.

COACH: I hear that. I can hear how much you care about Ms. Smith and those boys. And now we've arrived at the top of a new ladder. From the set of beliefs you just articulated, what actions might you take?

PRINCIPAL: Well, I'm not sure a tough behavior management system is the right approach anymore. For one thing, if relationships are the issue, strict discipline could only make things worse. I'm thinking about that comment you picked up on, about her always calling on girls. I'd like to know whether that's true and why.

COACH: It sounds like you'd like to go back to the bottom of the ladder and gather more data.

PRINCIPAL: [Laughs] Yeah. I suppose I would.

Reflect

How do you think the principal felt during this conversation? How do you know?

How do you think the coach felt? How do you know?

What assumptions do you hold about unpacking beliefs in a coaching conversation?

Round 2

Now that you've read through the scene and reflected a bit, reread the transcript. This time, label each of the coach's lines with the name of one of the six rungs of the Ladder of Inference. Notice how the Ladder provides a structure for the coach to support the principal to examine his beliefs and intended actions in this situation.

Reflect

What might be the impact for the principal of having used the Ladder with the coach to unpack his beliefs?

What might be the impact for Ms. Smith and other teachers at his school?

What might be the impact for students?

A final comment on the conversation that just unfolded. Notice that the coach did not say, "Wow, you are way up the Ladder of Inference. Stop jumping to conclusions." The purpose of this tool is not to diagnose or critique but to make thinking visible. When we are aware of the beliefs, biases, and assumptions that guide our behaviors, we see more possibilities and can choose to align our actions to our deepest values.

The Ladder of Inference Questioning Strategies

This activity will introduce powerful questions to help people reflect on their journeys up the Ladder of Inference.

The Ladder of Inference is one of the most powerful tools in Transformational Coaching, but it can also feel like one of the most challenging to use. We highly recommend developing a practice of using it yourself. Coaches also have beliefs worth unpacking. Getting comfortable examining your own thinking will better equip you to lead clients through the process.

Central to this process is the separation of fact from story. Facts are the raw data as a video camera would record them. Story is the intricate web of meaning we weave around those facts. Almost all conscious thought is story. A fact could be, "X said ___." We might tell ourselves the story that "X *rudely contradicted* me." (Hint: adverbs and adjectives are nearly always story.)

The following questions offer guidance in recognizing and, when appropriate, shifting our stories. It is not necessary to ask all questions at each rung of the Ladder. Use those that feel most helpful. As you build fluency using this tool, you might find yourself combining steps like assumptions and conclusions. Finally, we are presenting these sequentially even though traditional graphics of the Ladder (like the one on page 68) visually place data at the bottom to convey the idea of climbing up toward action.

Goal	Questions
DATA	
Separate fact from story by identifying the raw data.	• I hear that you saw/heard/experienced _____. (Paraphrase) • If you imagine that your mind is a video camera recording everything, can you name the specific data points that you latched onto? • What else might a camera have captured that we haven't named yet?

Goal	Questions
MEANING	
Notice our interpretations of what happened.	<ul><li>I hear that you saw _____ and the meaning you made was _____. Does that seem accurate?</li><li>Are there any other meanings you could make from this data?</li><li>How might the meaning you made be informed by your cultural and personal background?</li></ul>
ASSUMPTIONS	
Identify the characteristics we are assigning, which may be informed by past experience or our own existing beliefs.	<ul><li>What did you assume about _____ based on the meaning you made?</li><li>Can you identify the roots of that assumption? Where do you think it came from?</li><li>Are there any other assumptions you could make based on this meaning or the data itself?</li></ul>
CONCLUSIONS	
Name the judgments we are making based on the web of meaning we've woven.	<ul><li>Given everything you've named, what is your final verdict on this situation?</li><li>I hear that you've drawn a conclusion about_____. Can you identify the assumptions on which that's built?</li><li>Can you identify how your cultural and personal background have led you to the conclusion you've drawn?</li></ul>
BELIEFS	
Articulate a belief that has been formed or reinforced.	<ul><li>When you think these things about _____, what does that lead you to believe?</li><li>What assumptions or experiences might have led you to that belief?</li><li>Are there any other beliefs you might hold based on the meaning you've made and the assumptions you've drawn?</li><li>If this is the belief you hold, how will that affect the actions you take?</li></ul>
ACTIONS	
Connect the action we took or intend to take with the insights surfaced at other rungs of the ladder.	<ul><li>Can you identify the belief that's underneath that action?</li><li>What might be the consequences—intended or unintended—of acting out of this belief?</li><li>Do any other actions come to mind having now made your thinking visible?</li></ul>

Let's try out these questions and consider how to use the Ladder of Inference with clients.

1. Think of a recent situation in which you are certain that your reaction was the right one. Use the questions to trace your journey up the Ladder.

    Here's an example from Laurelin: *I was absolutely right that <u>my daughter should turn off the TV</u>.*

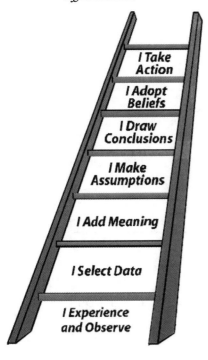

I take the remote and turn off the TV without a word.

↑ She can't regulate TV time on her own. I need stricter limits.

↑ She should turn off the TV immediately.

↑ Kids shouldn't watch more than 1 hour of TV per day.

↑ She's watching too much TV.

↑ Daughter has been watching TV for 75 minutes.

↑ Daughter is watching TV.

Your turn!

1. *I was absolutely right that* _____.

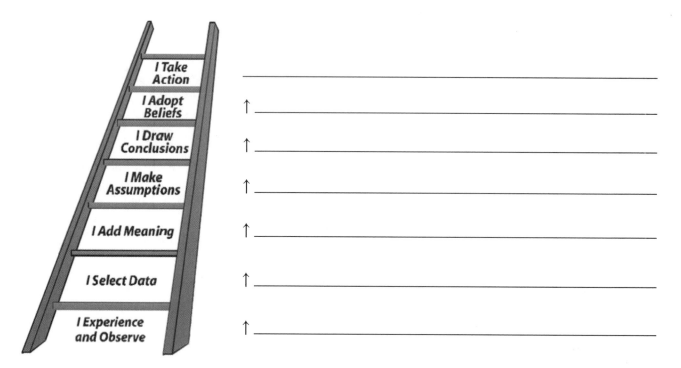

2. Now that you see your thinking laid bare, where along the way might you have thought something different?

3. Why might it be important to explore how beliefs are formed, and why we do what we do? You might reflect on the situation you just unpacked or more generally about the potential that lies in deconstructing your beliefs.

4. What is the value of exploring beliefs in the context of coaching?

5. How are you feeling about using the Ladder of Inference with your clients?

    a. If you feel ready and excited, what's your next step?
    b. If you don't yet feel ready or aren't excited, what are two low-stakes ways you could practice using it this week?

Exploring Beliefs About Equity

Do this activity to clarify your feelings and beliefs about coaching for equity.

There's so much to say about coaching for equity that Elena has written a whole book about the subject. She's also planning a workbook to accompany that book, but it'll take a minute before that's in your hands. A first step in coaching for equity is to get clear on your feelings and beliefs. Remember: A Transformational Coach always starts with themselves. Whenever we want to coach someone else on something—beliefs about their own efficacy as an educator or beliefs about racial injustice—we start by reflecting on our own beliefs on those topics.

Which of these statements do you agree with?

☐   It is a coach's responsibility to address inequities when they are observed.

☐   A coach shouldn't raise observation of inequities unless it's part of the teacher's coaching goals. If a teacher doesn't expect the coach to talk about these things, the coach shouldn't break that unspoken agreement.

☐   If a coach is going to talk about educational inequity, they should have training in how to do this. They need to know what racism is, how to create antiracist classrooms, and how to talk about inequities.

☐   A coach doesn't need to have extensive training in antiracism to address inequities that they observe.

☐   When a coach witnesses inequities, it's their responsibility to tell their principal and let the principal address the teacher.

☐   Coaching around issues of race and other biases is uncomfortable and hard.

☐   Coaching around issues of race and other biases can be healing for everyone.

Now it's your turn to further surface your beliefs about coaching for equity. Complete the following statements. Allow the sentence starter to help you dig into your feelings and beliefs.

Elena Reflects

When I think about coaching around issues of equity, I feel nervous, excited, hopeful, and anxious. I feel a lot of pressure to "do it right." I feel like it's my responsibility, however, and I know that I won't die from discomfort.

When I think about coaching around issues of equity, I feel. . .

When I think about having conversations about race and racism, I feel. . .

I believe that coaching for equity is. . .

I believe that talking about race and racism is. . .

If a coach is going to talk about educational inequity, then I believe they should. . .

For Further Learning

→ Read *Coaching for Equity.*

→ Enroll in a virtual *Coaching for Equity* learning experience and practice these skills with others (information at http://www.brightmorningteam.com).

Reflecting on Educational Philosophies

This activity will help you be explicit about the beliefs that inform your work in education.

While some coaching approaches advocate that coaches remain as neutral as possible, this is not an option for coaches seeking to transform schools into places that serve every student every day. The work of a Transformational Coach is inherently mission driven, and that mission is deeply rooted in what you believe to be the purpose of education.

Table 3.1 outlines the most common beliefs about the purpose of education. Reflect on how you feel about each one and whether it reflects your values and beliefs about education. Then consider which of these philosophies your school or district holds—either explicitly or implicitly.

Table 3.1: Educational Philosophies

Educational philosophy	My values **1** = very low value **2** = low value **3** = medium/neutral **4** = value **5** = high value	My district's values **1** = very low value **2** = low value **3** = medium/neutral **4** = value **5** = high value
Social reconstructionism. The purpose of education is to help students become good citizens who can help the world.		
Academic rationalism. The purpose of education is for adults to transmit a body of knowledge to children.		
Critical pedagogy. The purpose of education is to raise students' awareness so that they can be change agents in their own lives and in society.		

(Continued)

Educational philosophy	My values 1 = very low value 2 = low value 3 = medium/neutral 4 = value 5 = high value	My district's values 1 = very low value 2 = low value 3 = medium/neutral 4 = value 5 = high value
Self-actualization. The purpose of education is to bring out the unique qualities, potentials, and creativity in each child.		
Technologism. The purpose of education is to master skills, perform well on exams, and meet accountability expectations.		
Religious orthodoxy. The purpose of education is to teach the habits and values of a religious faith.		
Cognitive process. The purpose of education is to help students learn to think, reason, and solve problems.		

It may have been many years since you were last asked to articulate your educational philosophy—or you may never have engaged in such an exercise. Regardless, it is helpful to ask ourselves the following questions periodically because our philosophy of education can evolve over time.

I believe the purpose of education is to. . .

This is important because...

To reach this aim, we need teachers who _____ [verbs] and who are _____ [adjectives].

We need school leaders who _____ and who are _____.

We need schools that...

Return to these responses after 1–2 weeks. How do you feel reading them? If they don't light a fire in your belly, revise them. Repeat this process every week or so until you have an articulation of your educational philosophy that excites and inspires you. Coaches who hold a conscious understanding of their educational philosophy are more effective.

Once you're clear on your educational philosophy, represent it nonlinguistically in the form of a picture. You might include students, teachers, or classrooms in your drawing (or all of these) and symbolic representations of that philosophy. You're going to internalize and remember your educational philosophy much better if you take this time to draw it.

How can you remember to come back and do this last step? Maybe you can set a phone reminder or put a sticky note on your computer. Do something so that you'll remember to come back to this final step in a week or two.

From *The Art of Coaching Workbook: Tools to Make Every Conversation Count* by Elena Aguilar. Copyright © 2021 by Elena Aguilar. Reproduced by permission.

CHAPTER 4

Unpacking the Coaching Lenses

*T**his chapter will guide you through the application of the coaching lenses to deepen your understanding of them. Unlike the other chapters in this workbook, this one is to be engaged in as a whole. It won't make sense if you try to do just one activity. We suggest you read Chapter 4 of* The Art of Coaching *first.*

We're about to plunge you into an engrossing story about a coach who couldn't figure out how to work with an experienced teacher. But first, a few things.

Remember when we told you about thinking tools? (They were described in "Presenting the Three Buckets" in the introduction to this workbook). Well, the coaching lenses are like the meta, master set of thinking tools—in fact, all the other thinking tools that we're sharing with you could be mapped onto the coaching lenses.

This is a chapter that'll yield the greatest insights when engaged in with a learning community. Hearing how others understand, interpret, and apply the lenses will radically deepen your abilities to use them.

In this chapter, you'll first read a story. Then you'll explore how to apply the coaching lenses so that you can appreciate and understand the complexities of the situation. After that, you'll use the lenses to gain deeper insight into yourself. Finally, we'll share some additional reflections on the lenses. This content might feel dense: Take breaks, walk around the block, drink water. It'll transform your coaching.

A Story About a Teacher Who Just Wanted to Plan

Whitney, a Black woman in her early 50s, was a well-respected teacher in her suburban elementary school. She'd been on the fourth-grade team for more than a decade, serving intermittently as team lead for much of that time. While she wasn't known to be innovative, she was considered reliable and effective. Her colleagues liked her. Students learned. And the years went by.

It became clear, however, that Whitney had lost the spark she'd once had. She was becoming a complacent, and occasionally cynical, veteran teacher. She often graded work during the department meetings that she didn't lead. She didn't offer to share supplies or plans with colleagues as much as she once had. When the principal observed Whitney, he noted that lessons progressed smoothly and that students were focused and on task. But he also noticed the lack of joy in the teacher and students.

That year, the school hired Maren, a reading specialist, to work with teachers and grade-level teams to improve literacy instruction. Maren, a White woman in her mid-30s, had trained as a Transformational Coach. After a few weeks observing team meetings and teachers, Maren was delighted when Whitney asked for coaching.

"Is now still a good time?" Maren said, as she poked her head into the classroom. Whitney was behind her desk, staring at her computer screen.

"Yes. Sure. Come on in," she replied. Maren sat at a table near the front of the room. A few minutes later, Whitney shut her laptop, grabbed her planning book, and joined Maren. "I'm glad you were free today," Whitney said. "I've started planning my next reading unit and wanted to run some ideas past you."

Maren could have predicted that Whitney would want to discuss curriculum—it was all she *ever* talked about in department meetings—but she'd hoped to address student engagement. Maren had noted the low energy in Whitney's class. She knew from her own experience how much more she enjoyed teaching when she had deep relationships with her students and adapted lessons to their needs and interests. Although she felt disappointed, Maren said, "Sure. What have you got?"

Whitney spoke at length about the book choices she'd been mulling over, the standards she needed to address in that unit, and the materials she'd used in the past. She'd read two dozen new books over the summer and was excited to design units around them. Maren was impressed with Whitney's dedication. "So how can I help?" Maren asked.

"Well, I'd like a thinking partner as I backward plan the unit," Whitney replied. "I've pulled the seven target standards from the district's website. And I'd like to use these texts," she said, gesturing at three books nearby. "I thought maybe you'd have some new templates or processes we could use for planning."

"Oh!" Maren said, taken aback. "Well, no. I mean, that's not what I'm here for."

"Then what are you here for?" Whitney asked.

"Well," Maren took a long breath. She recalled how she'd practiced describing coaching to teachers. "I'm here to support your learning and leadership so that you can reach your professional goals and better support student learning. I'm here to help foster students' love of reading so that they can be successful in school and beyond. But I also like to think that I'm here to help nurture your love of teaching, so that you can feel successful and fulfilled in your role."

"But aren't you a reading specialist?" Whitney said. "Aren't you here to improve reading instruction? And doesn't that begin with planning?" Her brows were furrowed.

"Yes," Maren replied. "I *can* help with unit planning, especially if that's in service of a larger goal."

"Like what?"

"Well, why don't you tell me about some of your goals as a teacher."

"I really don't know what you mean," Whitney said, leaning back. "I've been doing this for 16 years. It's the same rodeo every year. What keeps things interesting for me is changing up the texts, coming up with new lesson ideas, varying my instruction. My performance evaluations are consistently good, so I don't really have *goals*, except perhaps 'keep it interesting.'"

She looks annoyed, Maren thought. *Maybe I should just go along with unit planning for now until we've built a better relationship.* Maren reflexively questioned her own competence. She'd been a kindergarten teacher and had only recently completed her reading specialist endorsement, so she felt a bit out of her league planning fourth-grade reading units. Moreover, she wasn't convinced that co-planning units was the best use of her role or her specific expertise—unless that planning was in service of a teacher's professional goals. The rest of the conversation progressed in a similarly awkward manner.

Toward the end of the conversation, Maren abruptly asked, "I'm curious—what do you look for in selecting new books for your students?"

"Since you ask," said Whitney, "I try to find something they'll connect with. You're new here, so you probably don't know that our student population has changed significantly over the past few years. There are a lot of immigrant families moving into the community, so I have a lot more English learners now. We used to be about 50-50 African American students and White students. Now I've got Latinos, African refugees, Pacific Islanders. It's the American melting pot in my classroom. It's hard to find books that everyone will like."

Maren saw an opening to explore Whitney's views toward her students, but she wasn't entirely sure how to proceed. She jotted down what Whitney had said in her coaching notebook and made a mental note to herself to come back to this.

Maren left the meeting with a long list of next steps that included, "Read *Esperanza Rising*" and "generate a 5-week unit template." Several items felt out of scope for her role, but she was grateful to have an inroad to working with Whitney.

The next morning, Maren saw Mr. Felding, the principal, in the hall. "Maren! How are you settling in?" he asked in his usual loud and jovial tone.

"Just fine, Mr. Felding, thank you. I think staff are starting to get used to me, and I've begun working with a few teachers."

"Wonderful! Say, are you working with Whitney yet? Something's been off in her room lately."

In her head, Maren replayed the coaching confidentiality agreements. "Yes," she answered. "We've started talking."

"About what?"

"That would be a great thing to check in with her on," Maren replied.

"Well, I don't care as long as you can bring a little life into that room! It's like a dead zone walking past her door every day," Mr. Felding lifted his arms in front of him and imitated a zombie walking.

Maren laughed nervously. "We'll see what we can do." And she hurried back to her office.

Maren and Whitney met several times to plan her upcoming reading unit. Once, hoping to learn more about Whitney's pathway into teaching, Maren asked an open question about her journey. Whitney responded briefly with, "My mother was a teacher." Another time, Maren tried to broach the subject of Whitney's professional learning goals, and again Whitney talked about trying to keep things interesting for herself.

Three weeks after they'd first met, Whitney passed Maren in the office. "Now that I'm starting the unit, I suppose we're done coaching. Thank you for your support. I think this is going to be a great unit."

"I'm glad you feel that way. I'd be happy to work together anytime." Maren replied, unsure of what else to say. Whitney smiled and turned back to the copy machine. As Maren walked back to her office, she became aware of her disappointment. *This isn't what I imagined I'd do as a Transformational Coach,* she mused. *But I don't know what I did wrong. I don't know what else to try.*

Putting on the Lenses

We're now going to guide you through a detailed analysis of the Maren-Whitney situation through the coaching lenses. The lenses expand our thinking and stretch us beyond what might naturally occur to us. They invite us into a richer, more multifaceted relationship with our clients and their dilemmas and move us beyond concluding that our client is "the problem" or that we are "the problem."

As a reminder, six of these lenses are described in detail in *The Art of Coaching* (pp. 49–62). The seventh, the lens of compassion, is not in *The Art of Coaching* but was added later by Elena to underscore the importance of empathy in Transformational Coaching. We also want to acknowledge that the first six lenses were created by the National Equity Project and are printed with their permission.

You can download the coaching lenses from our website, http://www.brightmorningteam.com.

As a reminder:

- Each lens is composed of a set of *assumptions* and *questions*.
- The assumptions are simple and memorable statements that represent the key ideas from the research and theory that inform each lens. Please note that sometimes we think of assumptions as being something bad, but they aren't. They're conclusions or summary statements.
- The questions arise from the assumptions. When we consider the questions in terms of a particular dilemma, we reflect on how they might direct our work with our clients. However, coaches can also turn the questions on themselves (and we'll show you what this sounds like).

First, you'll read the assumptions and questions associated with the lenses and do some digestion of them. Then you'll apply your understanding of each lens to the Maren-Whitney scenario.

Lens of Adult Learning

The lens of adult learning is foundational to how we view our clients, which is why we're starting here. People come to you for coaching to *learn* and *grow*. While their stated goals might be around improving student outcomes, taking on a new leadership role, or strengthening relationships, they will not reach their goals without learning. Viewed in this way, it becomes clear that the hurdles in the way of clients' goals can be overcome by *learning*.

Understand the Lens

Read the assumptions and questions for this lens and use these annotations:

 Ideas that spark new thinking

? Ideas you don't fully understand

In the margins, expand on your annotations and capture reflections. What thoughts and questions arise as you read these lists?

ADULT LEARNING
ASSUMPTIONS
<ul><li>Problems of change are problems of learning.</li><li>Adults (and children) must feel safe to learn.</li><li>Adults want to be the origin of our own learning; we want to control aspects of it.</li><li>People can be only where they are; we can meet adult learners only where they are.</li><li>Life experiences impact how we learn.</li><li>Adults come to learning with a wide range of previous experiences, knowledge, interests, and competencies.</li><li>Every human being is on a path from somewhere to somewhere; we must discover where people have been and where they're going.</li><li>We all enter the work of equity and justice from very different starting points.</li><li>If you don't acknowledge progress, you lose trust.</li><li>Adults want and need feedback.</li><li>The values that we hold around learning and education influence how we guide adult learners; we need clarity on what those values are.</li></ul>

- What is the gap between current reality and the goal?
- What is the goal or objective? What does exemplary performance in this role look like? How has that been communicated?
- What progress has been made toward this goal?
- What is going well? Which strengths can be built on?
- What are the gaps in ability? Skill? Knowledge? Will? Capacity? Emotional intelligence? Cultural competency?
- Is there evidence of prior learning?
- Does the will for learning exist? How do I know if it does or doesn't?
- Is this a safe space for learning?
- How is this person owning their learning? How can they own it more fully?
- What do I know about where this person is in their learning?
- What do I know about where this person is coming from? How can I more deeply understand their path?

Apply the Lens

Reread the story of Whitney and Maren. Imagine that you are wearing glasses that allow you to see only the elements that are relevant to the lens of adult learning. Complete your analysis in the table that follows the example.

The lens of adult learning	Example Analysis
An assumption that helps me understand the situation	*Adults want and need feedback.*
Insights about the situation when I consider this assumption	*I wonder what kind of feedback Whitney has gotten on her teaching over the past few years. She says her performance reviews have been good. Does she know that her principal has concerns?*
One or two questions from the lens that feel relevant	*Is there evidence of prior learning?*
Questions I could ask this client	*I could ask Whitney about the last time she made a significant change in her teaching. What prompted the change? How did she prepare for it? What did it feel like? What was the impact?*

Your Analysis	
The lens of adult learning	**Analysis**
An assumption that helps me understand the situation	
Insights about the situation when I consider this assumption	
One or two questions from the lens that feel relevant	
Questions I could ask this client	

Lens of Change Management

The lens of adult learning invites us to consider problems of change as eminently coachable problems of learning. While it is essential to relate to our clients as adult learners, we also acknowledge that what brings them to coaching is usually the desire to change something. The lens of change management compels us to consider the conditions in which learning and change happen.

Understand the Lens

Read the assumptions and questions for this lens and use these annotations:

  Ideas that spark new thinking

? Ideas you don't fully understand

In the margins, expand on your annotations and capture reflections. What thoughts and questions arise as you read these lists?

CHANGE MANAGEMENT

ASSUMPTIONS

- Beneficial change is possible in any situation.
- Building on strengths can lead to positive change.
- Change can be studied, understood, and influenced.
- These conditions need to be present for successful change: leadership, vision, skills, incentives, resources, and a clear plan of action.
- People need will, skill, knowledge, and capacity to change.
- An organizational identity conflict can be a step toward organizational change.

QUESTIONS

- What are the conditions for change in this situation?
- What's working in this situation?
- Which strengths can be built on?
- Where are the opportunities for leveraging change? What threats to change are present?
- What is the vision people that working toward?
- Which skills do people need to achieve the vision? What knowledge is necessary?
- Do people have the skills and knowledge necessary to implement change?
- Does the will for change exist here? Where?
- What incentives are in place for people to change?
- What resources are available to support change?

Apply the Lens

Reread the story of Whitney and Maren. Imagine that you are wearing glasses that allow you to see only the elements that are relevant to the lens of change management. Complete your analysis in the table that follows the example.

	Example
The lens of change management	**Analysis**
An assumption that helps me understand the situation	*People need will, skill, knowledge, and capacity to change.*

From *The Art of Coaching Workbook: Tools to Make Every Conversation Count* by Elena Aguilar. Copyright © 2021 by Elena Aguilar. Reproduced by permission.

Example

The lens of change management	Analysis
Insights about the situation when I consider this assumption	*I wonder which of these are present for Whitney and which might be gaps. Does she have the will to explore student engagement? Does she have the emotional capacity to do so?*
One or two questions from the lens that feel relevant	*What's working in this situation?*
Questions I could ask this client	*This question refocuses my attention from all the things that aren't working. The principal says students are on task when he observes, so management isn't an issue. Whitney puts a lot of thought into planning and tries to select books her students will enjoy. I'd like to ask, "What do you think is going particularly well in your reading instruction this year?"*

Your Analysis

The lens of change management	Analysis
An assumption that helps me understand the situation	
Insights about the situation when I consider this assumption	
One or two questions from the lens that feel relevant	
Questions I could ask this client	

From *The Art of Coaching Workbook: Tools to Make Every Conversation Count* by Elena Aguilar. Copyright © 2021 by Elena Aguilar. Reproduced by permission.

Lens of Emotional Intelligence

Our ability to recognize and navigate our own emotions and to recognize and navigate the emotions of others has enormous implications for how we navigate the complex social world in which we live. Though each of the Transformational Coaching lenses can be applied to both the coach and the client, it is especially important for coaches to practice looking inward through the lens of emotional intelligence. All too often, the challenges we face in a coaching relationship are tied to challenges we face in engaging with strong emotions—whether in ourselves or in others. Moreover, our ability to be emotionally resilient and to support clients to be the same depends on cultivating a high degree of emotional intelligence.

Understand the Lens

Read the assumptions and questions for this lens and use these annotations:

Ideas that spark new thinking

Ideas you don't fully understand

In the margins, expand on your annotations and capture reflections. What thoughts and questions arise as you read these lists?

EMOTIONAL INTELLIGENCE
ASSUMPTIONS
• We are all born with emotional intelligence and can further develop these skills and capacities.
• There are four areas of emotional intelligence: self-awareness, self-management, social awareness, and relationship management.
• An effective educator speaks about their emotions, welcomes feedback, and is aware of when they need help.
• An effective educator navigates their emotions with self-regulation.
• Adaptability and flexibility are indicators of high emotional intelligence.
• Emotional resilience is a reflection of high emotional intelligence.
• Empathy reflects social awareness.
• An emotionally intelligent educator understands power dynamics in an organization and how to navigate those while preserving and strengthening relationships.
• Emotionally intelligent educators build relationships between individuals and groups.

QUESTIONS

These questions can be asked of the inquirer themselves (of the coach), or they can be asked about the client. Here they are phrased as questions to ask about someone else.

Self-Awareness

- Does he recognize when he is experiencing emotions? Does he recognize how his feelings are affecting him at work and how his feelings affect others?
- How does she speak about her feelings? Does she have the vocabulary to describe her feelings?
- Can she recognize her strengths, areas for growth, and limitations?
- How does he invite or welcome feedback?
- Is he aware of when he needs help?

Self-Management

- How do they respond to strong emotions?
- How do they manage feeling stressed and triggered?
- Are they transparent about their feelings, beliefs, and actions? Can they admit mistakes or faults?
- How do they deal with change and new challenges?

Social Awareness

- Can he sense unspoken emotions in a person or group?
- Can he detect key power relationships?
- How does she cultivate an emotional climate that ensures that people are getting what they need?
- How does she monitor the satisfaction of those she serves?

Relationship Management

- How do they respond to the emotions of others?
- How do they create resonance and move people toward a compelling vision or goal?
- How does she model what she wants from others?
- How does she learn about other people's goals, strengths, and areas for growth?
- When there's a conflict, how do they understand different perspectives? How do they surface conflicts, acknowledge all perspectives, and redirect the energy toward a shared goal?
- How does she model respect, concern, and collaboration? How does she build relationships and spirit?

Apply the Lens

Reread the story of Whitney and Maren. Imagine that you are wearing glasses that allow you to see only the elements that are relevant to the lens of emotional intelligence. Complete your analysis in the table that follows the example.

Example	
The lens of emotional intelligence	**Analysis**
An assumption that helps me understand the situation	*Adaptability and flexibility are indicators of high emotional intelligence.*
Insights about the situation when I consider this assumption	*I wonder whether Whitney sees herself as flexible. On one hand, she is willing to plan entirely new lessons around different texts. On the other hand, she seems rigid in which aspects of her practice she's willing to critically examine.*
One or two questions from the lens that feel relevant	*Can she sense unspoken emotions in a person or group (social awareness)?*
Questions I could ask this client	*How aware is Whitney of the lack of student engagement in her classroom? How aware is she of how she is perceived in department meetings and by her principal? While I can't call this out directly, I might ask, "What's your sense of how students feel about being in your class? How do you want them to feel?"*

Your Analysis	
The lens of emotional intelligence	**Analysis**
An assumption that helps me understand the situation	
Insights about the situation when I consider this assumption	

| Your Analysis | |
The lens of emotional intelligence	Analysis
One or two questions from the lens that feel relevant	
Questions I could ask this client	

Lens of Inquiry

Coaches are eager to be of service to our clients, so we often jump to define solutions before we—and often, our clients—have fully understood the problem we are trying to solve. But, of course, the way we define a problem shapes how we define its solution. The lens of inquiry is a reminder to hold fast to the core coaching disposition of curiosity. It calls on us to look for evidence, to gather data from multiple sources, to question our assumptions, and to resist the temptation of appearing to be right. At the same time, it reminds us that, although we will never have all the answers, we must act anyway.

Understand the Lens

Read the assumptions and questions for this lens and use these annotations:

 Ideas that spark new thinking
? Ideas you don't fully understand

In the margins, expand on your annotations and capture reflections. What thoughts and questions arise as you read these lists?

INQUIRY

Apply the Lens

Reread the story of Whitney and Maren. Imagine that you are wearing glasses that allow you to see only the elements that are relevant to the lens of inquiry. Complete your analysis in the table that follows the example.

Example	
The lens of inquiry	**Analysis**
An assumption that helps me understand the situation	*Evidence and data are critical to making informed decisions.*

Example	
The lens of inquiry	**Analysis**
Insights about the situation when I consider this assumption	*I'm really curious how Whitney makes decisions about what to change and what to keep in her planning process. How does she assess how well students are connecting with the texts she's chosen and the lessons she's prepared?*
One or two questions from the lens that feel relevant	*From which perspective am I seeing this situation?*
Questions I could ask this client	*I'm realizing that, as I reread the story, I am assuming that the principal's assessment of student engagement is correct. And I'm judging Whitney a little for not doing more in that area. But is student engagement actually an issue? I'd like to observe an entire lesson and collect some data for myself.*

Your Analysis	
The lens of inquiry	**Analysis**
An assumption that helps me understand the situation	
Insights about the situation when I consider this assumption	
One or two questions from the lens that feel relevant	
Questions I could ask this client	.

From *The Art of Coaching Workbook: Tools to Make Every Conversation Count* by Elena Aguilar. Copyright © 2021 by Elena Aguilar. Reproduced by permission.

Lens of Systems Thinking

We live within countless complex and interconnected systems. Our bodies are systems that live within family and social systems. Individual schools are systems within a broader network of schools that are, in turn, part of larger educational system. The lens of systems thinking prompts us to explore how these layers of systems affect one another. Everything we observe is the result of a complex set of systems. Effecting change within such complexity can be confounding. Making the structure of these systems visible and exploring the interactions among them is key to intentional transformation.

Understand the Lens

Read the assumptions and questions for this lens and use these annotations:

★　Ideas that spark new thinking

?　Ideas you don't fully understand

In the margins, expand on your annotations and capture reflections. What thoughts and questions arise as you read these lists?

<table>
<tr><td colspan="1" align="center">SYSTEMS THINKING</td></tr>
</table>

SYSTEMS THINKING

ASSUMPTIONS

- Everything we observe is the result of a complex set of interactions.
- Whatever is happening in a moment is exactly what is supposed to happen in the system as it is. If we understand these interactions, we can intervene effectively to change them.
- If we understand a system's structure, we can identify possible leverage points to change it.
- Conflict and tension in a system are necessary and natural.
- To change systems, we must understand the big picture, consider an issue fully and resist the urge to come to a quick conclusion.
- We must consider the short- and long-term consequences of an action.
- All systems have delays. Change in one part of the system does not result in immediate change elsewhere.

- How is the current system designed to produce the results we're seeing?
- How did this system generate the behavior we're seeing?
- What are the relationships between things here?
- Where is the energy in this situation? Where are the stuck points?
- If I do this here, what would happen over here?
- If I do this now, what will happen immediately? What will happen in the long term?
- What are the unintended consequences of a particular action?
- If we shift our perspective, what might we understand about this situation?
- How can we summon the patience required for systems-level change?

Apply the Lens

Reread the story of Whitney and Maren. Imagine that you are wearing glasses that allow you to see only the elements that are relevant to the lens of systems thinking. Complete your analysis in the table that follows the example.

	Example
The lens of systems thinking	**Analysis**
An assumption that helps me understand the situation	*Whatever is happening in a moment is exactly what is supposed to happen in the system as it is.*
Insights about the situation when I consider this assumption	*Wow. This assumption gets me thinking about Whitney in a whole new light. What about her department, principal, and school is allowing Whitney to gradually disengage? How is the system designed to let her coast along on "good-enough" performance evaluations, despite low engagement?*
One or two questions from the lens that feel relevant	*Where is there energy in the system? Where are the stuck points?*
Questions I could ask this client	*This gets me wondering about Whitney in relation to her department. I'm curious to ask, "Are there teachers in your department, or perhaps in other grades, who you really admire? What to you admire about them? Would you be interested in opportunities to collaborate with or learn from them this year?"*

	Your Analysis	
The lens of systems thinking	**Analysis**
An assumption that helps me understand the situation	
Insights about the situation when I consider this assumption	
One or two questions from the lens that feel relevant	
Questions I could ask this client	

Lens of Systemic Oppression

If the lens of systems thinking holds that all systems produce the results which they are designed to produce, then we must pay particular attention to the design of systems that produce inequitable outcomes. Our educational system, like our judicial system, clearly produces such inequitable outcomes. If we are to create schools that enable all children to learn and thrive, we will need to dismantle the ways schools systemically oppress some groups of students. When we apply the lens of systemic oppression to our coaching, we hold ourselves accountable to name, analyze, and disrupt the patterns of power and privilege that deny a liberatory education to so many young people.

In the United States, race and class can determine how well a student will be served by the educational system. We acknowledge that the effect of systemic oppression looks different around the world; in addition to the role that race and class play, other factors can also contribute to inequities in our schools, including being a linguistic or a student's ethnic minority, gender identity, sexuality, religion, refugee status, and tribal affiliation.

Understand the Lens

Read the assumptions and questions for this lens and use these annotations:

 Ideas that spark new thinking

? Ideas you don't fully understand

In the margins, expand on your annotations and capture reflections. What thoughts and questions arise as you read these lists?

SYSTEMIC OPPRESSION
ASSUMPTIONS
• Inequities based on race, class, gender, and other identity markers are prevalent in our world and education system. • Oppression and injustice are human creations and therefore can be undone. • Systemic oppression negatively affects the educational process in countless ways. • Oppression and systematic mistreatment (e.g., white supremacy, racism, classism, sexism, and homophobia) is more than the sum of individual prejudices. • Systemic oppression has historical antecedents: it is an intentional disempowering of groups of people based on their identity to maintain an unequal power structure that subjugates one group over another. • Systemic oppression manifests in economic, political, social, and cultural systems and in interpersonal relationships. • Systemic oppression and its effects can be undone through recognition of inequitable patterns and intentional action to interrupt inequity. • Discussing and addressing oppression and bias will be accompanied by strong emotions.

QUESTIONS

- How are oppression, internalized oppression, and transferred oppression playing out right here, right now—in this relationship, classroom, school, group, organization, and district?
- Who has power here? What is that power based on?
- How are power relations affecting the truth that is told and constructed at any given moment? How do power relations reflect dominant systems of oppression?
- Who is at the table? Who isn't? How does this reflect dominant systems of oppression?
- How safe is it here for different people to share their truth? How safe is it for people from marginalized communities to share their truths?
- Whose safety is prioritized when there's space to share truths?
- How do I understand my practice as an educator committed to justice and liberation given how I am different or the same as my colleagues? As the people I am serving?
- How can I build my practice as a leader for equity starting with who I am and what I bring because of who I am?

Apply the Lens

Reread the story of Whitney and Maren. Imagine that you are wearing glasses that allow you to see only the elements that are relevant to the lens of systemic oppression. Complete your analysis in the table that follows the example.

	Example
The lens of systemic oppression	**Analysis**
An assumption that helps me understand the situation	*Inequities based on race, class, gender, and other identity markers are prevalent in our world and education system.*
Insights about the situation when I consider this assumption	*Whitney mentions that the demographics in her class have changed substantially in the last few years. I wonder how she feels about these changes. How does she feel about having fewer students who look like her? She refers to her classroom as a "melting pot." Does this mean she expects students to assimilate? If so, to what norm?*

Example	
The lens of systemic oppression	**Analysis**
One or two questions from the lens that feel relevant	*How safe is it here for different people to share their truth?*
Questions I could ask this client	*This gets me really curious about the composition of the staff and leadership at the department and school level. How well does it reflect the changing student body? Who has power at the school? Does Whitney, as a Black woman, feel empowered to advocate for what matters to her? Do her students and their families?*

Your Analysis	
The lens of systemic oppression	**Analysis**
An assumption that helps me understand the situation	
Insights about the situation when I consider this assumption	
One or two questions from the lens that feel relevant	
Questions I could ask this client	

From *The Art of Coaching Workbook: Tools to Make Every Conversation Count* by Elena Aguilar. Copyright © 2021 by Elena Aguilar. Reproduced by permission.

Lens of Compassion

An ethic of compassion underlies all of the other lenses: When we seek to understand, as we're doing when we're applying any of the other lenses, we're doing so because we care about a person and a situation. Creating an additional lens for compassion itself leverages its power. The lens of compassion is a reminder that creating schools that are places of liberation for all is only possible through a practice of love. This lens speaks to the worth and dignity to which we are each entitled for no reason other than because we are alive. It acknowledges the universality of suffering and summons coaches to act in service of healing and the greater good.

Understand the Lens

Read the assumptions and questions for this lens and use these annotations:

★   Ideas that spark new thinking

?   Ideas you don't fully understand

In the margins, expand on your annotations and capture reflections. What thoughts and questions arise as you read these lists?

COMPASSION
ASSUMPTIONS
• Compassion is the ability to suspend judgment of ourselves and others, appreciating that each of us makes choices based on the information and skills that we have at any given time.   • Compassion is the ability to act on a feeling of empathy for another living being.   • Compassion is our natural state. Sometimes conditions block us from feeling compassion, but we can find our way back.   • Compassion for another starts with compassion toward oneself.   • Cultivating compassion requires us to keep our eyes and hearts open even though what we see and hear might break our hearts.   • Gratitude, gentleness, and listening foster the development of compassion.   • It is an act of compassion to hold a calm and grounded presence in the face of another's suffering.   • If we pause and choose a response to a situation, we are more likely to feel compassionate.   • We can use compassion to dismantle destructive beliefs and behaviors.

- How are others experiencing this situation? What are things like from their perspective?
- How can we uncover the goodness and humanity in others despite their grief, anger, and exhaustion or despite our own?
- How do we support others to discover their best qualities? (And are we remembering to do so?)
- How do we create space for all voices to be truly heard? Whose voices are not heard?
- How do we help others explore the consequences of their actions and learn from them?
- How do we foster listening that leads to greater compassion and empathy in our communities?
- Where do we see people treating each other with kindness? How can we create more spaces where people treat each other with kindness?
- How can we return to a state of compassion when we notice we are triggered? How can we help others do this?
- How can compassion help us to dismantle systems of oppression?

Apply the Lens

Reread the story of Whitney and Maren. Imagine that you are wearing glasses that allow you to see only the elements that are relevant to the lens of compassion. Complete your analysis in the table that follows the example.

	Example
The lens of compassion	**Analysis**
An assumption that helps me understand the situation	*Compassion for another starts with compassion toward oneself.*
Insights about the situation when I consider this assumption	*I find evidence of Maren's own insecurities in this story— she hides her disappointment about discussing curriculum, she avoids the principal. I wonder how aware she is of her level of confidence in working with Whitney. Is Maren judging herself?*

Example	
The lens of compassion	**Analysis**
One or two questions from the lens that feel relevant	*How do we foster listening that leads to greater compassion and empathy in our communities?*
Questions I could ask this client	*Whitney seems eager to select texts that her students will connect with and acknowledge that they come from a wide range of backgrounds, yet she seems to be calling all the shots. I'd love to ask, "How are you inviting students into the decision-making process around what texts they'll read this year?"*

Your Analysis	
The lens of compassion	**Analysis**
An assumption that helps me understand the situation	
Insights about the situation when I consider this assumption	
One or two questions from the lens that feel relevant	
Questions I could ask this client	

Yes, You Can Use the Coaching Lenses

Having explored each of the seven lenses, we are able to consider how best to use them. Some coaches turn to the lenses to plan for coaching conversations, and others pull them out when they're reflecting on a conversation. Experienced Transformational Coaches are able to apply a coaching lens to a coaching conversation as it unfolds. That's an advanced skill—to process what you hear through the lenses during a conversation and quickly generate a question for your client. Being able to do this is a result of lots of practice. Every time you think about the lenses when planning or reflecting, you are internalizing them, as does talking to colleagues about the lenses. Each of the following ideas is an effective technique to practice using the lenses and making these powerful tools your own.

How will you remember to use the lenses? How will you keep them at your fingertips? Here are some suggestions:

- ☐ Make cheat sheets. Create a 4x6 notecard for each lens. On each card, list a few of the assumptions and questions that you find most useful. Use phrases that will help you remember the ideas, and embellish the cards with images or sketches if you want. Keep these in your coaching notebook or somewhere handy for easy reference.
- ☐ Personalize your copies. Paperclip a copy of the coaching lenses into your coaching notebooks. On that copy, highlight the assumptions or questions that are most helpful.
- ☐ Formalize the process. Use the process that Elena describes in Chapter 4 of *The Art of Coaching* for planning for a coaching conversation and using the lenses. Even if you only do this twice a year, you'll be amazed at what a powerful impact it has.
- ☐ Engage a protocol. Use the coaching lenses in a consultancy protocol (Chapter 15). This collaborative process is one of the most effective ways to deepen your understanding of the lenses.

Before we end this chapter, we've got three activities to help you practice the lenses. Because each activity will help you think about the lenses differently, we encourage you to do all three. The first activity simplifies the pages of assumptions and questions you've been working with and helps you distill what is most important about each lens. The second activity helps you extend your understanding of each lens as you apply it to yourself. Finally, in the third activity, we turn back to the story of Maren and Whitney as Laurelin and Lori apply the lenses fruitfully to the challenges of the situation.

From *The Art of Coaching Workbook: Tools to Make Every Conversation Count* by Elena Aguilar. Copyright © 2021 by Elena Aguilar. Reproduced by permission.

The Key Assumptions and Questions

Although the lenses in their entirety are invaluable, a handful of assumptions and questions drawn from across the lenses yield insight in almost any challenging situation. In Exhibit 4.1, you'll find the assumptions and questions that Elena considers to be key to identifying root causes and supporting growth. You can also download a copy of this handy one-pager from our website, http://www.brightmorningteam.com.

Exhibit 4.1: The Key Assumptions and Questions

	Key Assumptions	Key Questions
Adult learning	• Problems of change are problems of learning. • Adults must feel safe to learn.	• What is going well? Which strengths can be built on? • What are the gaps in ability? Skill? Knowledge? Will? Capacity? Emotional intelligence? Cultural competency?
Change management	• These conditions need to be present for successful change: leadership, vision, skills, incentives, resources, and a clear plan of action. • People need will, skill, knowledge and capacity to change.	• What are the conditions for change in this situation? • Do people have the skills and knowledge necessary to implement change?
Emotional intelligence	• An effective educator speaks about their emotions, welcomes feedback, and is aware of when they need help. • An effective educator navigates their emotions with self-regulation. • Emotional resilience is a reflection of high emotional intelligence.	• Do they recognize when they are experiencing emotions? Do they recognize how their feelings are affecting themselves and others? • How does he manage feeling stressed and triggered? • How does she cultivate an emotional climate that ensures that people are getting what they need?

(Continued)

	Key Assumptions	Key Questions
Inquiry	• The way we pose the question determines the nature of the answer. • The way we define the problem dictates how we define the solution. • The questions we ask are as important as the answers we find.	• What do I think is the problem? What do others think is the problem? • Who is defining the problem? From which perspectives am I seeing this situation? • Which other perspectives would help me understand this situation?
Systems thinking	• Whatever is happening in a moment is exactly what is supposed to happen in the system as it is. If we understand these interactions, we can intervene effectively to change them.	• What are the relationships between things here? • Where is the energy in this situation? Where are the stuck points?
Systemic oppression	• Systemic oppression negatively affects the educational process in countless ways. • Inequities based on race, class, gender, and other identity markers are prevalent in our world and education system.	• How are oppression, internalized oppression, and transferred oppression playing out right here, right now? • Who has power here? What is that power based on?
Compassion	• Compassion is the ability to act on a feeling of empathy for another living being. • Compassion for another starts with compassion toward oneself.	• How are others experiencing this situation? What are things like from their perspective?

Extend Your Learning

Pick one key assumption and one key question through which to think about your work and school for a whole week. Write these where you won't be able to forget what they are, and then spend a week analyzing your work and organization through this lens.

Looking at Yourself Through the Lenses

It's time to turn the lenses on yourself. There are two ways you can do this. You could select a situation in your work life that's perplexing you and do a deep dive into it, just as you did when analyzing Maren and Whitney. Or you can look at a number of situations, through what might be the most relevant lens for that situation. Given that you've just practiced using all the lenses to analyze one situation, we're offering you a chance to see how you can use just one lens at a time to gain insight.

The Lens of Adult Learning

Think about your learning journey as a coach. Reread the lens of adult learning and consider a couple of the questions:

- What are your current learning goals as a coach?
- What strengths and prior learning have you been able to draw on in learning to coach?

How do these, and the other assumptions and questions from this lens, help you understand your development as a coach?

The Lens of Change Management

Reflect on a change you've tried to make that you've struggled to sustain (e.g., learning a new language, starting an exercise regimen). Reread through the lens of change management, and adapt questions from the list to deepen your reflection. Consider these adaptations:

- What was the context in which you tried to make the change? What else was going on in your life at that time?
- How clear was the vision of success in implementing this change? What made it compelling?

How does the lens of change management help reframe the challenges you've faced in reaching your change goal?

The Lens of Emotional Intelligence

Reflect on a role you play that is important to you (e.g., educator, parent, volunteer). Adapt one question from each of the four categories in the lens of emotional intelligence to explore this role. For example, a person exploring what it means to be a parent might ask:

- Do I invite and welcome feedback from my children on my parenting? (*self-awareness*)
- How do I manage feeling stressed or triggered? (*self-management*)
- How do I monitor the well-being of my children? What makes it hard for me to do this sometimes? (*social awareness*)
- Am I modeling the emotional climate I want to be true in my family? (*relationship management*)

How does the lens of emotional intelligence support your understanding of yourself in this role?

The Lens of Inquiry

Reflect on a recent situation in which you feel confident that you were right or that you took the best course of action. Reread the lens of inquiry. Adapt any three questions from the list to explore the situation from a different angle. For example:

- How was I defining the problem?
- What other perspectives might have led me to define the problem differently or helped to give me a broader understanding?

How does the lens of inquiry help you understand the situation you were in as well as your own perspective on it?

The Lens of Systems Thinking

Reflect on your role as a coach as it fits within the larger systems of your school and school system. Review the lens of systems thinking, and adapt any three questions from the list to deepen your reflection. Here are some adaptations:

- How is the coach role set up at my school or in my district? What opportunities does this create? What limitations?
- What are the unintended consequences of describing coaching the way we do at my school?
- How does the lens of systems thinking help me identify places in the system where I could intervene to make my coaching more successful?

How does the lens of systems thinking help you understand your role as a coach?

The Lens of Systemic Oppression

Reflect on a system with which you feel a strong affiliation (e.g., your school, a family, a congregation, a community organization). How do inequities manifest in that system?

Reflect on the assumptions and questions in the lens of systemic oppression, and adapt questions from the list to deepen your reflection:

- Who holds the power in this system? What is that power based on?
- How safe is it for different people to share their truth? Who might be less inclined to be transparent?

How does the lens of systemic oppression help you better discern the patterns of power and privilege at work in this system?

The Lens of Compassion

Call to mind a story from your past whose outcome you regret—perhaps you wish you'd acted differently. Consider the lens of compassion and these adapted questions:

- Where in this story is there evidence of my goodness and humanity despite the outcome?
- How was this experience an opportunity for me to learn and grow?
- How does the lens of compassion help me view my role in a more loving manner?

How does the lens of compassion help you see that experience that you regret?

One Last Thing

To close up this chapter, we're including two analyses of the Maren-Whitney situation using the coaching lenses. Because they help each of us see what's beyond our initial perception, our insights vary given our experiences. In the first reflection you'll read, Laurelin used the essential assumptions and questions. In the second reflection, Lori takes a deeper dive into the situation by applying all the lenses.

As you read, we hope you'll get a sense of the power of using an individual lens to reveal key insights that might have been missed as well as how, taken together, the seven lenses intersect with and amplify one another. We hope you also see why it's so important to have multiple perspectives on any situation.

Laurelin Reflects

My heart really goes out to both Maren and Whitney in this situation (*compassion*). I can relate to Maren, as a new coach, seeing potential in Whitney but being unsure how to unleash it. She also seems a bit caught up in insecurities about her role, which is so common (*emotional intelligence*). I'm curious whether Maren has a community of coaches with whom she could discuss the challenges she was having in coaching Whitney (*adult learning*). I'm also curious how Maren's identity as a younger White woman influenced how she worked with Whitney, an older Black woman (*systemic oppression*).

I can relate to Whitney as well. I get the sense there's a lot happening beneath the surface that's leading her to focus so singularly on planning (*emotional intelligence*). Maybe she's getting bored and is looking for a challenge. I wonder what kind of professional development and leadership opportunities are available in her district for teachers with her level of experience (*systems thinking*)? Perhaps she feels sad about teaching fewer students who look like her, which makes me curious about what got her into teaching and how she ended up at this school (*inquiry*).

I'm curious whether Whitney would name student engagement as an issue. Is it off her radar because she has such a deep love of planning? Or is she aware but so uncertain about what to do that she's avoiding the issue (*adult learning*)? I also can't help but wonder how the shifting identity demographics in her classroom might be impacting Whitney's ability to build relationships with her students. What is the school doing to equip teachers to understand and navigate such a wide array of cultural differences in the student population (*systemic oppression*)? What kind of relationship does Whitney have with the principal, who seems to have such a strong presence in the school (*systems thinking*)?

If I were Maren in this situation, I might have done a few things differently. First, I would have held firmer to the importance of co-planning being in the service of a larger professional learning goal for the teacher (*adult learning*). I would have gently pushed to articulate a clear purpose for our work together and to identify the measures of success for our collaboration (*change management*). It's true that sometimes you have to take the opportunities where you find them. It's also important for new coaches to set clear boundaries around their time and the kinds of activities they take on.

Second, I would have asked Whitney's permission to observe her classroom to gather more data. Though this could have been in the service of planning a reading unit, I would have used the opportunity to gather evidence of students' levels of engagement throughout a lesson to help determine whether Whitney was unaware of or resistant to the need to do some work on engagement (*inquiry*). Looking at observational data together would also have given Maren the opportunity to hear how Whitney defines student engagement, which may differ from her principal's expectations.

Finally, I would have included time at the start of coaching conversations or in other settings to deepen my relationship with Whitney and earn her trust. I'd like to better understand what drives her as a teacher, which aspects of her identity are important to her, how she views her students, and how well she feels she fits in at the school (*compassion*). I would have named the differences in our social identities (like Maren, I am a younger, White woman), in addition to the perceived authority that comes with my role as a coach, so that Whitney and I could talk about these openly rather than having them play out, undiscussed, in the background (*systemic oppression*).

Lori Reflects

When I analyze this situation through each of these lenses, I see moments where Maren is earnest and eager and where Whitney needs a thinking partner. I also notice gaps in relationship building and trust, clearer expectations about coaching, an acknowledgment of one's identities and backgrounds (particularly in relation to race and age), and the impact of systemic forces that impede this relationship from becoming a strong coaching partnership.

Through the *lens of adult learning*, it seems like Maren dove right into coaching without considering what she knows about Whitney and how to meet her where she is. There were moments where Maren tried to connect with Whitney on her skills as a curriculum planner, and even though Maren did ask Whitney some questions about her background Whitney's terse responses suggest that Maren needed to spend more time developing trust with Whitney.

Through the *lens of change management*, it seems as though the desired outcome is for Whitney to revitalize her teaching. I wondered, though, does Whitney have this same goal? Has her principal communicated this to her? Through this lens I also wondered about what structures are in place for change to happen. Maren may not be well set up to support

Whitney, even though she's had training, and Whitney does not seem aware of the role of the coach, the definition of coaching, the need for change and incentives for change.

When I look through the *lens of inquiry*, it seems like Maren is hesitant in the questions she asks, and her questions don't yield what she hopes for. Maren's strongest question is when she asks Whitney about text selection and Whitney offers a lot of insights, including the changing demographics of the school. In response, Maren "saw an opening to explore Whitney's views toward her students, but she wasn't entirely sure how to proceed." Instead of probing more, she jots down notes in her notebook to come back to at another time.

I saw a lot in these interactions as they related to the *lens of systems thinking* and how all three players—Maren, Whitney, and Mr. Felding—have contributed to how this situation played out. Mr. Felding seems to support coaching. He (or some other power) supported Maren getting the training for coaching, but it's not clear if there is a shared understanding of both the definition of coaching and the role of coaching in their school. Mr. Felding also seems to believe that Whitney needs to change (e.g., "It's like a dead zone walking past [Whitney's] door every day"). However, Whitney shared that she gets good performance evaluations, and we've been told that Whitney is reliable and effective. This leads me to wonder where the disconnect is between the perception of Whitney's teaching and the reality.

Seeing this situation through a *systems thinking lens* overlaps with the *lens of systemic oppression*. Race is not explicitly addressed, and there are many coded behaviors, actions, and lost opportunities to explore race and identity. So much is unspoken in this narrative, which is often how race and conversations about equity play out in schools. Whitney is a reliable teacher whose students are learning in her class, yet she has lost the spark in her teaching. Has this been directly raised with her by the principal or anyone? What role does race play in Mr. Felding's perceptions? Is she an exception in the school, or are there other classrooms where students are not engaged? Does he hold all teachers to the same standard?

I also wonder to what degree Maren is aware of the role of race and cultural competency in her own experience and how that plays out in her interactions with Whitney. Does her hesitation and reluctance with Whitney come from fear? From the discomfort of coaching across lines of racial difference? And what role does age and experience play? Whitney is much older than Maren, and I wonder how this age difference shapes Maren's behaviors toward Whitney. Whitney seems to get what she wants from the relationship (curricular support), yet the relationship is transactional.

Continuing to look through the *lens of systemic oppression*, I wonder whose safety is prioritized in this situation. By staying silent about race, Maren privileges her own comfort. She doesn't seem to be interested in Whitney's comments about the shifting demographics in the school. If the school population used to be 50-50 African American and White, what was the race of the staff? Did that change? How does Whitney feel about the increase in immigrant communities at the school? Does she have some biases here? Although Whitney shared that she likes to vary her instruction, it seems that some aspects of her work haven't changed. Is that related to the shift in demographics and to Whitney losing her spark? And if so, then what's the impact on students?

When I consider this situation through the *lens of emotional intelligence*, I see that Maren seems self-aware, but I'm not sure how developed her skills are in engaging with her own insecurities and uncertainty. I also see that she's got some gaps in how she responds to Whitney's emotions. Maren seems to pick up on them, but she doesn't know how to engage with them.

When I view this entire situation through the *lens of compassion*, I feel compassion for Whitney and Maren. Maren does want to connect with Whitney, but it's not clear that she knows how to uncover Whitney's strengths, how to create space to dismantle limiting beliefs and behaviors, or how to have compassion for herself in this situation.

For Further Learning

→ Enroll in a virtual coaching workshop (information at http:// www.brightmorningteam .com).

→ On our website, you'll find a list of recommended resources to guide you in further learning about the theories and concepts from which these lenses are created.

CHAPTER 5

Beginning a Successful Coaching Relationship

Beginning a coaching relationship is exciting and scary, and coaches can feel a lot of pressure to "get it right." In this workbook chapter, we're going to lead you through a reflection on Chapter 5 of *The Art of Coaching* and ask you to make some decisions based on that content. Then we'll offer some additional examples of what's in *The Art of Coaching*, and we'll engage you in some activities around content that's only tangentially discussed in that book. We believe that between what you've read in *The Art of Coaching* and what you'll do in this chapter you'll be well prepared to launch your coaching relationships.

To get started, recall a time when you began a professional relationship. Perhaps with a new colleague, a principal, or if you're not brand-new to coaching, then with a client. In the following spaces, indicate what you were thinking and feeling as you began that relationship. Add hair or other identifying characteristics so that the figure looks a little like you.

Designing a Plan to Build Trust

Do this activity to process the content in Chapter 5 of The Art of Coaching *and to create your own road map for starting a successful coaching relationship.*

Ideally, you'd be working through this book in the summer before stepping into a coaching role. If that's not the case, then there are two ways to go about this plan: You could create a plan for the next time you start a coaching relationship (and think nonspecifically as if you were planning for any new client), or you could imagine that you can travel backward in time and plan for how you would have liked to begin a coaching relationship with someone with whom you're currently working. The latter will help you to reflect on a coaching relationship that you're in right now and could provide insight into what you might do to strengthen trust. You'll need to have *The Art of Coaching* next to you right now so that you can reference the description of these steps when necessary.

A Plan to Build Trust

I'm creating this plan and thinking about:

☐ New coaching relationships in general
☐ One specific person: _____

1. **Plan and prepare.**
   a. In your first meeting with a new client, what do you want them to think about you? When they go home that day and tell a friend or loved one that they met their coach for the first time, what do you want them to say about how they experienced you?

   b. Read through the questions in Exhibit 5.1 (*The Art of Coaching*, pp. 80–81). You can also download these from our website, http://www.brightmorningteam.com. Identify only four questions (out of all of the questions) that feel most important for you to ask. Write those down here:

2. **Cautiously gather background information.**
   If you plan to chat with someone else about a client that you'll coach, what will you ask? Here are a few suggestions:

   a. What do you see as their strengths?
   b. What do you think might be important for me to know so I can build trust with them?
   c. Is there anything about me that you know about, that might be worth sharing? What else might you ask?

3. **Establish confidentiality.**
   What will you say to your client when you discuss confidentiality? Write that down here:

   What will you share about how and when you'll communicate with your client's supervisor? (And does that supervisor expect any communication? If you're not sure—how can you find out?)

4. **Listen.**
   We will explore listening in-depth in Chapter 8 of this workbook. For now, based on what you know about yourself as a listener, what will be most important for you to keep in mind regarding your own listening when you first meet with a new client? Perhaps you know you have a tendency to interrupt, or that you space out sometimes, or that you sometimes want to offer solutions to problems before you've really heard someone out.

5. **Ask questions.**

   In addition to the questions you've determined that you want to ask, you'll likely need to ask follow-up questions. What phrasing feels most comfortable to you when asking questions? Elena begins many questions with, "I'm curious about. . ." What might be a go-to question starter for you?

6. **Connect.**

   What are a few things about you that you could share with a new client that might foster a connection? These could be about your professional experiences, your family, or your background. Identify three things you could share with just about anyone.

7. **Validate.**

   When you offer people appreciations or when you call out their strengths, what feels most comfortable for you to say? Identify a few phrases that work in general that feel authentic to you. These could include phrases like, "I'm really inspired by what you shared," or "Wow, that's awesome!"

From *The Art of Coaching Workbook: Tools to Make Every Conversation Count* by Elena Aguilar. Copyright © 2021 by Elena Aguilar. Reproduced by permission.

8. **Be open about who you are and what you do.**
   Script what you will share with a specific client, or in general, about who you are and what you do. You can draw on your mission and vision for yourself as a coach (see Chapter 2) or on other information that you feel needs to be shared.

9. **Ask for permission to coach.**
   After reviewing the examples in *The Art of Coaching* that describe what it sounds like to ask permission to coach, determine what you'll say.

10. **Keep commitments.**
    Reflect on your prior experiences with keeping commitments that you make. Do you tend to overcommit and struggle to fulfill those commitments? Do you overcommit to compensate for insecurities about yourself? What is important for you to be aware of when it comes to making commitments to new clients?

The Transformational Coach's Way of Being

Do this activity to get grounded in the mindsets and dispositions that will have the biggest positive impact on your coaching.

In the beginning of any relationship, we often try to figure out who the other person *really* is behind what they're saying and doing. How you show up in your first coaching conversations—who you are being—will have a tremendous impact on the quality of relationship you develop.

Think back to a recent coaching conversation that felt difficult. If you aren't coaching now, consider a similarly hard conversation with a friend or family member.

How do you think your client (or friend) experienced you in that conversation? Were you kind and patient? Curious and open? Now think symbolically: What kind of animal were you being in that conversation? Were you a gentle-eyed deer? Were you an owl? A prickly sea urchin? Jot down a brief reflection (or draw an image!) here:

Why did you choose that animal to represent you?

Is there another animal you wish you would have been? Why or why not?

A Transformational Coach's way of being makes all the difference between a transformational conversation and one that may not have such an impact on students. How a coach shows up, how they engage with their own emotions, and how they communicate are the key variables in a conversation. Elena has determined the following six ways of being that are critical for a Transformational Coach to embody:

1. Compassion
2. Curiosity

3. Trust in the coaching process
4. Humility and mutuality
5. Learner orientation
6. Courage

Call to mind someone you trust who has guided or supported you in some way—perhaps a mentor or coach or a school leader. Which of these ways of being do they embody?

In the following table, jot down the names of some other people you know from your professional or personal world who embody the Transformational Coach ways of being.

Way of being	Someone who embodies this way of being
Compassion	
Curiosity	
Trust in the coaching process (or trusting in a process)	
Humility and mutuality	
Learner orientation	
Courage	

The Six Ways of Being

As you read the following description of a Transformational Coach's way of being, highlight or underline phrases that resonate.

1. **Compassion:** Compassion is the ability to feel deep empathy for another being and to act on that empathy by, for example, communicating care, staying in relationship,

or speaking up or quieting down. A deep sense of interconnectedness allows us to have compassion for all people, which in turn gives rise to an unconditional regard for others. A Transformational Coach demonstrates unwavering compassion for a client, their students, the client's colleagues and supervisors, themselves, and all living beings.

2. **Curiosity**: Curiosity is, in part, an emotional state that allows us to move into the unknown while reducing our tendency to form judgments based on preconceived notions. Because fear shuts down curiosity, staying curious requires that we recognize and navigate our own fear. It also requires that we manage our discomfort when we don't know something. Curiosity also implies hope—that in staying open and curious rather than moving into judgment we express hope that what is not yet known will offer insight, answers, solutions. Curiosity makes us question our beliefs, assumptions, and ways of doing and being; it makes us question our world. A Transformational Coach is insatiably curious about others, about what is possible, and about one's own self.

3. **Trust in the coaching process:** Trusting the coaching process is about recognizing the many factors that play a role in personal transformation. It helps us remember that there will be times when we don't see evidence of change in a single conversation or even over a short period. By trusting the process, we remain open to possibility, recognize that the journey to transformation may be a long one, and refrain from acting on urgency in an unproductive way. A Transformational Coach understands that we might lay seeds of transformation that sprout in another season, and we become comfortable with the uncertainty of growth.

4. **Humility and mutuality:** Transformational Coaches know that we have made just as many mistakes as our clients and that we too have areas for growth. We do not expect perfection of ourselves or of others; we value growth. We hold that we can learn from anyone and that anyone can learn from us; we have the nimble skill to coach anyone. Humility generates a deep appreciation for ourselves, our clients, and the process. A Transformational Coach values the reciprocal nature of learning and the potential for our own improvement through the coaching process.

5. **Learner orientation:** Transformational Coaches regularly reflect on our own learning and development and actively seek out ways to develop our coaching skills, boost our knowledge about education and equity, hone our emotional intelligence, examine and interrogate our beliefs, and strengthen these dispositions.

6. **Courage:** A Transformational Coach aspires to create just and liberated communities and builds reserves of courage to do so. We think about courage as a muscle we can build. We learn about how others amass courage, we learn about what gets in the way

of acting with courage, and we understand how to engage with the fear that surfaces within us when we need be courageous. A Transformational Coach appreciates the power of courage and is committed to increasing their own.

Reflecting on the Ways of Being

For each way of being, reflect on how fully you feel you embody that disposition. If you want to rate yourself, of course—go ahead and do so. If rating yourself isn't helpful, then don't—you might just make notes in the margins to identify your strengths and areas for growth.

Compassion	1–5 Scale
I recognize that everyone is doing the best they can right now. I understand that people make choices that make sense to them, given their life histories and worldview.	
I know the difference between pity, sympathy, and empathy—and I know how I feel when I'm giving or experiencing these emotions.	
I feel empathy for people even when I disagree with their actions.	
When I feel empathy for someone, I take action.	
I recognize when it's hard for me to activate compassion, and I have strategies to help me do so.	
I feel compassion for myself, and I have strategies to act on those feelings of self-compassion.	
I see the interconnectedness between myself and others, and this deepens my compassion for others.	
TOTAL	

Curiosity	1–5 Scale
I am aware of underlying intentions behind the questions I ask.	
I am aware of how genuine my questions are (and that some might be more or less genuine than what I intend) and of how open I am to the way someone else responds to them.	
I'm aware of what's going through my mind when I ask questions and when I listen to the response.	
When listening to a client, I notice when my judgment arises, and I have strategies to manage that reaction so it doesn't obstruct my curiosity.	
I'm aware of my emotions when someone speaks, and I have strategies to engage with the emotions that surface that could block my curiosity.	
When someone says something that I disagree with, I get curious about my own values, beliefs, and experiences.	
I have strategies to engage with my fear.	
TOTAL	

Trust in the coaching process	1–5 Scale
I am patient.	
I have strategies to manage my impatience and anxiety.	

Trust in the coaching process	1–5 Scale
I recognize the many steps that lead to change, and I know we're on the right track because I see my client taking those steps.	
I can sense urgency in myself but don't act on it in a way that causes harm to others. I know that people can only be where they are and that I can't will them to be elsewhere.	
I recognize that I can't see every factor that plays a role in someone's learning journey, and I accept that positive change may occur when I can't see it.	
In my coaching work, I recognize my spheres of influence and control and can let go of what is outside of my control.	
I don't have personal desired outcomes or agendas when I'm coaching someone; I hold loose attachment to co-constructed outcomes and coach toward an organization's vision and mission.	
TOTAL	

Humility and mutuality	1–5 Scale
I learn just as much as my clients do within a coaching relationship.	
I recognize that my work as a coach furthers my own journey of growth and transformation.	
I know that I have made just as many mistakes as my clients and that I have just as many areas for growth.	
I don't expect my client to be perfect, and I don't expect perfection from myself.	
I know that I can learn from any client that I work with and I'm open to and eager for those learnings.	

Humility and mutuality	1–5 Scale
I know that any client can learn from me.	
I can be both humble and confident (and not insecure or arrogant).	
TOTAL	

Learner orientation	1–5 Scale
I plan for coaching conversations and practice them with colleagues.	
I invite clients to give formal feedback on my coaching a couple times per year, and I ask for feedback in conversations.	
I reflect on coaching conversations to analyze which coaching moves were effective and to determine how I can improve my coaching next time.	
I read books and articles about the content I coach in, about educational equity, and about the equity issues facing the students I serve.	
I interrogate my own beliefs about education, coaching, equity, race/racism and identity, emotions, and ways of being, and I find colleagues who help me do so.	
I recognize and reflect on my emotions regularly; I hone my ability to navigate my emotions and engage with them in a healthy and productive way.	
I reflect on how I show up and how I embody the Transformational Coach's ways of being; I identify how I can strengthen the way I embody these ways of being.	
TOTAL	

Courage	1–5 Scale
I know what I feel, look like, and sound like when I'm being courageous.	
I understand and appreciate how courage enables me to be a Transformational Coach, and I value building my courage.	
I know how to access my own courage and do so when I want.	
I recognize courage in others and draw inspiration from their courage.	
I have strategies to resist the pull to comfort and can manage my discomfort when I'm accessing courage.	
When I don't feel courageous, I have strategies to explore and remove the blocks to my courage.	
I value exploring fear and vulnerability as I know they are related to the courage I can access.	
TOTAL	

Way of being	Total score
Compassion	
Curiosity	
Trust in the coaching process	
Humility and mutuality	
Learner orientation	
Courage	

Reflect

Which way of being do you feel strongest in? Why do you think that's the case?

If you asked others which way of being they think you're the strongest in, would they choose the same one?

Which way of being do you find the most challenging? Why do you think that's the case?

Which way of being would you like to make the biggest growth in? Why? What might it look like and sound like for you to make growth in this area?

What do you think others would say about how you hold these ways of being? What would you want to change about that, and why?

Whose feedback could you solicit on how you demonstrate these ways of being? Why?

Whose feedback would you be afraid to ask for? Why? What could change that?

What's a next step you could take to continue developing these ways of being? Jot down a time-stamped commitment associated with that step.

For Further Learning

→ Read *Onward: Cultivating Emotional Resilience in Educators* and *The Onward Workbook*, which include an array of activities to know yourself and further develop your ways of being.

Reflecting on Trust

Do this activity to lay the foundation for building trust with others—Transformational Coaching always starts with personal reflection—so we've provided an opportunity to do so here.

On the following line, plot the names of 5–10 people whom you currently work with (or if you prefer, who are friends or acquaintances) according to how much you trust them. Feel free to use initials or a letter or symbol to represent them.

LOW TRUST   HIGH TRUST

⟵──⟶

What makes you trust the people who are on the high trust end? Describe behaviors or actions that led you to believe this about each of them.

If there are people in the middle space, what keeps you from fully trusting them? What barriers to trust seem most relevant, and what comes up for you as you name those things?

Think about one of the people on the low end of trust. What's happened that's made you feel like you can't trust them? Do you want that to change? What could happen to change that for both of you?

What are the factors that influence how you trust people? Do you notice a pattern when capturing those qualities here and where names have fallen above? Is there an opportunity here to shift or grow? Describe.

Now, think about a few colleagues. If they were doing this activity, where do you think they'd put your name? How much do you think they trust you? What factors do you think influence how much they trust you?

How comfortable would you feel right now asking your colleagues to share where they would place you? Why?

Think about a colleague with whom you feel you've built a lot of trust. What did you do to build trust with that person? What did you learn from this dynamic that can be applied to relationships with others?

Exploring Your Client's Identity Markers

This exercise will provide you with tips on how to ask your clients about their identity markers.

As you begin getting to know clients it's very important to understand how they think about themselves sociopolitically. In Chapter 1, you reflected on your own identity markers. Now we'll guide you in how to facilitate this exploration with your clients. For many coaches this conversation can feel uncomfortable. This is often because we don't talk openly about race in many places in the world. Race still feels like a taboo topic. It's something we must talk about, however, and we can make it less awkward by choosing to embrace the discomfort and engage in these conversations continuously and intentionally. A favorite student saying applies here: "It's weird only if you make it weird."

How to Open the Conversation: Part 1

Here are two ways to open this topic:

In addition to hearing about your experiences as a teacher, it's very helpful for me to understand how you think about your identity. The more I understand you, the better I can support you. So I'm curious how you identify in terms of your sociopolitical identity markers—race, class, gender, and so on. Of your identity markers, which ones feel most important to you? What role do those identity markers play in your daily experiences?

I don't want to make assumptions about you, so I'm curious how you identify in terms of your race or ethnicity?

In addition to offering insights about racial identity, opening this conversation can also surface important and otherwise invisible insights around a client's gender identity. If you ask directly about gender identity, then ask everyone you coach—not only people whose identity you're uncertain about. Again, we can begin to normalize talking about identity.

Engaging Your Client in an Identity Reflection Activity: Part 2

In addition to initiating the conversation with a general discussion about identity, it can be powerful to then engage your client in a more in-depth reflection. In Chapter 1, we provided you with an exercise to do just this (Exploring Identity Markers). You can offer that same activity to your client (and it's available for download from http://brightmorningteam.com). This is valuable for two reasons: it allows you to better understand your client, and it cultivates awareness in your client about their own identity and the impact that might have on their teaching and relationships with students, parents and guardians, and colleagues.

Here's how you can invite your client to do this reflection:

I know I'm officially your technology coach, so this might not feel like something you'd expect us to do together, but it's really helpful for me to have a deeper understanding of how you understand your identity. I have an activity that will probably take about 10–15 minutes to do, and we can do it now during our time together. It'll also be helpful as we talk about how you engage your class in integrating technology—so this will ultimately help students as well. How does it sound if we do this now?

As your client shares their reflection on the activity, follow up with coaching questions to deepen your understanding of who they are and to facilitate their self-understanding. You can simply say, "Tell me more about that." This is also an important conversation in which to use active listening and to pay attention to your own body language so that you're communicating curiosity, interest, and openness. If someone doesn't seem to want to talk about something, you might mentally note that and reflect on why that might be—but don't push.

Although we recommend this activity as a way to build trust with your client, we want you to manage your expectations. If you feel your client is guarded in their responses, you can come back to this again later. Sometimes elements of our identity may be very important to us, but we don't feel safe or comfortable sharing them at work, especially with someone who might be perceived as having authority. Follow your client's lead and express gratitude for what they chose to share with you.

Commit to Action

This activity is ideally done in the initial stages of getting to know a client. But if you're reading this at a time when that stage has passed, you can still invite a client to do this. You can simply say, "I'd really like to get to know you better, and I just learned about this activity that can help me do so. Would you be willing to do it?"

Identify a few clients with whom you would like to have a conversation about identity. List them here, and then print out the reflection exercise and commit to doing so. Bonus points for adding a date and time you'll make this happen.

1.
2.
3.

For Further Learning

→ Read *Coaching for Equity*.

→ Enroll in a virtual Coaching for Equity learning experience and practice these skills with others (information at http://www.brightmorningteam.com).

From *The Art of Coaching Workbook: Tools to Make Every Conversation Count* by Elena Aguilar. Copyright © 2021 by Elena Aguilar. Reproduced by permission.

Coaching Across Lines of Difference

Do this activity to deepen your understanding of the role that your identity markers play when coaching clients.

It's inevitable that you will coach clients who don't share some of your identity markers. You'll likely coach teachers who don't share your gender, age, race, sexual orientation, class background, and so on. It's critical that coaches hone an awareness of how difference impacts our coaching.

Reflect

If you've coached for a little while, take a moment to think about the people you've really enjoyed coaching. Jot down their names. What made it so enjoyable?

Can you identify any patterns or commonalities amongst this group of clients you've really enjoyed working with? Did they perhaps teach similar content? Was there something about their personalities or dispositions that resonated with you?

Can you identify any preference that you have in the kind of client you coach? Do you prefer to coach those who share your gender or age group? Or those who come from the same part of the country as you do?

Now think about the clients with whom you've had a harder time. Perhaps you've struggled to connect with them or to support them. When you think about their identity markers, do you see any patterns?

When you think about identity markers, are there people who hold specific identity markers whom you find it harder to coach? Perhaps you feel less comfortable with them? Perhaps you find it harder to coach teachers who are much younger or older than you? Or perhaps you find it harder to coach people who don't speak English as a first language?

A Case Study

Pick one client to reflect on more deeply. Perhaps a client whom you feel a little challenged by or you're just not as effective as you'd like to be in coaching them.

Step 1: Identify

List the similarities and differences that you are aware of between you and your client as they relate to identity markers. (You might want to look back at the activity in Chapter 1, Exploring Identity Markers, for a reminder of the many kinds of identity markers that we have). Refrain from making assumptions about what you don't know.

Similarities between me and my client	Differences between me and my client

Step 2: Reflect on a Conversation

Flag this page, and after your next conversation with this client come back here and consider how identity markers showed up in your interactions with this client. Reflect on your thoughts and feelings about them, observations of them, and communication with them. Jot down your responses to the following questions.

What was the purpose of this conversation? (Were you getting to know a client, analyzing data together, reflecting on an observation, or lesson planning?)

What role did my identity play in this conversation? How did my identity markers influence how I felt, thought, and acted in this conversation?

How might my identity markers have influenced my client? Why do I think that's the case?

What role did my client's identity markers have on my thoughts, feelings, and actions in this conversation? How might I have perceived or understood my client given their identity markers?

Was there anything I said as a result of the differences or similarities in our identity markers? What impact might that have had? What would I change if I could say it again?

Was there anything I refrained from saying because of the differences or similarities in identity markers? What impact might that have had? Why do I think I refrained from saying those things?

What conclusions did I come to today about my client? Is it possible that any of those had to do with of my client's identity markers? What is the impact on how I feel about my client based on these conclusions?

How were my emotions influenced by the similarities or differences between our identity markers? Was it harder for me to empathize with someone who has many different identity markers than I do? Did I feel more judgmental of someone who is different from or similar to me?

In my next coaching conversation with this client, what might be important for me to be aware of around coaching across lines of difference? If applicable, what intention or commitment can I set around this?

For Further Learning

→ Take our online course, Coaching Across Lines of Difference. For more information, go to http://www.brightmorningteam.com.

→ Read *Coaching for Equity.*

From *The Art of Coaching Workbook: Tools to Make Every Conversation Count* by Elena Aguilar. Copyright © 2021 by Elena Aguilar. Reproduced by permission.

How to Create a Coaching Agreement

Do this activity to understand and analyze the components of a coaching agreement and to inform the agreement you create.

A whole lot of unnecessary suffering and conflict happens between people when we're not on the same page about something or because we have different expectations of each other. A coaching agreement is simply a way for us to flesh out our shared or respective expectations, responsibilities, and commitments. It can feel a little awkward or like an unnecessary formality but creating this coaching agreement together will prevent a good amount of misunderstanding.

As described in *The Art of Coaching*, coaching agreements provide the who, what, when, where, and why of the work between you and your client. They can include a definition of coaching, the role of confidentiality, times you will be meeting, the role of your work plan, and the role of feedback. You—the coach—are responsible for writing most of the agreement, although there will be elements for which you'll want to get your client's input and engagement.

One consideration for the coach when writing the agreement is ensuring what we commit to is reasonable given the number of clients we have, the time we can offer each one, and our personal responsibilities. Overpromising and underdelivering (or simply breaking commitments captured in the agreement) can dismantle our client's trust. Craft your agreement in alignment with what you can realistically deliver versus what you think you *should* be delivering.

What follows is a portion of one of Elena's coaching agreements. It differs from the example in *The Art of Coaching* to provide additional insight and learning. As you read through it, note anything that you'd like to add into your coaching agreements.

This is for a client whom Elena coaches virtually—so you'll see some specific agreements about virtual coaching that might be helpful. After reviewing, use the questions to consider when designing your own agreement.

I'm honored that you've decided to engage in coaching with me. I am truly grateful to be a witness to growth and learning, and I look forward to this journey together. Please read through this mix of technical and substantive stuff that I need to share, and then we'll discuss your thoughts and questions.

Sessions

What we talk about is entirely up to you. Your coaching time is *your time,* and you bring the topics, questions, and concerns that you want to talk about. If you want to organize your coaching around goals, that's your choice. You can also focus your coaching on an inquiry question, and we can see where curiosity takes you. I encourage you to be as fully present as possible for your coaching sessions—to be in a place where you have privacy to speak, to put everything else aside, close down distractions, and to show up fully for yourself.

Confidentiality

Our coaching sessions are completely confidential. The fact that you are engaging in coaching is completely confidential. You are welcome, of course, to tell whomever you want that you are engaging in coaching, but I will never share that information with anyone.

Scheduling

We will schedule our sessions 6 weeks at a time. I will make every effort to accommodate your preference for a day and time to meet. If you need to change the time of your session, I can accommodate one reschedule per month. Beyond that, if you need to cancel your appointment, I am not able to reschedule your time. If you need to cancel your appointment, I'll be grateful for as much lead time as possible. I will schedule our meetings on Google calendar and will send you an invite.

On-Call Services

While we'll meet at our scheduled times, I am also available to you as needed, on call, if something comes up that you want coaching on. I will attempt to meet these needs as much as possible. I'll let you know if your needs and wants are exceeding my capacity—but usually, clients feel reluctant to reach out, so I encourage you to reach out if and when you want.

Where We'll Meet

You can choose whether we meet on Zoom or by phone. If we meet by Zoom, I'll send you the Zoom link. If we meet by phone, I'll expect your call at our agreed-on time. Regardless, my cell phone is _____. Please note that a text message is always preferred if you are trying to reach me outside our scheduled times.

Completing Coaching Services

Although you have made a commitment to engaging in coaching services for a year, if coaching isn't serving you you can break this contract. I encourage you to participate in a closing-out conversation with me before we finalize our work together.

Reflect

Which components of Elena's coaching agreement would you use in your own?

What additional content would you add to your coaching agreement? Why?

What feels most important for you to include in this agreement based on what's required to show up as your best self for your clients?

Does your coaching situation require any additional specific agreements? If so, how could you address those?

Next Steps

Use the template in *The Art of Coaching* (Exhibit 5.3, pp. 94–95) to create your coaching agreement and draw on your reflections from Elena's sample to inform what you include.

How to Build Even More Trust

This activity will help you connect the Transformational Coaching ways of being to how to build trust.

What are your typical go-to moves when trying to build trust with someone? List three here.

In his book *The Speed of Trust*, Stephen Covey talks about two dimensions of trust: character and competence. Character refers to your ways of being as a coach, and to your motives and integrity. Competence includes your knowledge, skills, follow-through, and results. Both character and competence are established over time.

Character

Earlier in this chapter, we looked at six core ways of being of a Transformational Coach. Take a moment now to consider how these dispositions build trust in coaching. Aim to identify two observable moves a coach might make to exhibit each way of being.

Way of being	"This way of being builds trust when. . ."
Compassion	*For example, "I acknowledge my client's unspoken emotions."*

Way of being	"This way of being builds trust when. . ."
Curiosity	*For example, "I name and question my own assumptions."*
Trust in the coaching process	*For example, "I clarify with clients the goals for our conversation"*
Humility and mutuality	*For example, "I ask a client's permission."*
Appreciation	*For example, "I tell my client how much I enjoy working together."*
Learner orientation	*For example, "I am realistic about who I am and what I can offer."*

From *The Art of Coaching Workbook: Tools to Make Every Conversation Count* by Elena Aguilar. Copyright © 2021 by Elena Aguilar. Reproduced by permission.

Reflect

Think of a conversation when you engaged in at least two of the actions you named in the table. What was the impact?

Think of a relationship where trust felt low. How might the actions you named in the table have supported trust between you and the other person?

Put a star next to two actions you named that, even though you know they're important, you don't often take. When in the next 2 weeks can you practice each action?

Competence

Our hope is that this entire workbook serves to deepen your competence as a Transformational Coach. The activities in this book can help you get crystal clear on the value you bring as a coach and equip you with the skills and practices needed to make good on that promise.

Competence is not just about the knowledge and skills you possess but also the results you achieve in applying them. Demonstrating your competence as a coach means gathering evidence of your impact, which is notoriously challenging. Here are five ways to make the impact of your coaching known:

1. *Formative feedback.* Ending each coaching session with a question that invites your client to identify what has been most helpful or useful that day is competence affirming for you both. The client ends by consciously acknowledging the value of the time you share, and you have the opportunity to understand how and where you have the greatest impact with them in each session and build on it.

2. *Referrals.* When a coaching relationship is going well or at the end of a successful engagement, ask your client to think of one to two colleagues who might also benefit from coaching. Then ask them to refer those people for coaching. Your client's story of how they've benefited will say more about your competence than you ever could.

3. *Artifacts.* Gather artifacts of your coaching work and modify them to share with a broader audience. Did you and a teacher co-plan a great math unit? Share it with the department or the district math specialist. Did you create a custom observation guide for a teacher struggling with student engagement? Offer it to the admin team.

4. *Testimonials.* Strong coaches end their coaching engagements by asking clients to reflect on their learning and progress toward their goals. Ask to record this conversation or write down powerful reflections that speak to the impact of coaching on the teacher or students. Capture these on the walls of your office for others to casually read.

5. *Data.* Whether or not your school or district collects data on coaching, you can create systems for measuring what matters to you. For example, you might ask teachers to complete a survey at the end of a coaching engagement in which you ask them, on a scale of 1 to 5, how likely they are to recommend coaching to others. Share this data with your supervisor during your performance review process and offer it to teachers who express skepticism about coaching.

Take a moment to reflect on opportunities in your school setting to expand and acknowledge your competence as a Transformational Coach.

What learning opportunities exist for me as a coach here?

How can I share with others the learning I have undertaken as a coach? (For example, create a "What I'm Reading" board or summarize a recent workshop you attended in the staff newsletter.)

What data do we gather on coaching? What opportunities exist for me to shape the data we gather and who sees it?

Of the four methods shared in this activity, which one will I experiment with in the next month? How?

An Initial Coaching Conversation

This activity will help you prepare you for successful first conversations with new coaching clients.

The beginning of a coaching relationship carries all the excitement and nerves of a first date. Who is this person I'm about to coach? Will I like them? What will they think of me? How will our relationship be shaped by the time and place in which we're coming together?

Even as we are stepping into the unknown, there is much we can do to prepare for a successful launch of a coaching relationship. The following transcript is of a conversation between a coach and her new client. As you read, use the following codes to engage with the text:

✓ = I have said this when I've coached someone.

! = This would be hard for me to say. It would feel awkward.

★ = I'd like to incorporate this into coaching conversations. I want to say this.

→ = I wish someone would ask me this question. I want to think about this for myself.

COACH: Hi, Kei. I've been looking forward to talking today. I'm really glad you reached out about coaching. I've heard such great things about you from the students here, and I'm excited to learn more about you.

KEI: Thanks for meeting. I've been meaning to reach out for a while. I hope it's not too late in the year for us to get started. I wasn't sure whether you worked with mentors or whether you were here to support only teachers; since my role is split between the two, I wasn't sure.

COACH: I'm glad you asked. Since my role is to improve student outcomes by elevating the leadership of all of our instructional staff, you definitely qualify!

KEI: So, where do we start?

COACH: Tell me what prompted you to reach out for coaching. What's been on your mind?

KEI: Yeah. . . [*sighs*] So, I think you know that this year I'm only teaching part time because of this new in-house mentorship program we're trying out. I think the administration has finally recognized that, given the amount of turnover we have, we need to do a better job supporting new teachers. Sometimes that's teachers new to the profession, and sometimes just teachers new to North [High School]. So there's a team of four of us doing this now. Three of us are still part-time teachers: my colleagues Kathy, Miguel, and I. And then Beatrice is kind of the lead mentor. She has a caseload like we do, but she also oversees the whole program, leads

From The Art of Coaching Workbook: Tools to Make Every Conversation Count *by Elena Aguilar. Copyright © 2021 by Elena Aguilar. Reproduced by permission.*

our professional development, and all that. [Coach: Uh-huh. . .] There's definitely some stuff around, I don't know, figuring out how to balance these new responsibilities. I mean, we all know that having half the classes doesn't mean having half the work!

COACH: [*Chuckles*] So true! Okay, so it sounds like you want to explore this question of balancing responsibilities as a teacher and a mentor. [Kei: Yeah. . .] And is that a time thing? Or are there other factors involved?

KEI: I mean, time is definitely part of it. But I suppose there are other issues, too. I mean, my relationships have shifted a little because of this. It's hard to put my finger on, but it's almost like some of the other teachers, people I've worked with for *years*, like they don't quite see me as one of them anymore. I don't know if this is all in my imagination or what, but it feels like sometimes I walk into the staff lounge now and the conversation shifts, like whatever people were talking about they'd rather not say in front of me. And I've always prided myself on having good relationships at work. I don't quite know what to make of that.

COACH: Okay, so there's the managing your day part, and you're feeling like you're being seen differently by others, maybe in a way that doesn't feel so good, and you'd like to understand what that's all about. Is that right?

KEI: Yeah, for sure. And part of me wonders whether it has something to do with Beatrice. Frankly, we were all a little surprised when she was put in charge of this program. I mean, she and I have always gotten along well enough, but she's not. . . er. . . well, let's just say she's not really the nurturing type. And I think so much of this mentor role is about helping people feel comfortable here, like they're part of the North family, like they belong. [Coach: Mm-hmm. . .] I mean, the woman knows her stuff. She went to this conference on mentoring over the summer and came back all fired up and with lots of great resources. She's been really helpful in that respect. But. . . [*pauses*] Well I think she's really invested in this program succeeding, and one of the ways that shows up is that she talks it up a lot. She did this whole presentation at the all-staff meeting at the start of the year, and she has the principal put little updates in her weekly e-mails.

COACH: And what does that make you think or feel?

KEI: I suppose, honestly, I feel a little embarrassed. There's so much that teachers are doing every day in this school that goes uncelebrated, I guess it feels like we shouldn't be so. . . visible. There are all these other dynamics at play in this retention and teacher-mentoring thing that she's

	either oblivious to or just doesn't want to take on. And I know some of the staff see that.
COACH:	Such as?
KEI:	So, it was a big adjustment for me when I got here. You know, I'm a Pacific Islander. I grew up in a pretty diverse neighborhood and went to school with all sorts of kids. I thought coming here to a mostly Black community and school—well I just kind of thought I'd fit right in. But it's not that simple. There's a lot I've had to learn about our community here, a lot of relationships I've worked hard to build over the past 7 years. And I see a lot of our new teachers. . . I mean, they're well-intentioned, and I know they want to be here. But a lot of them are White and pretty young. And part of helping them succeed here, part of helping them help *kids* succeed here, is about tackling those dynamics head-on. Our administration has done a bit on this front, and it's been okay. But so much happens in the informal conversations, in the ways teachers do or don't call things out in the staff lounge, or the ways people talk to and about students. I guess part of what intrigued me about this mentor role was the possibility of supporting new teachers in that way: helping them understand their own privilege, their own biases, helping them see how really amazing the kids at North are and how funny, and smart, and talented they are.
COACH:	And you don't feel like you're getting to engage with teachers in that way?
KEI:	Well, kind of. I mean, I definitely try to bring these things up when the opportunity arises. But Beatrice has this whole scope and sequence for mentorship that she developed at that training last summer, and she's pretty insistent that we follow it. She says it's just for the first year, that we'll be meeting in the spring to revise it for next year, but I guess I'm wishing we had more flexibility within it already or that as a team we could talk more about the reality of who the teachers are and who the students are at this school and how that's also a factor in retention and impact.
COACH:	Is that one of the things you'd like to explore through coaching—how you can raise these concerns with Beatrice and the other mentors?
KEI:	Is that the kind of thing we can do together? Is that your role?
COACH:	Well, the things you're naming sound deeply tied to both student outcomes and staff leadership, so yeah. And ultimately, this is *your* learning space. You determine what we work on together.
KEI:	Then, yes. I do think that would be helpful. I mean, I want to address the logistical pieces, how I'm using my time and just getting my systems in

place to manage two jobs, but I'd also love to think through my role on the mentor team and how to bring these concerns into our conversations.

COACH: Great! It sounds like we're starting to get some clarity on the goals for this partnership.

Imagine that Kei is your client. Skim back through the transcript, putting yourself in the place of the coach, and reflect on the following questions.

How have the foundations for trust been laid in this conversation? What considerations might be important in strengthening trust with this client?

What else do you want to know about this client? What are you curious about?

What challenges can you anticipate might surface if you were coaching this client?

While the dialogue between Kei and his coach demonstrates one approach to beginning a coaching relationship, there are a variety of things you may want to learn about your client as you get started. For each of the following categories, write two questions you would feel comfortable asking during an initial conversation with a client. For inspiration, see Elena's lists in *The Art of Coaching* (pp. 80–81), though we encourage you to write questions that feel natural for you.

To learn about. . .	I could ask. . .
My client's background	
How my client relates to others	
My client's experience with coaching	
What brought my client to coaching now	

CHAPTER 6

Enjoying the Exploration Stage

When you travel to a new country or city, do you prefer to read a dozen books about the place before you get there? Or do you arrive and sit in a central location and observe daily life? How do you like to get to know a new person? Do you have questions you regularly ask new acquaintances or colleagues? Or do you prefer to sit back and observe them and see who they are that way?

When we begin a new coaching relationship, we might draw on our tendencies or style in discovering new people and places. We will likely also need to take additional actions so that we acquire a meaningful and thorough understanding of our new client as well as of the context in which they work.

In Chapter 6 of *The Art of Coaching* you read a description of how to go about the exploration stage of coaching. In this workbook chapter, we'll provide you with a tool to keep yourself on track in the process of exploration. Then we'll give you a few new resources to build out your exploration toolkit.

The Exploration Project Plan

Do this activity to help you stay on track in learning about a new client.

In *The Art of Coaching,* Elena describes 10 steps in the exploration phase of coaching. After you've read those, use this project plan to determine which ones you'll do, when you'll do them by, and any next steps. We're including this here to help you stay organized because there are a lot of components within these 10 steps—plus, there are a few new tips here. For each item on the list, you'll find an explanation in Chapter 6 of *The Art of Coaching.* What's here is not meant to describe the steps but rather to help you get them done.

You'll need one of these project plans for each client you work with. You can download this template from our website, http://www.brightmorningteam.com. You could also use this one here to plan for one client with whom you want to really go deep. We know that the action steps here might seem like a lot to do, especially if you coach a dozen or more teachers. In that case, diving deep into one teacher's situation will yield learnings that may be helpful with others.

In the first column, check the items you want to do.

	Action steps	By when	My next steps or notes
1.	Gather relevant documents.		
	Determine organizing system (binder, digital folder).		
	Make a list of documents to collect.		
	Ask client about their understandings and feelings about these documents.		
2.	Gather and analyze formal data.		
	Collect data on student experience and outcomes.		
	Plan a conversation to talk to client about their thoughts and feelings about data.		
3.	Initiate informal conversations.		
	Identify a few times to walk around school and talk to parents, staff members, and students.		
	Identify specific people to talk to who might also have useful insights and talk to them and schedule a time to meet with them.		
4.	Uncover knowledge, skills, and passions.		
	Write up questions to ask the client and determine when this conversation will happen.		

	Action steps	By when	My next steps or notes
	Pick a page or two in the coaching notebook for the client on which to keep a list of things that are personal (e.g., they love chocolate, their uncle is a musician).		
5.	Explore beliefs about change.		
	Write up questions to ask clients about their beliefs about change and determine when to ask these.		
6.	Offer personality type test and other self-assessments.		
	Invite a client to take the Myers-Briggs personality type test (http://www.16personalities.com).		
	Plan a conversation to discuss the Myers-Briggs results.		
7.	Observe the client.		
	Talk to client about observing them and get their permission.		
	Observe client in a variety of contexts—not just teaching.		
	Observe staff meetings and other times when staff come together to get a sense of staff culture.		
8.	Conduct interviews and surveys.		
	Interview key stakeholders about their experience with the client.		
	Survey students, parents, or staff (when coaching a leader).		
9.	Look for the fires.		
	Create a page in coaching notebook for fires. Add to it as fires appear or are spoken about.		
10.	Engage in self-awareness exercises for coaches.		
	Decide how to track reflection and learning. Gather required items (a journal, for example).		
	Other (what else might be useful to do or gather to understand your client?)		

For Further Learning

Sometimes, we also use the following frameworks to get to know a client:

- Their strengths as determined by the CliftonStrengths by Gallup (StrengthsFinder) test (note that this is not free, but it's very useful) (find out more at https://www.gallup.com /cliftonstrengths)
- Their love languages (free): https://www.5lovelanguages.com/quizzes/
- Their tendency, according to Gretchen Rubin's Four Tendencies (free): https://quiz .gretchenrubin.com/
- Their Enneagram type (small fee): https://tests.enneagraminstitute.com/

Before you offer these to a client, make sure that you do them so that you'll understand what they encompass and so that you can discuss your client's results with them after. It's better to have a meaningful and reflective conversation about the results of one of these tools than it is to speak superficially about several, especially with limited time. It's great to then add tools as you and your client build trust and comfort or when different situations or challenges arise. Finally, there's no need to share your own results—unless your client asks.

Collecting Data: Reflecting on Our Own Attitudes

Do this activity to explore your beliefs about data and identify the types of data that will be most beneficial in your coaching relationships.

Before you explore your client's beliefs and attitudes about data, it is important to explore your own. If you are part of a professional learning community of coaches, it's really helpful to talk to each other about your beliefs around data and practice having the conversations that you'll have with teachers.

We define data as including all of the following—and more:

- Interviews with students
- Parent survey responses
- Detention and suspension rates
- Office referrals
- Video and photos
- Student work
- Standardized test scores
- Student grades
- Retention rates
- Attendance rates
- Classroom observation notes
- A teacher or coach's reflective journal
- Demographic information

Reflect

When you hear the word data, what comes to mind? Why?

From *The Art of Coaching Workbook: Tools to Make Every Conversation Count* by Elena Aguilar. Copyright © 2021 by Elena Aguilar. Reproduced by permission.

In the school you're in now (or the last school you worked in) what kinds of data are collected?

When you were a teacher, what kind of data did you find most useful and why?

How do you hope your clients feel about data you'll use by the end of your time together? What might you do to make that happen?

Knowing Your Community: Shadowing a Student for a Day

This activity will help you better understand the experience of students at your school and thus the strengths and shortcomings of the essential structures of the school itself.

We can learn most about schools through the student experience. Education researcher Grant Wiggins encourages educators to empathize with the learner by shadowing students for a day or two to best understand what happens during their school day. We believe that our schools would be different places if school leaders, staff, and teachers spent at least one day understanding the student experience by shadowing a student from the time they arrive at school until the time they leave.

Preparation

- Consider shadowing students from underrepresented or marginalized backgrounds (students of color, English learners, students with learning differences). You might actually learn the most from shadowing a student whose identity markers are in many ways as different as possible from your own.
- Depending on context, you may or may not want the student to know that you're shadowing them. Sometimes students who are aware of your presence may hyperperform or act in ways that are out of character.
- If the student is aware that you're shadowing them, make sure the student is aware of your role and purpose of your day; also make sure you've used the appropriate channels (e.g., permissions) to conduct your shadow visit.
- Depending on school culture and context, you may want to reach out to classroom teachers in advance and share about your goals for the shadow day. Sometimes making teachers aware of your shadow day in advance may shape their actions and they may teach differently knowing you are there. Use your best judgment about what feels most appropriate. If you do communicate with teachers in advance, your message could look like the following:

Dear [name of teacher],

In an effort to better understand the student experience, I will be shadowing [name of student] throughout their day. The purpose of this experience is so I can best understand the rhythms of a school day, know what the direct experience of a student is, and better understand the context for my role and responsibilities.

This experience is observational in nature and student focused and not meant to be evaluative. I will not be sharing my observation notes with anyone.

Even if your students are taking an exam or doing silent sustained work, it will be helpful for me to be a witness to the student experience.

If you have any questions, please feel free to reach out. Thank you so much for your time and consideration.

Table 6.1: Shadow Day Observation Tool

Course or subject	Time	Observations	Reflections or questions

On the Shadow Day

- When in classrooms, sit off to the side or in the back of the room, somewhere that isn't going to be a distraction. Some teachers may introduce you to the class; be prepared for students to ask why you're there.
- Document your experience; take notes of what you observe—both the teacher and student moves. You might create a tool to capture your observations using the simple headings in Table 6.1.

After the Shadow Day, Reflect

What were your primary observations of the student you shadowed? What were your primary observations of other students' experience?

What would you most like to celebrate about what you observed?

What were other important insights from your observation day?

When the student you shadowed goes home, how do you think they'd describe their day, and their experience in each class?

When teachers go home, how do you think they'd describe that class and the way that student showed up for it?

What was the day's most surprising insight? Why was it surprising?

What implications do these insights have for students?

What implications do these insights have for your role?

Who should I share my insights with and discuss what I learned? Administrators at my site? A grade level or department?

Knowing Your Community: Understanding School Culture

This activity will help you to understand the organizational culture of a school through conducting interviews with a range of school stakeholders.

To coach effectively, it is important not only to know and build trust with your client but also to understand the contexts your clients work within. An interview can be a useful tool to understand the ways organizational culture is lived within a school—and the impact that culture has on your client and their students.

The Process

Although interviews can be conducted at any time, the information you glean will be especially useful toward the beginning of a coaching relationship. If you work at the site where you coach, then you will most likely have an easier time identifying people to interview. If you work at multiple sites and time is a challenge, consider engaging in this process at one of the sites where you coach. While your sample size will be small, you can still learn much from several people's experiences. Among the school community members to interview, consider asking the following people for a 30-minute interview:

- A school leader (principal, assistant principal, dean)
- A teacher (different from the one you're coaching, preferably a different grade or subject area)
- A nonteaching staff member (front office person, maintenance staff, counselor)
- Students (either in a group, or a couple of different students from the student you shadowed, possibly from different grade levels, and across different demographics)
- Family members and caregivers

Choose about seven or so people to interview, so if a couple of people are unable to meet this commitment, you still have a range of people to draw upon.

Implications for leaders: If you are new to a school site, empathy interviews are a powerful way to learn about school community members and their experiences. Perhaps you conduct interviews with those you serve most directly first and, over time, interview additional community members as you are able.

At this stage, you need to introduce yourself and the purpose of the interview. The following language can be a helpful starting point, whether in person or via e-mail (you may need to adapt further for students):

My name is _____, and I am a coach at this site. To best support my client and learn as much as I can so my client can support students, I want to learn about this school from your experience of it. It is important to me that I can hear your honest reflections and stories so I can better understand the connections of different members of the community to this school's values and culture. The interview will take about 30–45 minutes of your time.

Setting Up

Once you have your list of interviewees, create a schedule that feels realistic to you. You can conduct interviews within the span of a couple days or over the course of a week. Devote about 60 minutes to each interview, which will allow you to review your notes and write any immediate reflections from the conversation.

Preparing Your Questions

To understand organizational culture, focus your questions around connections, beliefs, and values. Here are some questions to ask:

- What are you most proud of in your work here?
- Where and how do you think you make the biggest impact in this school?
- When you walk into this building, what do you see? What stands out?
  - ☐ What don't you see?
  - ☐ What do you wish you could see more of?
- What is this site's motto or core values?
  - ☐ How do you know?
- Who do you feel most connected to here? Why is that the case? Describe the quality of your connections here:
  - ☐ What is your connection to school leaders?
  - ☐ To colleagues?
  - ☐ To students?
  - ☐ To families?
- How is information shared in the community? Who shares it?
  - ☐ How do you learn about school events?
  - ☐ About what's happening in the classroom?
- How do leaders interact with people here?
  - ☐ How do teachers interact?
  - ☐ How do students interact?

- How do families interact?
  - [ ] How do families interact?
  - [ ] How do you know?
- Tell me about a time...
  - [ ] when you felt really proud to be part of this school. Why?
  - [ ] when it was hard to be a part of this school. Why?
- If you had a magic wand and could make one improvement to the school, what would it be?
- Think about someone you spend time with outside of school that you talk to about your work. If I asked them, what would they say makes you happiest here? What would they say you'd like to change or improve?
- How do people currently outside the school (peer schools, prospective families, alumni) describe their experience here?

The Interview

Because you are a Transformational Coach, you can easily apply your coaching dispositions to this context. Here are some additional reminders, particularly if you have little to no rapport or trust with the people you're interviewing:

- Build rapport with a brief check-in. A good starter question could be, "Tell me about something you recently did that brought you joy." Spend no more than 5 minutes checking in.
- Ask one question at a time. Probe more deeply for questions that seem interesting to your interviewee. You may not get to all your questions.
- Look for inconsistencies and contradictions; what people say and what they do can be very different.
- Observe nonverbal cues, such as use of hands and facial expressions.
- Ask neutral questions like "What do you think about...?"
- Explore emotions. "What's coming up for you right now?" "What do you feel about...?"
- If you get stuck, ask, "Can you say more about that?" or "Tell me more."

After the Interview

Thank your interviewee for their time, of course, and when possible send a brief follow-up or thank-you. You may also consider sharing some of the themes of your day with those you interviewed.

Knowing Your Community: Classroom Learning Walks

Do this activity to learn how to conduct a learning walk so you can better understand classroom culture.

Learning walks, a process used for quick classroom observations, can be useful experiences when identifying what learning and culture looks like in learning spaces. The goals of a learning walk are to capture snapshot data to better understand teaching and learning—from instructional practices to student engagement to classroom environment. The following process can help you make the most of your time during the walk.

Prior to the Walk

Clarify the goals of a learning walk with your client and coordinate timing of visit. If you and your client are doing a learning walk of other classrooms, coordinate with the teachers you're visiting. Make sure to communicate that your intent is not evaluative but rather that you're wanting to understand classroom culture. Also be sure to review confidentiality agreements. The teacher you'll visit might be wondering if you'll share your observations with the principal, so be sure to clarify who you'll be talking to about what you see and hear.

Walking: The Class Visit

- Spend about 10–20 minutes in the classroom.
- Take in all available data:
  - ☐ What is the teacher doing?
  - ☐ What are the students doing?
  - ☐ What artifacts are on walls, student desks, and teacher desks that might help us understand the learning process?
  - ☐ If virtual, what do you notice students doing? How is the teacher using technology tools or virtual considerations (e.g., cameras, mute).
  - ☐ Who is doing most of the talking and work? How is time being used?
- If you can do so without being disruptive, ask students about what they're working on and what they are learning.
- Take lots of notes. Capture as many specifics as you can.

After the Walk

- Review observation notes and do some interpretation:
  - ☐ What do your observations tell you about the class, the teacher, the students? What questions remain?
  - ☐ What are the implications of this learning walk for the student experience?
  - ☐ What did you learn about yourself from this learning walk?
- Send the teacher a quick note. A protocol like "Wows and Wonders" is a quick way to offer feedback (Wow: what was impressive; Wonder: something you are curious to learn more about—the more specific, the better). Be mindful of anything that comes across as constructive feedback or criticism in your note. If you saw something concerning, plan to ask about it in your conversation from a space of curiosity. If you're unsure, make time to observe again—and for a greater length of time if you are able. Offering "drive-by feedback" in a note can break down trust or feel disempowering from the teacher perspective and make your conversation later more difficult.
- Plan for your coaching conversation based on the data you gathered. What questions might you ask your client? What do you anticipate your client might say?
- Sometimes when we observe a teacher, we can walk away feeling like, *There's so much this teacher needs to work on!* That might be the case, but be careful when you meet with them not to turn on the feedback firehose. You'll need to determine what's most important to start with and what the teacher might be most willing to work on, and take it one conversation at a time.

In Table 6.2, you'll read an example of a coach's learning walk notes. When you do your own walk, create a template based on this one or come up with your own.

Table 6.2: Example of a Coach's Learning Walk Notes

Observations What I see, hear, and experience	Reflection What this tells me about this classroom community	Questions
26 fifth-grade students: 18 students I perceive as students of color (4 Black students, 3 Asian students, 11 Latinx students), 9 who present as White. 14 boys, 12 girls. Teacher is a White female.	Class is racially and ethnically diverse with an almost even gender balance. Class is representative of the demographics of the school.	What are implications for students with predominantly White teachers in a school that has a majority of students of color?
Desks arranged in groups of four with class materials in the center of each table (pens, glue sticks, construction paper). The far side of the room is the "reading corner" with rugs, a bookshelf of books, and beanbag chairs. The words Reading Corner are on the wall above the area. Three computer stations against the far wall. Teacher's desk in the far corner with a bulletin board behind desk. Bulletin boards with student work around the room. This week's poetry includes a poem by William Carlos Williams and is surrounded by student poems that mimic his style.	Classroom culture encourages collaborating and literacy based on what I see on the walls and the ways the desks are arranged. There is a lot of visual stimulation in the class, and the poetry bulletin board seems to be updated weekly. Teacher's corner takes up very little space. There seems to be intention in how this teacher wants students to move around the classroom, and the reading corner invites a cozy vibe.	How does the classroom environment shape classroom culture? I didn't see class norms anywhere, and it seems this class promotes a lot of student voice. I wonder how the teacher creates and fosters classroom culture?
Students doing collaborative jigsaw group work (eight groups of four, one group of three) are discussing and creating storyboard for *Esperanza Rising*. One set of instructions is in the middle of the table for each group. Teacher circulating and crouching down with each group. When she comes by, students are attentive. Two groups seem to be struggling and have their hands raised as teacher is talking to another group.	Teacher seems to be spending more time with some groups than others. There seems to be a reliance on the teacher. Some groups are working quietly, and a couple of groups have had their hands raised for several minutes.	What are the procedures for asking questions? How does the teacher check for understanding? How clear are students about their expectations for this assignment?

From *The Art of Coaching Workbook: Tools to Make Every Conversation Count* by Elena Aguilar. Copyright © 2021 by Elena Aguilar. Reproduced by permission.

CHAPTER 7

Assembling Your Basic Coaching Toolbox

At some point almost every coach starts to feel overwhelmed by the endless complexity of coaching. If you are beginning to feel like it's time to organize an overwhelming amount of material, if you are looking for some clarity about what you really need to know, what resources you really need at hand, you'll appreciate this chapter.

The activities gathered here are the key tools we think you'll need in any coaching relationship. We like thinking about a toolbox because it's something handy, something that you can carry with you. However, we also want to caution you that this analogy could be problematic if you think about your clients as *fixable*. Generally, that's how we use our tools, right? We build, fix, and assemble objects. We feel compelled to issue this warning because many schools and organizations are transactional places where teachers feel disempowered. We don't want to contribute to that by implying that coaches run around schools with tools to fix teachers. We offer *resources* for coaching—tools that can refine your listening, deepen how you hear and understand clients, and help you focus conversations.

In this chapter, we've compiled key tools—most of which are not found in *The Art of Coaching*. The first four activities introduce new content and they might feel a little dense. You're really getting a sneak peek at what will likely be in the second edition of *The Art of Coaching*. These concepts can be powerful elements of successful Transformational Coaching.

In addition to the tools we've chosen to include in this chapter, we encourage you to determine which tools (or resources) in this workbook and in *The Art of Coaching* you're finding to be essential in your coaching work. Though we know that many coaches will benefit from using the resources in this chapter regularly, we also know that many of us have unique needs. Consider what's in this chapter to be the hammer, screwdriver, tape measure, and wrench for coaching, and then think about what else you need, given your unique circumstances, to be successful as a coach. Perhaps a level or a putty knife or a clamp?

Finally, before we dive in, we invite you to reconsider our use of metaphors. If the idea of tools and a toolbox isn't resonating for you, how would you like to think about your essential coaching resources? As keys on your key ring? As a menu of resources? If you've got some preliminary ideas, jot those down or draw them in the space that follows before continuing in this chapter.

How to Structure a Coaching Cycle

This activity will help you map out how to design a coaching cycle.

You can't build a house without a blueprint. The equivalent for a coach is a plan that describes the overarching sequence of actions. This is a tool that sets you up to be intentional and systematic and therefore successful. You might think about this process as a blueprint for what you do in a *coaching cycle*, or over a period of working with a client.

Elena conceives of this process as being composed of four phases, shown in Figure 7.1. These phases are more or less sequential, although at any point in a coaching cycle we may draw strategies from other phases. In the beginning of a coaching relationship, more time is spent in the *surfacing* and *recognizing* phases. After a coach has worked with a client for some time, and after they've spent meaningful time in the first phases, it's likely that they'll often be working in the *create* phase.

Interestingly, this essential tool is scalable. Just as it can shape a coaching cycle that plays out over weeks and months, it also provides a map for a single conversation. In any conversation, a Transformational Coach frequently moves through all four phases.

Figure 7.1: Phases of Transformational Coaching

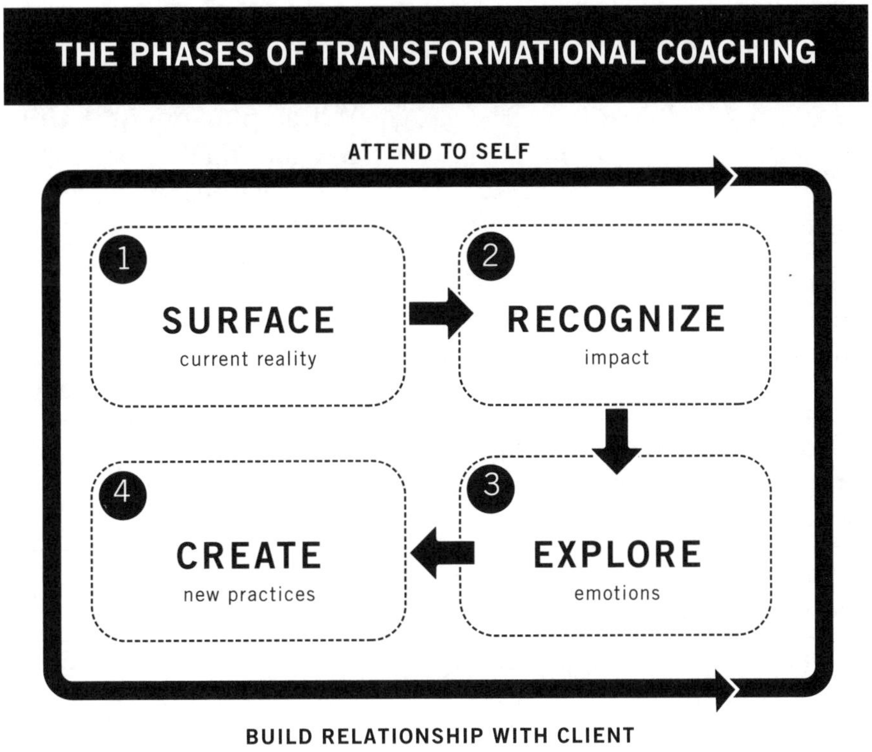

From *The Art of Coaching Workbook: Tools to Make Every Conversation Count* by Elena Aguilar. Copyright © 2021 by Elena Aguilar. Reproduced by permission.

Appendix B provides an in-depth look at these four phases, and in *Coaching for Equity* Elena goes much deeper into them. Here's an overview.

Phase 1: Surface. We surface what's happening in a classroom, school, or organization by seeking to understand the teacher or leader, the students, the community, the institutional history, as well as current contexts. We consider both strengths and challenges.

Phase 2: Recognize. We guide a client to unpack the root causes of the challenges they're facing and explore the underlying mental models that contribute to the problems. We support our clients as they identify and reflect on how those problems impact students, their communities, and themselves.

Phase 3: Explore. We coach our client to acknowledge, name, accept, and understand emotions. This allows the client to release emotions and access deeper levels of courage, commitment, and confidence.

Phase 4: Create. We coach to create new beliefs and ways of being, which in turn create new behaviors.

To deepen your understanding of these phases, the following list provides snapshots from a coaching cycle. As you read through these randomly listed snapshots, consider which phase you would guess they belong to. You can also reference Appendix B if you're stuck.

Snapshot	Which phase might this be found in? S = Surface R = Recognize E = Explore C = Create
A coach models how to redirect off-task student behavior. Then the teacher practices and receives feedback.	
A coach uses the ladder of inference to help a client reflect on the assumptions that they made about a student's abilities.	
A coach asks a teacher about what attracted her to this profession and what her core values are.	
A coach gathers and disaggregates office referral data with a teacher.	

From The Art of Coaching Workbook: Tools to Make Every Conversation Count by Elena Aguilar. Copyright © 2021 by Elena Aguilar. Reproduced by permission.

Snapshot	Which phase might this be found in? S = Surface R = Recognize E = Explore C = Create
A coach guides a teacher's reflection on office referral data.	
A coach facilitates a conversation about the teacher's racial identity and the role that plays in how the teacher responds to the off-task behavior of students who don't share his racial identity.	
A coach notices that her client is upset by the office referral data and asks the client, "What's coming up for you right now?"	
A coach and teacher visit the classroom of another teacher to observe how he responds to off-task student behavior. The coach and teacher debrief, and the teacher determines two things he'll try with his students.	
A coach co-plans the opening of a lesson for a new unit with a teacher.	
A coach asks a teacher what her fears are about trying out stations with her students.	
A coach and teacher survey students about their interests and skills.	
A coach and a teacher are reflecting on a semester of working together and the coach asks the teacher what she's feeling she did well.	

How Long Is a Coaching Cycle?

Now that you have a better idea of what happens in each phase, let's consider what this might look like in a coaching cycle. In some schools, a coaching cycle could be 6 weeks, 8 weeks, or a semester or a school year. The length of a coaching cycle is usually determined by a coach and their supervisor and is connected to how coaching is defined at that school and what role coaching plays. A coaching cycle is often really determined by how long you'll work with a client in combination with established coaching structures. Perhaps, for example, you'll work with a client for a year, but you're expected to engage in two cycles, each one around a different area of instructional practice.

Additional Resources

This question about how the length of a coaching cycle is connected to a much bigger conversation about how schools define and organize coaching. One place to start to take action on clarifying these is "You Can't Have a Coaching Culture without a Structure," by Elena Aguilar. *Educational Leadership*, Nov. 2019. Volume 77, No. 3.

What follows are some suggestions for how to plot the phases of Transformational Coaching.

Phases	8-week cycle	12-week cycle	Semester (20 weeks)
Surface	Weeks 1–3	Weeks 1–4	Weeks 1–5
Recognize	Weeks 2–4	Weeks 3–6	Weeks 4–8
Explore	Weeks 3–5	Weeks 4–7	Weeks 6–10
Create	Weeks 4–8	Weeks 5–12	Weeks 8–20

While we hope this helps to give you a starting place to think about how to move through the phases, you also need to understand that this is a rough description of what happens in a cycle. It's very likely that in a 12-week cycle, after you guide your client through the Recognize phase, you go back and surface more information. It's likely that when you're in the Surface phase, you might have an entire conversation in which you're helping your client process emotions that are coming up. For example, imagine that the veteran teacher that you're coaching begins describing what brought her into teaching and then expresses strong and painful emotions about what her teaching journey has been like. It might be that the next time you meet with her, you spend the entire conversation helping her process those emotions. It's also very common that when we're in the Create phase, we take mini cycles back through the Surface, Recognize, and Explore phases. And when we're just starting to work with a teacher, it's also quite possible that in that first or second meeting we begin to help them create new practices.

From *The Art of Coaching Workbook: Tools to Make Every Conversation Count* by Elena Aguilar. Copyright © 2021 by Elena Aguilar. Reproduced by permission.

These phases are intended to be used as a blueprint. They provide some guidance and direction, but their success depends on the coach's judgment in applying them.

Reflect

Now think about how you've organized coaching in the past or how you've sequenced your coaching now. How does this blueprint—the phases of Transformational Coaching—help you think about how to modify your coaching work? What might you change or do differently in the way you're pacing your coaching?

Make a few notes about how you'd like to engage in the process.

Phase	An activity I've done in this phase	A new activity I'd like to do in this phase
Surface		
Recognize		
Explore		
Create		

How to Focus a Coaching Cycle

Do this activity to understand how to use inquiry questions to focus a client's learning.

Who decides what a teacher focuses on in coaching? Does a teacher set their own goals in coaching, or is that something a principal determines? Does all coaching have to be focused on goals? These are some of the most common questions we hear from coaches.

In Chapter 7 of *The Art of Coaching,* Elena lays out how to create a work plan that guides coaching. A work plan is a key tool for your coaching box. It outlines what you will focus on with a client and is usually co-constructed with the client. We recommend you read that chapter before continuing with this activity.

In the time since she wrote *The Art of Coaching,* Elena has expanded her thinking about crafting the goals section of a work plan. This came about after working with a number of clients for whom the structure of goals was not useful. The clients weren't motivated by goals, they felt that setting goals limited what they might be able to learn, and they also raised some important considerations around how goals can be oppressive. Elena's client Alejandro explained that being asked to set professional growth goals further forced him into a linear, sequential, and transactional way of thinking. This was, he explained, a sharp contrast to the ways of thinking and being in the indigenous family and community to which he belonged. "As a school principal, I have to set many goals," he said. "When it comes to my professional goals, I would love to take an emergent or iterative approach." Elena was compelled by Alejandro's explanation and during the three years that they worked together Alejandro's learning was guided by *inquiry questions.*

Organizing a coaching cycle around inquiry questions is an alternative to developing goals. The idea is simple: The client generates open-ended questions about themselves and their teaching or leadership practice. Here are some examples:

- How could I develop better relationships with students and parents who don't share my racial background?
- How can I better understand why students don't master parts of a standard? How can I use a variety of formative assessments so that I have a better understanding, every day, of the progress they're making?
- What would happen if I managed my stress better in terms of the climate in my classroom? How could I better manage my stress so that I don't get triggered by student behavior?
- How can I scaffold my science lessons so that my English learners can access the content? How can I better understand their language needs so I set them up for success?

Whether you and your client choose to organize your work around inquiry questions or goals depends on personal preference. Assuming your client isn't mandated to have goals, you can talk to your client about how they'd prefer to structure their learning. Coaching toward goals and coaching toward questions proceeds similarly.

Reflect

To more deeply understand how inquiry questions can focus the learning in a coaching cycle, imagine that you are being coached. If your coach gave you the choice to determine your own inquiry questions, what would those be?

Write four open-ended questions—these generally start with "how" or "what." They should be meaningful; answering them would help you become the coach you want to be. After generating four questions, select one that feels most compelling. Write that one in the center of the bubble chart in Figure 7.2; then generate five subquestions, and write those in the surrounding bubbles. This is the same process you can use with a client to help them determine an inquiry question for a coaching cycle.

An Example of Coaches' Inquiry Questions

- How can I be more effective with teachers I think are resistant? How can I help them to be open to working with me?
- What can I do when I get really triggered by things that teachers say? How can I be sure they don't feel like I'm judging them?
- How can I have a better relationship with my principal and get him to work together on teacher professional development? How can I communicate more clearly with my principal so he understands me better?

Write Your Own Inquiry Questions

1.

2.

3.

4.

Figure 7.2: Your Inquiry Question

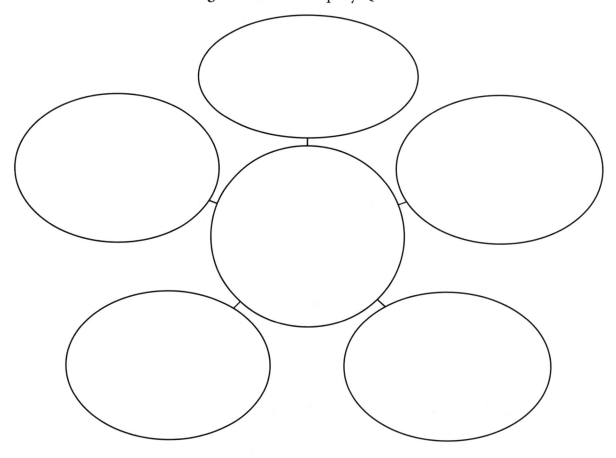

From *The Art of Coaching Workbook: Tools to Make Every Conversation Count* by Elena Aguilar. Copyright © 2021 by Elena Aguilar. Reproduced by permission.

Three Goals in a Coaching Conversation

Do this activity to understand the goals that you, the coach, will hold for how you coach in every conversation.

In a coaching cycle, ideally the client sets their learning or professional goals or determines their inquiry questions in partnership with the coach. In every conversation, the coach keeps these goals or questions at the front of their mind. They are like the goal posts for the work that the coach is doing with the client.

In addition, a Transformational Coach brings goals to every conversation—these guide what the coach says and does. As described in Chapter 1, a Transformational Coach attends to a client's behaviors, beliefs, and ways of being. Therefore, in any coaching conversation a Transformational Coach has three goals: (1) to increase the client's emotional resilience, which cultivates a *way of being*; (2) to strengthen the client's reflective abilities, which expands *beliefs*; and (3) to build the client's skills, which builds *behaviors*. Let's look at the connection between these goals in a conversation and the larger commitment to coach behaviors, beliefs, and ways of being.

Increase Resilience

Resilience shifts and expands our way of being, so when we coach to build resilience we coach a way of being. We increase our resilience when we explore our emotions, deepen our self-awareness, and tap into positive feelings including hope, purpose, curiosity, and empathy. Resilience expands when we focus on what we can influence and when we are learning and growing. Coaching toward resilience can sound like:

- I can hear some emotions in your voice when you describe that experience. Do you want to unpack those?
- What do you think that frustration was about?
- What do you think she felt in that situation?
- What did you notice about how you responded to their behavior?
- I hear how frustrating that was. Given what's within your sphere of influence, what could we focus our conversation on?
- How do you want to be remembered?
- What would you do if you had nothing to fear?

Strengthen Reflection

Strengthening reflective abilities can shift our beliefs, so when we coach to build reflective abilities we coach around beliefs. The ability to reflect is strengthened when we unpack our thoughts, understanding the processes through which we make decisions. The capacity to reflect is enlarged as we recognize the underlying mental models that form our beliefs. Coaching toward reflection can sound like:

- I'm curious about how you came to hold that belief.
- What assumptions were you operating under?
- I hear that you interpreted her behavior as meaning. Are there any other ways you could interpret her behavior?
- If you could go back in time and do that again, what would you do differently?
- I hear that was hard. What did you learn about yourself from that experience? How did that experience shift your thoughts about yourself as a teacher?

Build Skill

Because building skills results in more effective behaviors, when we coach to build skill we create new behaviors. Skill is built when learning is scaffolded, when the desired or needed skill is within our zone of proximal development, and when the skill we're building is the right size and the right piece. Sometimes to buy into building skill, it helps to see evidence that we need to build that skill set. Helping a client to build a new skill might sound like:

- Let's script what you'll say to introduce this concept.
- What are the instructions you'll give kids for this activity?
- What vocabulary will they need to know to access this content?
- When you greet students at the door, how might you respond to a student who ignores your welcome?
- What are the learning objectives for this lesson? How will you know if students met them?

The art of coaching is the ability to weave together coaching of behaviors, beliefs, and ways of being in a way that doesn't feel contrived. It is possible that in a coaching conversation focused on resilience you guide your client to develop new skills to build their own resilience or into deeper understanding of how their mental models undermine their resilience. In another conversation, you might focus on beliefs about students, which will likely raise emotions and therefore provide an opportunity to coach around resilience. Sometimes we might provide what seems like straightforward instructional coaching that builds skill, and we might wonder how we're coaching around resilience. If we end that conversation with an opportunity for the client to name what they've learned and how they feel at the end of the conversation—and they say, "I'm excited to try this tomorrow with my students!"—then they bring a moment of awareness to the positive emotions that come up from learning, and they've increased their resilience.

Plan

Identify an upcoming coaching session in which you'd like to be intentional about coaching toward resilience, reflection, and skill building.

Client	Topic of an upcoming conversation or client's goals	What you might say
Coaching toward increasing resilience		
Coaching toward strengthening reflection		
Coaching toward skill building		

The Arc of a Coaching Conversation

Do this activity to get concrete tips on how to navigate any coaching conversation.

A coaching conversation is like a story: There's a beginning, a middle and an end. Let's look at what a coach says and does in these stages to move a conversation along.

Beginning Stage

This usually takes about 5 minutes or less. It's a brief check-in on how the client is doing and an invitation to share something that might be outside of the main topics of conversation. It can also help the client to transition into the coaching space.

The very first time you meet with a new client, share that every conversation will begin with a quick check-in. We often say, "So that you don't have to think about it, I'll keep track of time." This prevents the check-in from extending too long. You can also say, "If the timer goes off and you're in the middle of a story that may not be directly related to the plan for that time together, but that's important, then of course you can have more time to talk about that."

These are the kinds of things we say at the beginning of every coaching session:

- I'm glad we're meeting. I've been looking forward to this. As always, let's take a few minutes to check in. How are you doing today?
- Last week we talked about a conversation that you wanted to have with a student's parent. Do you want to share how that went before we move into the rest of our conversation?
- What's been a bright spot from this last week?
- Is there anything you want to say so that you can feel fully present for our conversation today? Anything you need to get off your chest?

Now it's your turn. How could you open up a coaching conversation? Jot down a couple of your go-tos and perhaps a new question or two.

Middle Stage

Coaching conversations generally focus on a client's goals, the areas they've determined that they want to improve in, or an inquiry question that they want to explore.

After the brief check-in that opens a coaching session, a coach uses their critical judgement to decide when to shift into the main part of the conversation. This can sound like:

- I'm hearing that the conversation you had with the student's parent raised many questions for yourself about who you are as a teacher. Would you like to continue exploring those questions, or would you like to move into discussing the items we'd agreed to discuss today?
- It sounds like you might need a little more time to process the fight that just happened in your class before we move on to talk about the last reading assessments. How about if we take another 5 minutes and then check in to see if you are ready to move on?

Now, your turn. How could you shift the conversation into the client's goals or the areas that you're working on? Jot down anything you've said to facilitate this shift and perhaps a new question or two.

It's critical that you give your client choice. However, if you notice a pattern that could indicate that your client is avoiding the main topics for the session, you might need to raise that with them, or just shift the conversation and see what happens. When you move into the main topics for the conversation, you can say something like:

- Today we'd planned on talking about the last reading assessment. I'm hoping that we can review that data and identify implications for your next unit. Does this still feel like the most useful thing for us to talk about?
- I'm hoping that today we can debrief my visit last week. Is there anything else you want to make sure we talk about?
- Last time you said you wanted to explore your beliefs about yourself as a White woman teaching in a Black community. Where would you like to start?

From *The Art of Coaching Workbook: Tools to Make Every Conversation Count* by Elena Aguilar. Copyright © 2021 by Elena Aguilar. Reproduced by permission.

End Stage

The last 5–8 minutes of a coaching session are for reflection, agreement on next steps, and confirmation of the next meeting. Here are some of the things we say to help shift clients into this last stage:

- I'm hearing that we need more time for this topic, so I've noted that. Our time always goes by so fast and we're going to need to wrap up now. What's an insight you've gained in this conversation that you want to be sure to remember?
- I want to honor your time and I know you have another class coming soon, so let's move into our closing. What was helpful today?
- Let's review our next steps. What did you jot down that you're going to do before we meet next?
- So I've got two things I'm going to do by the end of the day tomorrow. What were the agreements you made?

Finally, at the end of a coaching session, we thank our client and appreciate who they are. Be genuine and say something simple like, "Thank you for your deep engagement today. I'm grateful that I get to work with you."

Now, it's your turn. What have you said, or what would you like to say, to close up a coaching conversation? Jot down some phrases and perhaps a question or statement or two.

The Spheres of Influence

This activity will help you appreciate the power of the spheres of influence, a key Transformational Coaching thinking tool.

Figure 7.3: Spheres of Influence

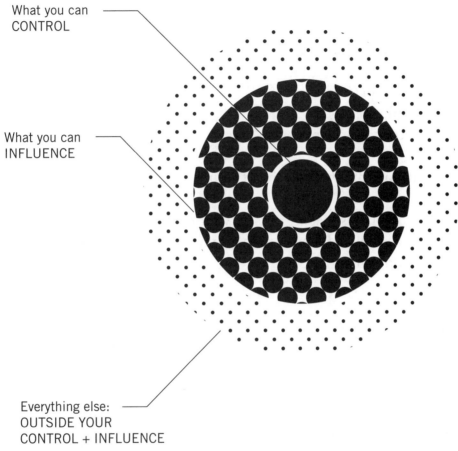

What you can
CONTROL

What you can
INFLUENCE

Everything else:
OUTSIDE YOUR
CONTROL + INFLUENCE

One of the best ways to understand the idea of the spheres of influence (Figure 7.3) is to experience it yourself. Make a quick list of things you've complained about (or wanted to complain about) in the last week—the big stuff and the little stuff, at work or at home. Include at least 10 items.

1.
2.
3.
4.
5.
6.
7.
8.
9.
10.

Now, code each of these complaints as:

- within my control (C)
- within my influence (I)
- outside my control and influence (O)

Which category did the majority of your complaints fall into?

Read the complaints that are outside your control and influence and notice how your body feels as you read them—perhaps your shoulders tighten or your breathing shallows. What do you notice?

Of the complaints outside your control, are there any that you can look at differently so that you can have more influence over them? For example, if you were just told that you will be required to attend a biweekly evening meeting on new assessment procedures, you might feel as though you have no control over this mandate. But perhaps you could talk to your principal about a rotating schedule where you'd attend some but not all the meetings. Or perhaps you could request a stipend for attending. Sometimes we can find ways to influence what feels like something outside our control, or at least to have a voice in it. What could you do?

Of the complaints outside your control, are there any that you'd like to let go of? Imagine putting them into a helium-filled balloon and then watching the balloon rise into the sky and disappear. Draw a balloon here. Inside of it, write the complaint that you want to let go of. Draw as many balloons as you want.

Look at the complaints that are within your spheres of influence and control. What concrete action can you take to address one of these complaints? For example, I haven't been eating enough vegetables lately. If I signed up for a veggie box to be delivered each week, I'd probably eat more because they'd be in my refrigerator already. Identify actions you could take to address at least three of your complaints.

Using the Spheres of Influence in Coaching

This activity will guide you in how to use this key Transformational Coaching tool.

The spheres of influence tool is invaluable for coaches—and easy to internalize and use. The concept is simple: We can classify our complaints into those we can control, those we can influence, and those we can't control. The clarity that can emerge from this sorting activity frees up a lot of emotional energy and helps us see that we have more agency than we think. Figure 7.3 is a visual representation of this concept.

The first way to use the spheres of influence in coaching is as a mental framework through which to understand your client and to help them. Imagine this: A coach has just arrived in Ms. Greenwood's classroom for their weekly coaching session. It's Friday afternoon, and as soon as they sit down Ms. Greenwood shares this:

> *You know I like you and all, but I wish we could cancel this session. I'm just exhausted. I got to school late this morning, so I was reprimanded by our principal. Then, during morning recess, Michael decided to hide in the play structure, and everyone panicked when they realized he was missing. So I was frazzled when we started math, and of course this was the day that my university supervisor decided to stop by unannounced. And I know I've said this before, but I hate this new math curriculum we adopted. Well, I didn't adopt it—it was forced on me. I know, last time we talked about how maybe I wouldn't hate it so much if I just organized all the manipulatives because I can never find the ones we need for a lesson. I know, I'm a mess. And I didn't have time for lunch again. I had to staple the reading packets we used this afternoon—and it was so hot in this room this afternoon. I thought I was going to melt. So I wish we could cancel, but I know I have no choice but to meet with you today.*

Now reread this passage, and code each sentence or statement as being within Ms. Greenwood's control (C), (C) within her influence (I), or outside her control (O).

How many items did you find that are within Ms. Greenwood's control or influence?

When you listen to a teacher complain, vent, or share, if you hear them express a lot of frustration about things that might be within their control or influence, you have an easy next step. You can say, "I'm hearing that you're frustrated about many things. Of the things you just mentioned, which ones are outside of your control?" In asking this, you invite your client to acknowledge what's outside their control. They might then shift into discussing what's within their influence or control, or you might need to prompt them by saying something like, "I hear frustration in things that are outside your control. Do you want to talk more about those, or would you like to talk about the things that you can influence?" This is a question that gives your client choice. Anywhere we can offer people choice, we do that.

Let's say Ms. Greenwood wants to keep talking about her principal and Michael and her university supervisor. Sometimes when people vent, they need for us to recognize and acknowledge the emotions they're expressing. This can sound like, "I hear your frustration. Do you want to unpack that emotion? What's that frustration about?" Frustration, you should know, is a form of anger. And anger often masks sadness and a sense of injustice—we feel angry when our boundaries are crossed or when something we value feels violated. Imagine we've asked Ms. Greenwood if she wants to unpack her frustration, and she sighs loudly and says, "No, that's a waste of time. I can't do anything about what my principal does or how Michael behaves." In this statement, she's accepting what's outside her control. Now, you can say something like, "Okay, that sounds wise. So what would be helpful for us to talk about?"

If Ms. Greenwood had continued venting about the things that are outside of her control, you could also say, "I'm hearing you complain about a lot of things that might be worthy of complaining about. I agree that this room is very hot! Is that something you want to take action on? And it does sound like your principal was unfair in his reprimand of you—it's not your fault that there was an accident on the bridge and you were late. Do you want to follow up with him about how he treated you? The thing is, Ms. Greenwood, you have a limited amount of energy. So where do you want to put that energy?"

Another way to use the spheres of influence is to give your client a copy of the graphic (Figure 7.3) and share this concept with them. You can engage them in the sorting activity that you did in the last exercise and invite them to make a decision about which (if any) complaints they want to let go of. Here's how we introduce this to clients: "I'd like to share a concept with you that I find really helpful. It's called the spheres of influence. It basically suggests that we can sort things into those we can influence and control, and those we can't control. And this can help us figure out how we can deal with the frustrating things we can experience. Do you think this could be helpful to you?"

Once you've explained this concept, and your client now understands this terminology, then it's easier at times to say to them, "I'm hearing that you're talking about things that seem outside of your control. If I've got that wrong, tell me. But I'm wondering if you'd like to shift to talk about the things that are within your influence?"

Let's be real: Schools are frustrating places. There's a lot that's outside our control and influence—in schools and in life. A Transformational Coach can help someone process the emotions that come up and can kindly guide someone back to a place of agency and power, back to what's within our influence and control. We all feel better when we're using our energy in those spheres.

Strengths-Based Coaching

Do this activity to practice using one of the most important thinking tools and to hone your ability to see your client's strengths.

We're willing to bet that the people you've trusted the most have been those who saw your potential and your strengths—even when you didn't. We all have admirable parts of us. One of a coach's primary jobs is to see those parts in someone and to remind them of their strengths. We consider this thinking tool to be one of the most important to regularly and skillfully use as a coach.

Think about someone you're coaching now (or even someone you work with), maybe someone with whom you're struggling a little bit. What makes them hard to work with?

Now, think about their strengths. Refer to Table 1.1, and then group those strengths into the head, heart, and hands categories in Figure 7.4. If you can't categorize some strengths, drop them in the Other space. Please add some hair or something to the head so that it doesn't look so generic and so that it resembles your client!

Figure 7.4: Head, Heart, Hands

Reflect

What, if anything, has shifted in your thinking about this person after thinking about their strengths?

How can you get deeper insight into your client's strengths? What might you ask them, or what could you do to see more of their strengths?

Understanding Strengths-Based Coaching

Let's be clear. Strengths-based coaching is *not*

- pretending someone has no weaknesses or is perfect
- avoiding giving hard feedback
- overestimating someone's competence
- trying to be a friendly or likeable coach

Strengths-based coaching is about seeing every situation in life as an opportunity for learning and growth and calling on our client's reservoirs of knowledge, skills, experience, and attitude to ensure a successful outcome. Strengths-based coaching means we don't make excuses for our clients. It means we see them for the whole, resourceful, creative beings they already are, and we help them to draw on those qualities when challenges inevitably arise.

How and When to Use Strengths-Based Coaching

The graphic in Figure 7.4 helps you slow down your thinking to be more intentional in identifying another's strengths, especially when conflict, mistrust, or hurt are clouding your ability to be positive or productive.

Strengths-based coaching is also invaluable when starting a coaching relationship. You can download the Celebrating Strengths graphic from our website, https://bright morningteam.com and use it when you begin coaching someone. After a couple of conversations, or perhaps after an observation, capture your perception of your new client's strengths.

Another way to use this when building a coaching relationship is to invite your client to fill it out about themselves. While it's affirming when other people see our strengths, it's also critical that we see our own strengths. If you invite your client to identify their own strengths, it's a reflective activity for them, and it helps them share parts of themselves with you that they might not otherwise find a way to share.

Mind the Gap

Do this activity to learn how to use an invaluable thinking tool for understanding your client as a learner.

It's hard to plug the hole we can't see. All too often in coaching we focus on the solution (the plug) without adequate attention to the root cause (the hole). We ask, "How can this person change?" when we should be asking, "Why haven't they changed already?" When we surface the root causes of a person's inabilities, the how often becomes obvious. The mind the gap framework, depicted in Figure 7.5, compels us to slow down and deeply analyze a situation before jumping into potential remedies.

When you're learning a new coaching tool, start with yourself. Think about a change that you are struggling to make right now. Maybe you'd like to exercise regularly, sleep 8 hours, or spend more time with friends, but it's just not happening. Maybe you want to learn to play the piano. Maybe you consistently get feedback about your communication style that you don't know what to do with. Jot down your change challenge.

Now ask yourself: What's getting in the way of change? Put a star next to possible root causes from the following list, using the space to add additional thoughts about how this might be playing out in your situation.

Knowledge? "I'm realizing I don't know how to learn an instrument. Maybe I can find a methodology to follow."

Skill? "I've tried a few yoga classes, but it's not something I can lead myself through yet. I wonder if there's a class I can take online or at a local studio."

Capacity? "I want to spend more time with friends and family, but I've got a ton on my plate right now. I'm having a hard time prioritizing, figuring out what I need to stop to be more available for them."

Figure 7.5: Mind the Gap Framework

MIND THE GAP:
Identifying Learning Needs

Ability to take action, to do what we need to do

SKILL
The ability to execute the technical elements of a task. Can be the application of knowledge.

KNOWLEDGE
The theoretical or practical understanding of a subject. Can also be information.

CAPACITY
The time and resources to do something. Can also be emotional and physical capacity.

WILL
Desire, intrinsic motivation, passion, or commitment. Usually has an emotional tone.

CULTURAL COMPETENCE
The ability to understand, appreciate, and interact with people from cultures or belief systems different from one's own; the skill to navigate cross-cultural differences.

EMOTIONAL INTELLIGENCE
The ability to be aware of, manage, and express one's emotions; the ability to recognize, empathize with, and manage other people's emotions.

brightmorningteam.com

brightmorning
every conversation counts

From *The Art of Coaching Workbook: Tools to Make Every Conversation Count* by Elena Aguilar. Copyright © 2021 by Elena Aguilar. Reproduced by permission.

Will? "Sleep seems like one of those things I should prioritize, but the fact is that I value my downtime in the evenings more."

Emotional intelligence? "My co-teacher says I've been distant lately. I can sense that I'm irritated with her but can't put my finger on why."

Cultural competence? "I come from a large family, where people were constantly talking over one another. If I didn't interrupt, I didn't get heard! Yet some of my colleagues seem offended when I interrupt them in meetings."

Each of these questions invites us to explore a different possible gap in learning. In Figure 7.5 you'll see the graphic that represents this concept.

Practice

Here's how you might use this framework. Imagine a teacher says one day, "Samantha is such a rude student. She's always rolling her eyes during my lessons!" When we hear something like this, a few possible gaps come to mind:

Knowledge: Does the teacher know what Samantha is reacting to when she rolls her eyes?
Will: Is this teacher curious enough to ask Samantha why she's rolling her eyes?
Emotional intelligence: Does this teacher recognize how upset she gets when Samantha rolls her eyes? How does she manage this feeling in Samantha's presence?
Cultural competence: How might the teacher's identity (or Samantha's) be influencing the interpretation of eye-rolling as rude?

After this quick analysis, we are better prepared to unpack the statement with the teacher to identify what sort of learning might be possible or needed. In this situation, we might ask:

What do you imagine is going on in Samantha's head when she rolls her eyes?
What associations do you have, from your own background, with eye-rolling?

Now you practice. Imagine a teacher says the following. Look at the mind the gap graphic and explore how each gap might be at play for this teacher. Take notes on what each gap makes you wonder and think.

I was actually excited to come back to school this year. I went to this incredible PD this summer and got so many ideas for my drama class and felt so rejuvenated. And then I get here, and I'm told that I have to teach reading intervention, which I've never taught before, which I don't know how to teach, which I just don't want to teach. Our admin used to listen to us. They thought about our needs as well. Why don't we get any say in these big decisions? I feel like all the excitement has been drained out of me. I don't know how to teach reading intervention for English learners! I had like 2 days of training on working with English learners, and that was 15 years ago; now we have all these kids coming in from countries where they're having wars and stuff. How am I supposed to do this?

Skill	Knowledge
Capacity	Will
Emotional Intelligence	Cultural Competence

Now what are three questions you could ask the teacher to test your hypothesis?

1.

2.

3.

What to Say When You're Stuck: Survival Coaching Phrases

Do this activity when you just need to learn a few phrases you can use in a coaching conversation.

At some point, you need to say something to your client—probably pretty soon after you sit down with them for the first time. What follows are a list of five coaching survival phrases that Elena has determined are the most useful and relevant in almost any context. These are the five phrases she encourages coaches to memorize and draw on at any moment. As you read through these, identify the one or two that you think would be most useful for you to remember and put a big star by those.

Tell me more about. . . or I'm curious about. . .

Reason for using
- when someone is not forthcoming or doesn't say much
- when you have no idea how to respond to what they've shared
- so you can hear more and then determine a meaningful direction for the conversation
- when someone is disengaged in the conversation

What would be most useful for us to talk about right now?

Reason for using
- when someone tells you a whole lot and you don't know where to go
- when someone is rambling or venting
- when you want to put the responsibility for the conversation on the speaker—to empower them

So what I'm hearing you say is _____. Did I get that right?

Reason for using
- to demonstrate that you've listened carefully and thoughtfully
- to reflect back what you've heard for the speaker
- when someone is expressing strong emotions

What do you hear yourself saying?

Reason for using
- when you're working with a highly reflective learner
- when someone is emotionally distressed
- when someone isn't emotionally distressed as a way to cultivate metacognition

Can you think of a question I could ask you right now that would be helpful?

Reason for using
- when you feel like you've tried everything and you're really stuck
- when someone pushes back on every suggestion you make
- to help the learner feel more empowered

Now, before we look at some more coaching sentence stems, we have two big warnings for you:

MAKE THESE SENTENCE STEMS SOUND LIKE YOU!

BE MINDFUL OF YOUR TONE AND BODY LANGUAGE!

When we train coaches, in our virtual and in-person workshops, we spend a lot of time modeling these, practicing them, and giving each other feedback. That's because, as you can imagine, these can be said and delivered in a wide variety of ways. Can you imagine a coach saying to you, "What do you hear yourself saying?" in a snide, mocking tone of voice? Can you imagine hearing it (or saying it) in a kind, thoughtful way?

First, you've got to practice saying these and modifying the language so they feel like you. For example, Elena is prone to saying, "I'm curious. . ." before just about everything else she says. It's just her way of talking. She also says, "Wow" and "Hm" a lot. (You can see Elena demonstrating coaching conversations in all of our online courses.) In addition, as we've said, your tone of voice and body language will carry a tremendous amount of information about how you are feeling and thinking about your client. It takes practice to find the right tone and corresponding nonverbals.

Reflect

Recall a time when you felt someone was speaking to you using scripted language (or imagine someone talking to you this way). How did that feel? What did it make think about the person speaking?

Recall a recent challenge you dealt with at work. If you'd had a coach to talk to, which of these questions do you wish they'd have asked you?

Now, jot these sentence stems down in your coaching notebook so that you can use them in an upcoming coaching conversation.

Transformational Coaching Stems

Do this activity to powerfully expand your repertoire of what you can say in a coaching conversation.

We're about to offer you a lot of coaching stems and questions organized into three categories:

1. **All purpose:** These work with almost anything, anywhere, anytime.
2. **Facilitative and directive stems:** These are questions aligned to the content in Chapters 9–12. We're including these here because once you read those chapters, you'll recognize that they belong in your basic coaching toolbox.

Here are some important considerations regarding coaching sentence stems:

- The categories are fluid. A clarifying question can also be a question that coaches a way of being, and it can be a cathartic question.
- How you classify the question has a lot to do with the coach's intention when using it. That means that you can use these questions for different purposes. So don't get hung up on how sentence stems are classified.
- You must make these questions sound like you—you have permission to modify them (in fact you probably should) so that they feel authentic. It's unsettling when someone sounds like they're reciting a script in a coaching conversation, so modify.
- Your tone of voice, pitch, pace, volume, and nonverbal communication will be just as important in how your question is received as the words that you utter. We'll return to this aspect of communication in Chapter 8, but it's important to remember as you read these.

Finally, you may notice (if you're doing a close comparison) that these questions are updated and expanded from those in *The Art of Coaching*.

> You can download these lists of questions from our website, http://www.brightmorningteam.com

As you read through these questions, code them in the following way:

✓ I already say this, or something like it, when I coach.

☆ This is a good one. I want to use this.

? I don't know about this one. I want to learn more or hear it being used.

All-Purpose Questions	
General reflective (or active listening)	**Clarifying**
• So, in other words. . . • What I'm hearing, then, is _____. Is that correct? • What I hear you saying is _____. Am I missing anything? • I'm hearing many things. . . • As I listen to you, I'm hearing _____. Is there anything else you feel I should know? • I'm curious to hear more about. . . • What would be most useful for us to talk about right now?	• Let me see if I understand. • I'd be interested in hearing more about _____. • It would help me understand if you'd give me an example of _____. • So, are you suggesting _____? • Tell me what you mean when you _____. • Tell me how that idea is like (or different from) _____. • To what extent is _____? • I'm curious to know more about _____.

Facilitative and Directive Stems

Facilitative coaching	Directive coaching
Supportive stems	**Informative stems**
• I noticed how when you _____ the students really _____ [to identify something that worked and why it worked]. • It sounds like you have a number of ideas to try out! It'll be exciting to see which works best for you. • What did you do to make the lesson so successful? • I'm interested in learning (or hearing) more about _____. • Your commitment is really inspiring to me. • It sounds like you handled that in a very confident way. • You did a great job when you _____. • I'm confident that you'll be successful.	• There's a useful book on that topic by _____. • An effective strategy to teach _____ is _____. • You can contact _____ for that resource. • _____ is very effective at teaching that skill; maybe you could observe him. • Some teachers do _____. You might see if that works in this situation. • I'll share some resources with you that will be useful.
Cathartic stems	**Prescriptive stems**
• What are you hearing in what you're sharing? • I'm noticing that you're experiencing some feelings. Would it be okay to explore those for a few minutes? • What's coming up for you right now? Would you like to talk about your feelings? • Wow. I imagine I'd have strong emotions. What are you feeling? • What's another way you might look at this situation? • What would it look like if _____? • When has something like this happened before?	• I would like you to discuss this issue with your supervisor. • You need to know that the school's policy is _____. • Have you talked to _____ about that yet? Last week you said you planned on doing so. • Would it be okay if I share some advice that I think might help you? You're welcome to take it or leave it, of course. • I'd like to suggest _____.

From *The Art of Coaching Workbook: Tools to Make Every Conversation Count* by Elena Aguilar. Copyright © 2021 by Elena Aguilar. Reproduced by permission.

Facilitative and Directive Stems	
Facilitative coaching	**Directive coaching**
Catalytic stems	*Confrontational stems*
• Tell me about a previous time when you _____. How did you deal with that? • What do you think would happen if _____? • I hear you're really struggling with _____. How do you intend to start? • It sounds like you're unsatisfied with _____. What would you do differently next time? • You've just talked about five different things you want to work on this week. The last thing you mentioned is _____. How important is this to you? • How was _____ different from (or similar to) _____? • How do you want your students (or a particular student) to remember you? • How do you want to remember this time or situation in 15 years? • Is there a question you think I could ask you right now that would be helpful?	• What do you hear yourself saying? • Would you be willing to explore your reasoning (or assumptions) about this? • I'd like to ask you about _____. Is that okay? • What's another way you might _____? • What would it look like if _____? Is there any other way to see this situation? • What do you think would happen if _____? • What sort of an impact do you think _____? • I'm noticing _____ [some aspect of behavior]. What do you think is going on? • What criteria do you use to _____? • Who do you want to be in this situation? • How do you want others to see you in this situation? • How did you come to that conclusion?

Reflect

If you had to choose your two favorite questions from all of these lists, which would you pick?

If you had a coach and were meeting with them today, what are two questions you'd want them to ask you?

How did these questions help you think about your role as a coach?

For Further Learning

→ Enroll in the virtual Essentials of the Art of Coaching course so you can see these sentence stems modeled in a coaching conversation and can practice using them in guided activities.

The Core Emotions

Do this activity to practice addressing emotions—and remember that one distinguishing thing about Transformational Coaching is that we coach emotions.

Naming emotions is much harder than it seems, and the way you label an emotion influences how you express it. A Transformational Coach recognizes when a client is experiencing emotions and invites them to acknowledge, name, and process those emotions. Because many of us have undeveloped vocabulary sets to talk about our feelings, the core emotions resource is invaluable. We always have it (literally) in our bags when we meet with clients.

Practice

PART 1

Identify a recent time when you experienced strong emotions. Perhaps they were unpleasant or uncomfortable. Once you've recalled that experience, read through the list of core emotions and see if you can identify what you were feeling.

PART 2

When we hear a client expressing a strong emotion—usually some kind of distressing feelings—here's how we introduce the core emotions:

- I'm hearing some strong emotions. Let's take a look at this resource. (Place the document in front of client.) Which words do you see that reflect how you are feeling?
- I'm hearing a lot of sadness. How about if you look through this resource and see if there are any secondary emotions?
- What's coming up for you right now? How are you feeling? (If the client seems at a loss for words, then we offer them the document.)

Your turn. Recall a time when a client, colleague, or friend was expressing strong emotions. What could you have said, in your own words, to introduce the core emotions to them and to invite them to use it for reflection?

Core emotion	Fear	Anger	Sadness	Shame
Common labels for this emotion	Agitated Alarmed Anxious Apprehensive Concerned Desperate Dismayed Dread Fearful Frightened Horrified Hysterical Impatient Jumpy Nervous Panicked Scared Shocked Shy Tense Terrified Timid Uncertain Uneasy Worried	Aggravated Agitated Annoyed Antagonized Bitter Contemptuous (other than for self) Contentious Contrary Cranky Cruel Destructive Displeased Enraged Exasperated Explosive Frustrated Furious Hateful Hostile Impatient Indignant Insulated Irate Irritable Irritated Mad Mean Outraged Resentful Scornful Spiteful Urgent Vengeful	Alienated Anguished Bored Crushed Defeated Dejected Depressed Despairing Despondent Disappointed Discouraged Disheartened Dismayed Dispirited Displeased Distraught Down Dreary Forlorn Gloomy Grief-stricken Hopeless Hurt Insecure Isolated Lonely Melancholic Miserable Mopey Morose Neglected Oppressed Pessimistic Pitiful Rejected Somber Sorrowful Tragic Unhappy	Besmirched Chagrined Contemptuous (of self) Contrite Culpable Debased Degraded Disapproving Disdainful Disgraced Disgusted (at self) Dishonored Disreputable Embarrassed Guilty Hateful Humbled Humiliated Improper Infamous Invalidated Mortified Regretful Remorseful Repentant Reproachful Rueful Scandalized Scornful Sinful Stigmatized

Core Emotion	Jealousy	Disgust	Happiness	Love
Common labels for this emotion	Competitive Covetous Deprived Distrustful Envious Greedy Grudging Jealous Overprotective Petty Possessive Resentful Rivalrous	Appalled Dislike Grossed out Insulted Intolerant Nauseated Offended Put off Repelled Repulsed Revolted Revulsion Shocked Sickened Turned off	Agreeable Amused Blissful Bubbly Cheerful Content Delighted Eager Ease Elated Engaged Enjoyment Enthusiastic Euphoric Excited Exhilarated Flow Glad Gleeful Glowing Gratified Harmonious Hopeful Interested Jolly Joyful Jubilant Lighthearted Meaningful Merry Optimistic Peaceful Pleasure Pride Proud Relieved Relish Satisfied Thrilled Triumphant Up Zealous	Acceptance Admiration Adoring Affectionate Allegiance Attached Attraction Belonging Caring Compassionate Connected Dependent Desire Devoted Empathetic Faithful Friendship Interested Kind Liking Passionate Protective Respectful Sympathetic Tender Trust Vulnerable Warm

For Further Learning

→ Read *Onward: Cultivating Emotional Resilience in* Educators and *The Onward Workbook.*

→ Enroll in our online course, The Art of Coaching Emotions (information at Http://www.brightmorningteam.com).

Filling Up Your Toolbox

Flag this page and come back to this activity after working through this book so you can complete your toolbox. We know that we could have put this at the end of the book, but we want to keep tools with tools.

Now having completed this workbook, and having read *The Art of Coaching*, what else would you place in your basic coaching toolbox? The concepts and tools that are *always* useful in any coaching conversation?

Your toolbox will likely look different from other coaches' toolbox because everyone is different—with different needs at different places on the learning journey. Go through the resources in this book and complete Table 7.1. You'll also see Elena's toolbox following the blank template (Table 7.2). We suggest you have no more than three or four key tools for each section (with some tools in multiple sections). You can download this template from our website and add rows if you want. You might also revise what's in your toolbox every year as you deepen your understanding of Transformational Coaching.

Table 7.1: Toolbox Inventory

Toolbox Inventory: My Key Coaching Resources	
Phase	**Tool**
All phases	
Building trust	
Surface	
Recognize	
Explore	
Create	

From *The Art of Coaching Workbook: Tools to Make Every Conversation Count* by Elena Aguilar. Copyright © 2021 by Elena Aguilar. Reproduced by permission.

After you've compiled a hearty list of resources, then reproduce this page and post it on your office wall or your computer's desktop, so you can easily be reminded of your coaching tools. Of course, you could take this a step further and make copies of pages from this workbook, download tools from the website, revise tools to make them yours, and then assemble them all together in whatever way works best for you—as a packet or in a digital folder. This resource repository, when organized and accessible, can shift your work into greater efficacy and create the conditions for you to do Transformational Coaching.

Table 7.2: Elena's Toolbox

Toolbox Inventory: My Key Coaching Resources	
Phase	**Tool**
All phases	Listening to your listening
	Sphere of influence
	Celebrating strengths
	The core emotions
Building trust	Core values
	Personality types
	Celebrating strengths
Surface	The lens of adult learning
	Mind the gap
	The lens of systemic oppression
	The equity rubric (published in *Coaching for Equity*)
Recognize	Catalytic and confrontational approaches
	The lens of systemic oppression
	Teacher-student interactions
Explore	Cathartic and catalytic approaches
	The lens of emotional intelligence
	The legacy question
Create	The lens of adult learning
	Mind the gap
	Ladder of inference

CHAPTER 8

Deepening Your Listening Skills

*D*o this activity to appreciate the value of this key coaching strategy.

This chapter might be the most important one in this book. Listening is a foundational skill for a coach and one that we need to practice year after year. When someone listens to us well, all of their attention is focused on us and we feel held. Seen. Accepted. We sense our value as we recognize that the other person has put aside demands for their attention.

Who has listened to you well? To more deeply understand the power of listening, think about that experience and write a short thank-you note to that person in the space provided. Tell them how it felt when they listened to you and perhaps what that listening meant to you. Let them know what implications that listening had for you in that moment or beyond.

If trust is the foundation of a Transformational Coaching relationship, listening is the material from which that foundation is built. Listening is expressed in the things we do and in how we show up—in who we are *being*. Most of us have an intuitive sense when we are being listened to well and when we are not. Often, this is fueled by our subconscious attunement to the other person's nonverbal cues. In this chapter, we'll explore different kinds of listening, including attending to nonverbal communication.

Dear

Who I Am as a Listener

This activity will help you take stock of yourself as a listener. Think of it as a pre-assessment that will help you establish a baseline from which to develop.

Be honest. What do you know about yourself as a listener? What have people told you about how you listen?

What do you remember about how people around you listened when you were growing up? Were there people who you recall were good listeners?

Who do you find it easier to listen to? Friends? A partner? Your students or your children?

Who do you find it harder to listen to? Friends? A partner? Your students or your children?

What do you know about the conditions in which you listen well? Are there times of the day when you feel better able to listen? Are there places where it's easier to listen? Do you listen better on the phone or in person?

Draw your head on this page and what your face looks like when it's listening. In the thought bubbles, write some of the common things that go through your mind when you are listening. Add more thought bubbles if you'd like.

Quiet Listening

Do this activity to gain more insight into how you listen.

Listening is best practiced live with a partner, but you can also practice listening while watching television, enjoying music, or listening to the radio or a podcast. In all cases, aim to:

- *listen with your head*—let distracting thoughts float away
- *listen with your heart*—attune to the emotions within you and in the other
- *listen with your body*—fix all your senses on the object of your listening

Try this today. Choose a setting in which to practice listening for 5 minutes. Turn on the radio or call up a friend and tell them, "I'm practicing listening and am going to try to talk as little as possible in this conversation." Ask your partner or housemate, "Could you talk for 5 minutes? I want to see if I can be quiet and listen."

After you do this, reflect. What was that practice like? What did you learn about yourself?

To master quiet listening, you'll need a deeper understanding of your experiences with and feelings about listening. Take some time to think and write about the following prompts.

I know that someone is fully present with me and listening when they. . .

When they do this, it makes me feel. . .

I know that someone is not really listening to me when they. . .

When they do this, it makes me feel. . .

When someone interrupts me, I feel. . .

I'm most likely to interrupt someone when I. . .

I know that I am fully present with and listening to someone when I. . .

When I do this, I feel. . .

Reflective Listening

Do this activity to understand one kind of listening and to practice it.

Early in a coaching relationship, and when we are listening to build trust or to identify the focus of a conversation, it's important to use what's often called *active listening* or *paraphrasing*. We call it *reflective listening* because a coach can be like a mirror, helping clients see who they are. This is a powerful listening strategy to build trust, communicate empathy, and show your client that you're there for them.

When we use reflective listening, we ensure that we are hearing precisely what the other person wants to communicate. We do this by using phrases like:

"What I'm hearing is _____. Is that correct?"
"I'm hearing a few things: _____. Did I miss anything?"
"As I listen to you, I'm hearing _____. Is there anything else you feel I should know?"

Notice that there are two components of these phrases: reflecting back what you've understood and creating an opening for the coachee to correct or build from that understanding. To do this effectively, the coach listens not only for what is said but also for feeling, tone, and subtext.

Reflective listening is a very intuitive form of listening, and, when done well, it makes people feel seen and valued. If it feels natural, you can reflect strengths in what the client has shared or acknowledge their emotions. This can sound like:

"I'm really hearing your commitment to finding a win-win solution in this conflict you're having with you co-teacher."
"Wow, that sounds like a hard situation that you handled well."
"I hear a lot of sadness in what you're sharing. Is that part of your experience?"

Although it can feel awkward at first, paraphrasing is an effective way to build trust and to demonstrate your intention to listen deeply. Like any skill, it gets less awkward with practice. And of course, you can practice active listening in *any* conversation with anyone—we use it with our children and significant others.

A few tips:

- Paraphrase what the speaker says without overinterpreting their words.
- Be cautious not to parrot what the speaker has said.
- Follow up by inviting the speaker to clarify anything you might not have understood or have missed.
- Craft a few reflective listening stems that feel comfortable and sound natural for you.

Reflective Listening Stems

- So, in other words. . .
- What I'm hearing then is _____. Is that correct?
- What I hear you saying is _____. Am I missing anything?
- I'm hearing many things. . .
- As I listen to you, I'm hearing _____. Is there anything else you feel I should know?
- I'm curious to hear more about _____.
- What would be most useful for us to talk about right now?

Practice

Read the following conversation snippets, and script a possible response. Take this practice all the way by saying these lines aloud and revising them until they feel natural.

Scenario 1

The teacher says: "I'm so glad you're here. My gosh, what a day this has been. I'm at my wit's end with my department chair right now. We're supposed to be using our department meetings to co-design lessons for this new curriculum, and it feels like she spends half the meeting just rehashing what's already been communicated in the week's all-staff e-mail. I've been working weekends trying to make sure I understand the curriculum and have engaging lessons for my kids. But it just keeps feeling like they fall flat. I felt so much more comfortable with the materials we had last year. Dionne, down the hall, seems to love it. I keep meaning to make it over there to ask what she's doing or even see her in action, but I never seem to have the time. And my English learners—gosh, I just know there's more I could be doing for them, but, again, where do I find the time?

So I'm really hoping you're coming today with some of what you're seeing work in other people's classrooms because we're sure as heck not going to get to talk about *that* in our department meeting on Thursday!"

> I might say. . .

Scenario 2

The teacher says: "It's interesting that you ask about the purpose we established as a department at the start of the year. You know we spent half a day on that during in-service week, and we haven't revisited our norms or purpose statement once since then. I wonder if our chair even has them anymore. I mean, we talked a lot in August about wanting to collaborate more as a department, especially knowing we were getting a new curriculum and that two of our teachers were brand-new. It really makes me wonder about our district's obsession with having the latest curricula. Surely it would be better for kids to have teachers who really knew what they were doing and who had had a chance to fine-tune their lessons rather than feeling like the rug is constantly getting pulled out from under us. But, you know, collaborating with my colleagues sure would go a long way. If we could just get *that* dialed in."

> I might say. . .

Scenario 3

The teacher says: "I suppose I just feel really frustrated. I'm upset with our department chair for what I perceive as a real lack of leadership. I'm upset with the administration for giving us a new curriculum yet again. It feels like we never get a chance to really settle in. And I'm so hungry to just feel settled and not feel like a brand-new teacher year after year. And I suppose I'm upset with myself. I know I could be doing better by kids, and I want to! I'm just so exhausted all the time running myself ragged trying to stay on top of everything."

> I might say. . .
>
>
>

Scenario 4

The teacher says: "Hmm, hearing you reflect that it's so obvious that I need to be taking better care managing my energy during the week. All this weekend planning means I haven't been taking the walks in the woods that I normally would this time of year. And I'm so tired in the evenings—I'd usually rather veg out in front of a show than to read or call my mom or do any of the things that actually fill my cup. [*long sigh*] And I know I shouldn't put all the blame on our chair. I have a copy of our norms. Who's to say I can't bring them to our next meeting to review? I mean, number three on the list was, 'Stick to the agenda,' which is what's leading us to waste the first half of every meeting. Okay. I think I'm ready to take a little more responsibility here—both for my own attitude and well-being and also for what happens in those meetings."

> I might say. . .
>
>
>

Now read how Laurelin thought about these scenarios and how she'd respond.

Scenario 1

Laurelin might say: "Wow. I'm just taking that all in. I can really hear your commitment to making this curriculum work for your kids and your frustration that the department meetings don't feel helpful right now. I can hear how hungry you are to learn from your colleagues. Did I miss anything?"

Rationale: This teacher is coming into the conversation with a lot of energy. She's all over the place, talking about department meetings, her weekends, Dionne, her English learners. In reflecting back what I'm hearing, I want to help connect her with her emotional experience, tease out some themes in what she's shared, and begin to identify what will be most useful in this conversation.

Scenario 2

Laurelin might say: "It sounds like your department planted the seeds for stronger collaboration this year, but maybe they haven't been watered as the school year's gotten underway. Does that sound right?"

Rationale: I can sense this teacher sitting on the fence between taking action to create the department she wants and miring herself in blame and frustration, which will keep her squarely in the victim role. I opt to use the metaphor of planting seeds here to reflect what I've heard and create an opening for her to explore what watering those seeds could look like.

Scenario 3

Laurelin might say: "[*Long, slow breath*] Yeah. I really hear your frustration, and I hear how tired you feel. And underneath it all, I hear sadness. You really care about your students and about your role as their teacher. It's hard to care so much and not feel successful."

Rationale: Now we're getting to the heart of things. All this blame and shame is wearing this teacher out! Yet I still don't hear her tapping into the emotional root of her frustration, which I'm sensing is sadness. I want to acknowledge that sadness and the care it's tied to and invite her to accept that it's okay to feel sad. We can't shift what we can't accept.

Laurelin might say: "It sounds like it would be helpful to get back into some of your self-care rituals. Like they say on the airplanes, put your own mask on first. And I hear you considering whether you could be the one to bring up the norms again with your department as one way of getting those back on track. So what commitments do you want to make coming out of this conversation?"

Rationale: As often happens when we use reflective listening, the coachee has found her own path toward resolving this challenge. She's identified the need to better manage her energy throughout the week, and she's connecting that to how she shows up in meetings. My goal at this point is to reflect the ideas she's brainstorming so she can get clear on what action steps she wants to take coming out of the conversation.

Honing Your Intuition

Do this activity when you want to explore intuition and refine this superpower.

Quiet listening and reflective listening rely heavily on your ability to pay attention to your intuition. Intuition—when it's running strong—can almost feel like a kind of psychic power. Experts tell us that what we call intuition is really an ability to take in a lot of data points—especially the nonverbal cues that others communicate—match those up to previous experiences we've had, and come to a quick conclusion. But intuition can feel deeper and more powerful than that explanation. It's often experienced as a gut feeling, a sense of deep knowing. Elena explains that it's probably her deepest and truest secret power as a coach and one that can feel nebulous to teach others to hone. Although it may be true that intuition is a part of our personality (see Chapter 1), we can all become more intuitive.

Neuroscientists tell us that intuition sits predominantly in the nondominant hemisphere of the brain and, as such, is often more connected to images, feelings, physical sensations, and metaphors than it is to language or quantitative data. To hone your intuition, you need to exercise that nondominant part of your brain. Here are some ways to strengthen your intuition. Read through these, and then pick one or more to try for the next week. This is not a comprehensive list, so please add to this list with the ways you already know of that heighten your intuition.

- **Meditate**. Meditate every day—or almost every day—for a few weeks, and you'll see your intuition sharpen quickly.
- **Keep a journal**. Write a stream of consciousness. Start with an open prompt to get you going, like "Lately, I've been wondering about _____." Or "All the feelings passing through me these days are _____."
- **Write yourself a letter about an issue you're dealing with**. Write in great detail and then at the end of it, finish by completing this sentence: "The action I need to take is _____."
- **Focus your thinking.** Yes, this is what you're doing when you meditate, but extend that practice into other activities like taking a walk or doing dishes. Engage in those activities, and don't listen to anything or talk to anyone else—just sharpen your awareness of whatever you are doing.
- **Pay attention to your dreams**. Before you go to sleep, tell yourself that you want to remember your dreams. When you wake up in the morning, before you open your

eyes or move, try to remember your dreams. Get up and write about them. Just before you go to sleep, you can also ask yourself a question that you want to dream about, like, "I can't decide whether to take that other job." See what happens if you ask a question that you're trying to figure out right before going to sleep.

- **Draw, paint, scribble, work with clay, or color mandalas** (circular or geometric patterns).
- **Hone your body awareness.** Sometimes we experience intuition through our bodies—our body might tense slightly when we're feeling anxious even before our mind has registered the same stressor.

Exploring Mental Detours

Do this activity to hone awareness of the ways your mind wanders when you are in a conversation.

Sometimes you're hearing what someone says, but are you really listening? When we listen, our minds can take detours. They charge off on their own journeys, sometimes thinking about their own experiences with what the speaker has shared: *Oh, yeah, that same thing happened to me during my first year of teaching and I remember. . .* Other times our minds start to plan what they'll say when the person stops talking: *She really needs to just _____. I'm going to suggest that she _____.* Sometimes a surge of empathy can be a detour if it takes our mind to get off the highway of the conversation: *Oh, that's awful! My heart aches hearing what she's going through. Now I understand why she's feeling so despondent.*

Our minds take detours. Some of these can have a more detrimental impact on the conversation than others. For example, if we are prone to detours where we experience a lot of judgment about our client, that'll likely have a significant impact on how we respond to them. If we are prone to wanting to ask clarifying questions, we may not listen closely enough to hear what the client is trying to express.

One of the first steps in building our listening muscles is to cultivate awareness of which detours our minds take and what prompts them to take those detours. Then we can consider the impact of this wandering on our client and on a coaching conversation. A detour into empathy will not have the same impact as a detour into spacing out. Once we recognize the detours our minds take and the impact those have, then we can get around to kindly redirecting our thoughts and to teaching our minds to stay present. But first, we need to know where these fickle minds of ours can travel and what sends them off-track.

Reflect

1. Skim the following list. Put a check mark next to those that you know you do sometimes.
2. Fill in the right-hand column to reflect on the circumstances in which your mind takes detours.

I do this	Mental detours	I'm most likely to do this when. . .
	Connecting I want to interject with a connection to what the speaker is saying. I want to feel closer to the speaker by sharing a similar thought or experience.	
	Fixing I want to offer a solution or some advice or suggest something that can be done. I want to fix it.	
	Disagreeing I want to interject with a disagreement, to discuss or debate something the speaker is saying or how they are saying it.	
	Questioning I want to ask a clarifying question for more information or so I can better analyze the situation. Or I want to ask a probing question so the speaker can explore their thinking more deeply.	
	Feeling uncomfortable I am experiencing an uncomfortable emotion because of what the speaker is saying. I'm feeling annoyed, impatient, judgmental, bored.	
	Feeling comfortable I am experiencing a comfortable emotion because of what the speaker is saying. I'm feeling caring, excited, enthusiastic, appreciative.	
	Spacing out My mind is wandering to an unrelated topic. I'm spacing out or distracted by unrelated thoughts or stimuli in our environment.	
	Planning an exit I'm considering options for how to get out of this conversation.	
	Other (describe):	
	Other (describe):	

Understanding what can prompt a mental detour is a critical step in redirecting your mind.

Elena Reflects

My mind can take major detours when I am emotionally activated in a conversation. If a client uses a phrase like *these kids* or seems to hold low expectations of children, my mind can take a sharp right turn out of the conversation and into feeling uncomfortable. In that place I stew in anger and create barriers between myself and my client.

When I notice that I've taken this detour, I ask myself what I'm feeling. It's taken practice, but I now recognize that I'm often experiencing sadness and anger. These emotions arise from my personal experiences and from those of people I love. I also remember that my anger can fuel my commitment to social justice when I work with it in a healthy way. And I know that my sadness deserves attention. When I tell myself, *Ah, you're hurting. I hear this. I promise we'll come back to this later, and we'll attend to this pain,* then I'm often able to return to the conversation. Once I'm mentally back with my client, I can see their pain—even when they say disparaging things about kids—and I see how they're speaking from unhealed hurt. And then I can respond to that suffering with compassion.

There are many ways to redirect your thoughts back to the conversation when they take a detour.

Laurelin Reflects

I think about staying present in coaching both proactively and reactively. On the proactive side, it's easier for me to stay present when I'm well rested, when I'm clear on my intention going into a conversation, and when I've minimized distractions in the coaching environment.

On the reactive side, there are a few tricks I use when I catch my attention wandering. First, I take a long, slow breath and really feel into my body. While our minds can wander into the past and future, our physical sensations live only in the present. When I bring my awareness to my body, I'm more present with my client. Second, I call to mind all the things I love about my client. When I connect with my sense of care, there's nowhere I'd rather be than right here, right now, listening to this person.

Finally, I acknowledge what pulled me away from presence. My most common mental detours are Fixing and Questioning. When I notice these arising, I use the mantra, "I'm not here to fix. I don't need to know." This brings my listening back to my client.

Reflect

When you catch your mind taking a detour, how can you bring your attention fully back to the person you are listening to? Draw on what you've learned in *The Art of Coaching* and in earlier chapters of this workbook—perhaps on your coaching mantras (Chapter 2) or insights into how you want to be as a coach.

For Further Learning

→ Enroll in a virtual Essentials of the Art of Coaching workshop and practice these skills with others (information at http::/www.brightmorningteam.com).

From *The Art of Coaching Workbook: Tools to Make Every Conversation Count* by Elena Aguilar. Copyright © 2021 by Elena Aguilar. Reproduced by permission.

Listening to Your Own Listening

Do this activity to practice cultivating awareness of your mental detours.

This activity is best done if you have a partner. You could have anyone engage in this practice with you—they don't need to be a coach or an educator. Your partner will read the monologues aloud, and you'll use the mental detours tracking log (Table 8.1) to document where your mind goes. Use the same log for all the practice monologues so you can see your overall tendencies. This is a good time to listen like you normally do (rather than trying to be an exemplary listener) so you can understand your mind's tendencies.

Table 8.1: Mental Detour Tracking Log

Mental detours	Tally marks for each detour
Connecting I want to interject with a connection to what the speaker is saying. I want to feel closer to the speaker by sharing a similar thought or experience.	
Fixing I want to offer a solution, advice, or a suggestion of something that can be done. I want to fix it.	
Disagreeing I want to interject with a disagreement, to discuss or debate something the speaker is saying or how they are saying it.	
Questioning I want to ask a clarifying question for more information or so I can better analyze the situation. Or: I want to ask a probing question so the speaker can explore their thinking more deeply.	
Feeling uncomfortable I am experiencing an uncomfortable emotion because of what the speaker is saying. I'm feeling annoyed, impatient, judgmental, bored.	
Feeling comfortable I am experiencing a comfortable emotion because of what the speaker is saying. I'm feeling caring, excited, enthusiastic, appreciative.	

Mental detours	Tally marks for each detour
Spacing out My mind is wandering to an unrelated topic. I'm spacing out or distracted by unrelated thoughts or stimuli in our environment.	
Planning an exit I'm considering options for how to get out of this conversation.	
Other (describe):	
Other (describe):	

Monologue 1

Did you get that e-mail? About the emergency meeting after school? I can't believe she's doing this again. It's probably something like, "On my walk-through today, I counted only 15 classrooms that had learning targets posted on the board. And 27 classrooms did not have the correct blackboard configuration." I'm here until 6:30 every night, and I get here at 7:00 a.m. This is crazy making. How can we be asked to do anything else? I spend most of the afternoon cleaning up the mess that admin doesn't take care of—calling the parents of kids who cut class. Of course, those parents never answer the call. I just don't understand. Don't they care about their kids? I've just about had it.

Monologue 2

I am so excited about this year! I had a great summer—I hope you did, too. I hope we'll have time to share stories because I love hearing about your adventures with your kids, but I know that you want to talk to me about the new curriculum. I did get those boxes. They're over there in the corner; I just don't know when I'm going to have a chance to unpack them. I'm really trying to get this bulletin board up, and you know I'm not really onboard with this new program. I just don't think it's right for our kids.

Monologue 3

I've been teaching here for 18 years, and I've done a good job. Everyone knows that. I get kids coming back for years after they graduated thanking me and telling me how much they loved my classes, that I was their favorite teacher, that I was so much fun. And now I'm on an improvement program?! What is that about? Now I'm being told that I won't be able to coach football anymore unless my kids' test scores go up? I can't help it if some of these kids don't want to learn. That's just a handful of kids, and we all know that some are little delinquents. I mean, this neighborhood has changed so much since I started teaching here. I'm a good teacher.

Monologue 4

I was actually excited to come back to school this year. I went to this incredible professional development week this summer and got so many ideas for my drama class, and I felt so rejuvenated. And then I get here and I'm told that I have to teach reading intervention, which I've never taught before, which I don't know how to teach, which I just don't want to teach. Why don't we get any say in these big decisions? We used to have admin who listened to us, who thought about our needs as well. How can they make this switch without even consulting us? I just feel like all the excitement has been drained out of me. I don't know how to teach reading intervention for English learners. I had like 2 days of training on working with English learners. That was 15 years ago, and now we have all these kids coming from countries where they're having wars—how am I supposed to do all of this?

Monologue 5

I really like you and all—I mean we've taught together for 12 years—but I just don't feel like I need a coach. I hope you don't take it personally, but I'm doing good and I think our new teachers really need a coach. You can just walk past their classroom and hear the kids bouncing off the walls. We get kids now who don't even know how to sit on the floor and be quiet for 1 minute—I really think you need to work with those teachers. I don't want to see so many of our teachers burning out and quitting. Why are you supposed to work with me anyway?

Reflect

What are your overall tendencies in terms of the mental detours you make?

Were you surprised by the data you gathered? Why or why not?

Are there any mental detours that you want to set an intention to take less frequently? Which ones?

How would your coaching relationships (and perhaps other relationship in your life) be different if you didn't take those detours?

What needs to happen so that you can take those mental detours less often?

Nonverbal Communication: Focusing on Ourselves

Do this activity to cultivate a foundational understanding of the role of nonverbal communication.

It's said that some 65% of communication is delivered and received nonverbally—in our posture, gestures, facial expressions, and eye movements. (See Figure 8.1 for a list of common nonverbal cues.) These typically subconscious behaviors clue us in to someone's attitude or state of mind, so good listeners constantly scan the nonverbal presence of others. We know you know it's important to pay attention to body language, but let's name some reasons it's especially important for coaches to be aware not only of the nonverbal communication of their clients but also of their own body language:

- When we talk with someone and perceive a mismatch between their selection of words and their nonverbal communication, our trust in the other person diminishes.
- When our own body language doesn't match what we're saying, others won't trust us as much.
- If we can't read a person's nonverbals, we feel uncomfortable around them.
- When we misinterpret someone else's body language, we can miss an opportunity for connection, or we can even take actions that have a negative impact.

It's critical that we are aware of our body language so that we can build and maintain trust. And it's critical that we pay attention to our client's body language so that we can better understand them.

Figure 8.1: Common Nonverbal Cues

Nonverbal communication can be expressed through the following (and many other cues):

- breathing patterns including sighs and loud exhales
- yawning
- leaning forward or backward
- head movement such as nodding
- furrowed brows
- a set jaw
- pinched lips
- eye contact or lack of eye contact
- hunched shoulders
- crossed or uncrossed arms
- hand movements like clasping, fidgeting, or rubbing

Reflect

What kind of feedback have you received from others about your body language? Have people commented on the amount you smile or on whether you look upset often or seem angry?

How do you think others perceive your body language? How do you think they interpret some of your nonverbal cues?

How do you feel about the way your nonverbal cues are interpreted? Are they accurate? Do you wish your cues were interpreted differently?

Extend Your Learning: Solicit Feedback

Identify a few people you trust within your personal and professional circles. Explain that you're working on honing your awareness of your nonverbal communication and that you want to know how they experience you. Ask them the questions here, and record some of their responses. Appreciate their honesty.

What do you remember about my body language when we first met? How did you interpret my body language?

How do you experience my nonverbal communication now, while we're talking?

When it comes to my nonverbals, is there anything I could do that would make you feel more comfortable?

What do you think someone who doesn't know me as well as you know me would say about my nonverbal communication? What do you think others perceive in my body language?

For Further Learning

→ Enroll in an Essentials of the Art of Coaching workshop to continue learning about nonverbal communication.

→ Read Elena's blog: https://brightmorningteam.com/2013/12/the-importance-of-listening-to-non-verbal-messages/.

Nonverbal Communication: Understanding Our Clients

Do this activity to hone your awareness of how you interpret other people's body language.

Now that you've reflected on your own body language, you can start thinking about other people's. Think about this as how you listen to nonverbal communication.

Our listening (both to verbal and nonverbal communication) is profoundly influenced by the cultural group with which we identify as well as by dominant culture. For example, if you believe (as our dominant culture does) that women should usually smile, then you might be unsettled if you have a female colleague who doesn't smile all the time. Dominant culture holds beliefs and values around how men and women should communicate nonverbally, and it also holds beliefs and values about how people of different races or ethnicities should communicate. For example, it's acceptable for White men to raise their voices, loudly proclaim their opinions and beliefs, and express their rage, but it's not acceptable (or even safe) for men or women of other ethnicities to do this.

There's a lot more to unpack about how we interpret the nonverbal communication of those who are different from us and to recognize how dominant culture distorts our ability to listen and causes us to have problematic interpretations. To begin an exploration of these ideas, reflect on your own perceptions.

Reflect

What kind of body language in others makes you feel comfortable and relaxed?

What kind of body language in others makes you feel uncomfortable?

Think of a nonverbal cue that makes you uncomfortable. How do you interpret it? (For example, "If someone doesn't make eye contact with me, I've interpreted that as disinterest in the conversation.") See if you can identify a few nonverbal cues and how you interpret them. (Reference Figure 8.1 for a list of cues.)

Think of someone you perceive as being different from you. Perhaps this person is of a different ethnicity, religion, sexual orientation, or gender. Can you identify some nonverbal ways that this person communicates that you don't understand?

Are there any nonverbal cues that you communicate that you suspect are reflective of your ethnicity or culture? How do you think those are interpreted?

Elena Reflects

Katia was a novice coach I trained who had a lot of potential, but when I observed her coaching I was surprised by her responses to her client, Jack. She didn't seem to notice that Jack was upset or that each question she asked seemed to heighten his distress. The conversation felt awkward. Later, when we debriefed, I brought up an exchange she had with Jack about a parent interaction. "What did you notice about Jack when you asked how the phone call went?" Katia looked at me blankly. "What do you mean?" she asked.

"What did you notice about how he responded?" I said.

"Well. . . I . . . I mean he answered it, right?" Katia said. She shifted uncomfortably around in her chair.

From *The Art of Coaching Workbook: Tools to Make Every Conversation Count* by Elena Aguilar. Copyright © 2021 by Elena Aguilar. Reproduced by permission.

"I'm noticing right now that you're shifting around in your chair," I said.

"I'm sorry," she interjected. "I can get squirmy."

"I see that. What are you feeling right now?" I asked.

"I'm nervous," she said. "I feel like I got the wrong answer."

"Okay, I can see you're nervous. That's what I'm reading in your body language. When you were in conversation with Jack, and when you asked him the question about the parent, what did you notice about his body language?"

Katia looked at me. "I . . . umm. . . I didn't notice anything. What do you mean?"

"I saw his face get red, he rubbed the palm of his hand vigorously with one thumb, and he looked down at the table."

"Oh," Katia said. "I didn't notice that." Katia dropped her head.

"I thought you didn't notice," I said, "And that was important information he was giving you. I think that's why your conversation didn't go where you'd hoped it would go."

Katia and I spent a long time talking about this. Like a handful of coaches I've worked with, Katia wasn't tuned in to body language. She needed to learn to see it, to pay attention and register body language, and to learn how to interpret it. If you're like Katia, there's nothing wrong with you—it's just a skill you need to acquire and refine.

Extend Your Learning: Observing Coaching Clients

Step 1

Next time you meet with a client, capture notes on their body language. Try to capture as many as possible. It's important that these notes are simply descriptions of what you see, for example:

- He's sitting at desk, legs crossed, leaning forward over the table, elbows propping up head.
- When I ask, "Tell me about your day," her eyebrows rise, eyes get big, and she sighs and looks out the window.

It can take careful attention to capture descriptive notes without interpreting your client's body language. Interpretation sounds like, "He crossed his arms *defensively* over his chest." Capture descriptive notes for a couple of sessions.

Step 2

After a couple of coaching sessions when you've focused on taking notes on your client's nonverbals, reflect on these questions:

What insights did you get into your client from paying attention to their body language?

What did you notice that you might not have noticed had you not been doing this activity?

Were there any points when you said or did something because of what you noticed in their nonverbal communication? What happened?

When You Get Triggered

Do this activity to learn strategies for when you are emotionally activated in a conversation.

Like it or not, there's a good chance you'll feel triggered in a coaching conversation now and then. This is simply because you are a human being and humans have emotions.

Notice

The first step in dealing with this situation is to recognize that it's occurring. That might sound confusing or simplistic, but often we get triggered and we don't even know it. We might find ourselves on a mental detour from the conversation, or we might find ourselves in an argument with a client. Anytime your coaching conversation turns into an argument (or when you're trying to convince someone else that you're right and they're wrong), you are no longer coaching them.

So how do you know you're triggered? Sometimes your body gives you cues—you might feel physically uncomfortable, or you might get a stomachache or slight headache or whatever your body does when it's distressed. You might also notice that the thoughts going through your mind have become uncomfortable: maybe you're casting judgment on the other person or maybe you're thinking, *I can't believe she's saying this again. Why do I have to coach her?* You might be thinking, *Is she saying this just to get a rise out of me?* Finally, your emotions will let you know that you're triggered (after all, to be triggered is to have strong uncomfortable emotions). So perhaps you notice a surge of irritation or disgust or fear—those feelings might travel through your body and thoughts as a way to let you know that they're arising. And then you can say, "Aha! I'm triggered!"

How to Engage with Triggers

1. Notice that you're triggered and name it: I'm triggered!
2. Pause to acknowledge your sadness, fear, and anger.
3. Investigate and tend to the emotions that are calling for your attention.
4. Ask yourself, *Who do I want to be?*

Pause

When you're triggered during a coaching conversation, it's best to recognize the sadness, fear, and anger that's coming up and reflect on them later. This promise to yourself will allow you to reenter the conversation and know that you're not just brushing these feelings aside. It's also really good to take a couple of deep breaths in this step.

Investigate

Later that day, or whenever you can, you've got to dig into that sadness, fear, and anger. In Chapter 1, you reflected on "The Things That Get Under My Skin." Reread what you wrote there. How does that exercise help you understand why you get triggered? Also return to the "Exploring Mental Detours" activity in this chapter. Does that give you additional insight into why you get triggered? Almost everyone has unhealed pain, and each person's journey to healing is different. We encourage you to pursue that journey—you deserve it. There's also a correlation between the amount of healing you do and the impact you'll have as a coach. You'll likely continue to be frequently triggered if you have a lot of unhealed parts of yourself.

Be Who You Want To Be

In any situation, all you can do is be who you want to be. This is firmly within your sphere of control. So who do you want to be as a coach? Go back to the activity in Chapter 5 about the Transformational Coaching ways of being. Go back to your core values in Chapter 1. Go back to your coaching mission and vision statement and your manifesto from Chapter 2. Who do you want to be as a coach? Reminding yourself of this will help you when you get triggered. Turn this sense of who you want to be into self-talk phrases, and run those tapes through your mind when you get triggered.

Elena Reflects

When I first became a coach, I worked with a couple of clients whom I felt like triggered me a dozen times an hour. While I investigated why I responded to them in the way I did, I found it useful to use the following self-talk phrases:

- *Who are YOU to judge someone, Elena?*
- *Be here now. Stay in the conversation.*
- *Be curious.*
- *Be kind.*
- *How would you want someone else to treat you?*

After a while, after I healed some of my achy places, and as I practiced noticing and pausing, I found myself triggered less and less. I also noticed that when I was triggered, I felt an immediate kindness toward myself—I knew that the trigger meant I was experiencing strong emotions that deserved attention. And I'd come to trust myself that I'd attend to those later. Making that shift to being able to send my own compassion resulted in a tremendous shift in my coaching. I am now very rarely triggered (something I never thought would happen).

Reflect

Recall a time when you felt triggered in a conversation, either a coaching conversation or any professional conversation. What did the other person say? What were you thinking? Fill in the speech and thought bubbles.

How did you know you were triggered? What did you think, feel, or notice physically?

What were you feeling underneath the trigger? (Use the core emotions in Chapter 7 as a resource.)

Where did those feelings come from? What were they trying to tell you? What is the unhealed pain that is asking for attention?

Who do you want to be as a coach? What could you say to yourself in the middle of a coaching conversation if you get triggered? (Return to your core values, mission and vision, manifesto, and coaching mantras for ideas).

Return to that time that you were triggered. In the thought bubble, write what you wish you'd thought and said to yourself—what you want to think and say to yourself next time you're triggered. Below the thought bubble, draw what you'd look like in a conversation where you aren't triggered.

Common Mistakes Coaches Make in Conversations

Do this activity to identify what not to do in a coaching conversation.

In this book, we're emphasizing what you should do as a coach—because we know that's what you want. Sometimes it's also helpful to know what not to do. We've all made the mistakes that you're about to read about. The key is to be aware of your tendencies so you can correct your own course.

Read each description of common communication mistakes that follow, and reflect on your tendency to do it. Even if you're a new coach, you'll recognize which mistakes you tend to make, as the list applies to all kinds of settings, from personal relationships to classroom interactions with students, not just to coaching conversations. Mark an X on the line in the spot that reflects your tendency to make this mistake.

Asking Closed Questions

Ask yes or no questions, or questions that invite only a short response.

Example: Do you do projects on a regular basis?

Never   Sometimes   Often

⟵————————————————————————————————⟶

Asking Questions That Disguise Advice

You ask a question when you really want to give advice. The question is subtly manipulative and might begin with, "Should you. . . ?" or "Could you. . . ?" or "Will you. . . ?"

Example: Do you think it would work better if you gave students an example of the project before they start?

Never   Sometimes   Often

⟵————————————————————————————————⟶

Asking Rambling Questions

When you're trying to ask the perfect question or you're just unclear on what you want to ask, you might ask a question three different ways or string together sentence fragments. You ramble. Sometimes we do this when we're trying to lead a client in a particular direction.

Example: I'm hearing that you're having a hard time, which is common for new teachers. I mean when I think about my first year—oh, I won't go there, but I'm really thinking about different ways you could get support, or maybe it would be better for you to talk to your principal, but I guess what I'm wondering is. . . ?

Never   Sometimes   Often

Asking Leading Questions

You know what these are, right? Teachers often ask students leading questions. These are the questions that subtly point toward the answer—usually one that the coach wants to hear.

Example: Given what happened on the last field trip when students got on the train and you lost track of them and then we got a panicked call from a parent, do you think you should do something different this time?

Never   Sometimes   Often

Asking Why Questions

Why questions put people on the defensive. It can feel like they're being asked to justify their actions.

Example: Why do you think you reacted to that student with so much anger?

Never   Sometimes   Often

Interrupt

Sometimes we're not even aware that we interrupt others. You might talk over people, finish their sentences, or flat out interrupt.

Never   Sometimes   Often

⟵───⟶

Fill Every Second with Talk

Your client says something, and you jump in right away with another question or comment. You feel uncomfortable with silence.

Never   Sometimes   Often

⟵───⟶

So What Do I Do Instead?

If you find that you make some of these common mistakes, here are some things you can do instead.

If you. . .	Then try. . .
Ask closed questions	Start with the word *what* or *how*. That will open up a question.
Ask questions that disguise advice	Recognize that you are wanting to give advice or a suggestion. Either give the advice or rephrase the question so that it's open and allows the client their own answer.
Ask rambling questions	Taking a few seconds of quiet time to figure out what you want to ask and to formulate a question. You can even say, "Give me a moment to think. I want to be clear about what I'm asking."
Ask leading questions	Ask questions with multiple solutions. For example, "Would you say you were feeling discouraged? Or would you say you were feeling sad?"
Ask why questions	Rephrase the question and start it with "What. . ." For example, rather than saying, "Why do you think that student responded like that?" You can say, "What might the student be leaving unsaid?" Or rather than saying, "Why did you do that?" You can say, "Can you tell me how you made that decision?"

From *The Art of Coaching Workbook: Tools to Make Every Conversation Count* by Elena Aguilar. Copyright © 2021 by Elena Aguilar. Reproduced by permission.

If you. . .	Then try. . .
Interrupt	Count to two after the client has stopped speaking before you reply or ask a question. Also remember that your goal as a coach is not to interject your ideas but to help the client explore theirs.
Fill every second with talk	Increase your tolerance for being in silence with your client. Recognize the emotions that come up for you—anxiety, fear, uncertainty—and remind yourself that you'll be okay. Also remember that silence is when your client might be thinking and your job is to give them space to think.

Reflect and Plan

Which are two mistakes you make most often?

Write two statements that make the connection between a change you want to make, and the impact you'll then have on your client. The basic structure for this statement is, "If I _____, then _____, and this will _____. Here's an example:

If I count to three after a client speaks, then I will interrupt less often. This will give my client space to think and increase her trust in me.

Write two statements that make the connection between the common mistake you want to stop making and the positive impact that will have on your client.

Draw a symbol (whose meaning is apparent only to you) on the front of your coaching notebook (or a sticky note for your computer) to remind you of what not to do or what to do in a conversation.

Six Tips That Will Transform the Texture of Your Conversations

This activity will help you internalize a handful of the most important communication strategies.

When watching Elena demonstrate Transformational Coaching, observers frequently comment on how calm she seems and on the slow, even measured pace of the conversation. Quiet pauses, often another remarked on element of these demonstration conversations, are one of the tools that transform the texture of a Transformational Coaching conversation.

What follows are six tips to integrate into your own coaching communication. We think about them as strategies that make the texture of a conversation one that is light, spacious, soft, and inviting. Read the short descriptions, and then on the following page, draw a symbol or sketch to help you remember the concept.

Talk less: Talk much less than your client talks. Aim to talk for less than 1/3 of the time. Your job is to ask some good questions. Give your client space to think. Trust that they can find the solutions to their problems.

Speak slowly: When you say something, speak slowly. Don't hurry your questions.

"Tell me more": Often the best response is, "Tell me more." Speak these words from a place of wide-open curiosity.

Think: Give yourself permission to think. Know that you can tell your client, "I need a moment to think about what you just said." It's honorable to think.

Relax the body: Soften the space between your eyebrows, relax your arms, let your jaw drop, and smile slightly. Also breathe.

Listen from love: Listen from a place of love.

From *The Art of Coaching Workbook: Tools to Make Every Conversation Count* by Elena Aguilar. Copyright © 2021 by Elena Aguilar. Reproduced by permission.

| Talk Less | Speak Slowly |

| "Tell Me More" | Pause to Think |

| Relax the Body | Listen From Love |

CHAPTER 9

Practicing Facilitative Coaching Conversations

In this chapter, we'll dive into what a coach can say during coaching conversations—to the responses we make. We've explored listening skills and a range of thinking tools, and now we're getting to the third bucket of Transformational Coach skills. We know you're excited. We sense it. But, first, in the following speech bubble, write a phrase or question (or two) that you think you often say in coaching conversations. These could be ones that you're proud of or that you're laughing at yourself about saying. For example, one of Elena's go-tos is, "Wow." She says that a lot when she's coaching. This is not her favorite coaching stem, but she says it a lot. What do you often say?

(Re)Introducing the Coaching Stances

In *The Art of Coaching*, Elena divides the moves a Transformational Coach makes into two categories—our language and the activities we use with clients, she explains, can be categorized as either facilitative or directive. Like all categorization systems, this one is imperfect: Lots of the things we say and do fall into both categories at the same time. But starting off with categories can be helpful.

When you take a facilitative stance in coaching, you are guiding someone with a light touch, gently coaxing them toward finding their own insights and understandings. You hold up a mirror and ask them what they see.

When you take a directive stance in coaching, you're applying a bit more pressure, a firmer nudge. You're holding up the mirror in front of them and saying, "Look at this funny hair sticking straight up right here! What do you want to do about it?"

This is really important, so we're going to write it in big bold letters:

A TRANSFORMATIONAL COACH USES

BOTH

FACILITATIVE AND DIRECTIVE COACHING STRATEGIES.

One stance is not better. Both are needed.

Perhaps think about it this way. Imagine that, as a coach, you had an internal dial you could fiddle with during coaching conversations. Turned all the way to the left, you become 100% facilitative, meaning that you share no expert knowledge but rather support clients to learn new ways of thinking and being through reflection, observation, and experimentation. Turned all the way to the right, you become 100% directive, meaning that you lead the conversation from your own expertise and may make suggestions, model lessons, or teach clients how to do something.

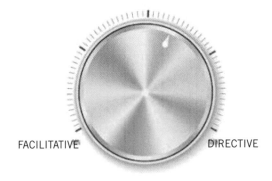

FACILITATIVE   DIRECTIVE

Part of the artistry of Transformational Coaching lies in recognizing that this metaphorical dial exists and adjusting it strategically during the conversation. Directive coaching and facilitative coach each has a place in your repertoire, but they are not equally transformative.

Directive coaching is frequently practiced by those who coach in a particular content, discipline, or instructional framework. For example, a district might adopt a new curriculum and provide coaches who will help teachers master the material. Or a school might take on a behavior management program and hire coaches who can support its implementation. In these models, the coach is seen as an expert who is responsible for teaching a set of skills or sharing a body of knowledge.

Directive coaching is relevant and necessary at times; however, these strategies are also limited. Directive coaching alone is less likely to result in long-term changes of practice or deep internalization of learning. A coach may notice that they return to a teacher they worked with, only to find that the teacher has given up using the strategies they appeared to have adopted in coaching. This is because directive coaching alone does not expand the teacher's *internal* capacity to reflect, make decisions, or explore ways of being.

For coaching to have deep, lasting impact, coaches need a broad range of modalities. In facilitative coaching coaches do not share expert knowledge. They work to build on the client's existing skills, knowledge, and beliefs to construct new skills, knowledge, and beliefs that will form the basis for future actions. For example, in facilitative coaching, a coach might guide a teacher to reflect on their own experiences as a student to better understand the assumptions they make about what good teaching looks like. Or a coach might support a new administrator to craft a tool for gathering staff feedback and then explore what she hears back. The facilitative approach is all about growing a client's autonomy as a learner and leader.

It can be helpful to further dissect facilitative and directive coaching to identify six different approaches a coach can take during a coaching conversation. Usually, in a coaching conversation, we use most, if not all, of these stances. Let's briefly review these six stances, from the far left of the dial to the far right.

Facilitative Stances

- A supportive approach provides confirmation, offers encouragement, and helps the client maintain focus and motivation.
- A cathartic approach allows the client to express and release powerful emotions.
- A catalytic approach elicits self-discovery and problem-solving, encouraging the client to take responsibility for their learning and future actions.

Directive Stances

- A confrontational approach raises awareness of behavior, beliefs, or being; challenges the client's assumptions; helps the client see the consequences of an action; and interrupts "rut stories" (see *The Art of Coaching*, p. 198).
- An informative approach imparts knowledge and information, provides resources (e.g., curriculum, lesson plans, templates), or directs clients to them and supplies missing facts.
- A prescriptive approach gives directions, recommendations, or advice and directs behavior (not beliefs or being).

Many new coaches will ask when to use each stance and how often. Facilitative approaches are more consistent with the ultimate aim of Transformational Coaching, which is to build resilient, self-directed, equity-minded learners and leaders. The one exception, perhaps, is the confrontational approach, which is a directive stance but that we use to disrupt problematic beliefs and ways of being.

The allure of the informational and prescriptive stances is that they can feel very satisfying for the client (who gets a fix for a sticky problem) and for the coach (who gets to feel helpful). The risk is that clients can become dependent on us playing this role. Remember, directive approaches are less effective in building someone else's long-term capacity. If we find our clients wanting us to engage in this way, it can be helpful to use a gradual release model to support the development of their autonomy.

Over the next four chapters, we'll explore what it means to coach from both facilitative and directive stances and when to use one stance or the other. But before we get to the decision-making around what stance to use, you need to know a bit more about what facilitative and directive coaching entails.

This chapter explores coaching from a facilitative stance. To understand and effectively use the approaches that comprise facilitative coaching, we need to start by taking a look at emotions. We often coach from a facilitative stance in a conversation when our client is experiencing emotions or when we know it would be useful for our client to explore their emotions. So we'll begin with a brief exploration of emotions.

Why Deal with Emotions?

This activity will help you use your own experiences to illuminate the rationale for using facilitative coaching stances that acknowledge emotion.

One of the things that makes Transformational Coaching different from most other coaching approaches used in schools is that we pay attention to and value emotions. We know that emotions are information, and we seek to understand this information. We know that emotions are the keys to our resilience, and we work to unlock this resilience in ourselves and our clients. Although we might feel uncomfortable at times with our own and others' emotions, we know that having and expressing emotions is part of being human. We accept this humanity, we grab a box of tissues, and we coach on.

To get you into the mindset of this chapter, we ask you to engage in a few activities to recall your first year of teaching. This will help you understand why we have to deal with emotions, and it'll save us all a lecture about why it's important to ask about feelings.

Part 1: Peaks and Valleys

First, using the rest of the space on this page, draw a line that represents your first year of teaching—or any early tumultuous year that you remember clearly—and include at least three mountain peaks (to represent highs) and three valleys (to represent lows). Label those peaks and valleys with your memories from that year. Of course, if you want more room, use another paper. You could take a photo of your completed creation and paste it in here.

From *The Art of Coaching Workbook: Tools to Make Every Conversation Count* by Elena Aguilar. Copyright © 2021 by Elena Aguilar. Reproduced by permission.

Part 2: Storyboarding

In the following boxes, storyboard your first year of teaching, showing the expression on your face at different points in that year. You're also welcome to add thought or word bubbles or add captions. Remember, this is not an art class, so slide those fears to the side and allow yourself to have fun!

From *The Art of Coaching Workbook: Tools to Make Every Conversation Count* by Elena Aguilar. Copyright © 2021 by Elena Aguilar. Reproduced by permission.

Part 3: Coach Your First-Year Self

Now that you've spent some time recalling that first year, it's time for you to engage your coaching skills. Pick out one of the peak or valley moments, and say what you wish a coach would have said. Then select a couple of the scenes that you storyboarded and do the same. For example, perhaps you depicted a difficult afternoon when, as soon as the kids had left, you sat at your desk and sobbed. What do you wish a coach might have said had she walked in at that moment? Don't worry about being super "coach-like" right now—just write from your heart, from who you are, and from what you already know.

Moment:

What I wish a coach would have said:

Moment:

What I wish a coach would have said:

Moment:

What I wish a coach would have said:

Moment:

What I wish a coach would have said:

Part 4: Here's Why We Deal with Emotions

Given what you've just recalled about your entry into teaching, we wonder how you'd make the case for why a Transformational Coach attends to emotions. Jot down some thoughts.

Here's why a Transformational Coach recognizes, accepts, and coaches emotions:

- We are human beings. Human beings have emotions.
- Teachers experience lots of emotions, perhaps even more than folks in other professions, in part because we're dealing with children all day long, and they have lots of emotions. Also: Teaching is a service profession. Emotions such as care, commitment, and love are at the root of why we teach. Emotions brought us to this field.
- When we coach around emotions, we access the powerful, energizing forces of care, commitment, and love. These are inner resources that help us mitigate the stress and challenges we face every day in schools.
- When we don't acknowledge, accept, and process unpleasant emotions, they come out anyway, and they can come out in ways that hurt people, including the children we teach.
- A healthy workplace is one to which we can bring our full humanity, including our emotions. A school that is committed to retaining teachers values coaching emotions as much as coaching instruction.
- When teachers engage in coaching around emotions, they are far more likely to be effective in every sense: They navigate unexpected changes, respond calmly to student behavior, build positive relationships with children, plan engaging lessons, and so on.

What resonates with you in this list? What would you add to this list of reasons we coach emotions?

What Is an Emotion?

Do this activity to get a clear understanding of what an emotion is—because it's really useful to know exactly what we're talking about.

How would you explain what an emotion is? Is it a physical experience? Something that goes on in your head? Your heart? Take a quick stab at a definition of an emotion. (Seriously: Do this before you go ahead. Activating prior knowledge is a good thing, remember?)

What follows is an excerpt from Elena's book *Coaching for Equity*. As you read it, highlight information that is new to you. We're including this here because you won't find it in *The Art of Coaching*, and we think it's useful to know.

Excerpt from Coaching for Equity

An emotion is information. An emotion is a message that something matters. An emotion is the primary way that your body and mind send you signals about what you need. An emotion is a portal to wisdom. . .

Emotions occur in our bodies and often have a mental or psychological component. Something happens and our bodies respond, and our minds create meaning: A friend smiles at you and says, "Good morning," and your body produces dopamine (a feel-good hormone) and you think: *I'm glad to see her. I'm grateful for her friendship.* Or a seventh-grade student rolls her eyes at you, your body produces stress hormones, your heart beats a little faster, your breath gets shallow, and you think: *She's so disrespectful. I'm sick of teaching ungrateful kids.* Sometimes the mind creates meaning first, and then body responds. This is what an emotion is: a cycle of mind-body experiences. How we respond in this experience, when it reaches the point of story-making, is what matters. And how we respond can take two directions: the path of liberation or the path of suffering.

Emotions are trying to give us information. The first monumental shift we could make in how we engage with emotions would be to see them as our friends. In so much of the Western world, we see the unknown as something scary, so we push it away. But what if we could welcome whatever emotion shows up? It would be a different world if we greeted an emotion warmly, invited it in for tea, and sat down with it and said: "Hi! I'm listening. What do you want to tell me?" To do that, we'll need to recognize *when* we're experiencing an

---

emotion, and we'll need to hold a value that emotions are worthy. After that, we'll need resources for how to interpret what the emotion says and how to respond.

When emotions show up, our response can be found along a continuum. On one end, we experience emotions as a flood that sweeps us away. We can hurt people when we speak impulsively and lash out. In contrast, on the other end of this continuum, we suppress emotions. We ignore or avoid emotions, fearing that they will overwhelm us or could damage our relationships. We pretend they're not happening and try to work around them. Some people repress emotions indefinitely, or the emotions explode out. Emotions demand to be seen and heard, and they can come out unproductively in our words or in our silence, directed harmfully inward or outward.

For emotions to lead us down the path of liberation, we must welcome them, identify them, learn from them, and express them without blame or judgment. When we are open to emotions, we'll not only be more equipped to respond to uncomfortable or unpleasant emotions, but we'll be more responsive to the pleasant emotions. In shutting ourselves off from emotions, we're denying ourselves a whole lot of enjoyable emotions.

Summarize Your Learnings

What are three key ideas you're taking away from this passage? Summarize those in short statements.

-

-

-

Articulate Your Own Definition

How would you now define an emotion? Try to use simple phrasing. Imagine defining an emotion to middle school students.

The Cycle of an Emotion

This activity will give you a deeper understanding of what an emotion is—and will set you up to be able to coach emotions even more effectively.

When Elena was doing research for her book *Onward,* she learned about the cycle of an emotion, and she got very, very excited. She realized that, in understanding the sequence of events that creates an emotion, we can pinpoint precisely where resilience can be cultivated. When she gets around to writing the second edition of *The Art of Coaching,* the cycle of an emotion—and this opportunity to build resilience—will be included, but we don't want to make you wait for that.

Let's start here again: An emotion is a reaction to an event. Something happens, your mind processes it, your body responds. (Sometimes it feels like your body responds first, but the experts say that our mind has interpreted the event first.) Then you behave in accordance with your mind's interpretation and your body's response. So emotions are physiological, cognitive, and behavioral experiences. This cycle is illustrated in Figure 9.1

Prompting event. This is the stuff that happens outside you, in your environment, such as an unexpected fire drill, a canceled meeting, or a crying child. Prompting events can also happen within you; they can be thoughts, memories, or even emotions.

Interpretation. Your mind makes sense of what happened. The event is filtered through your evaluation, understanding, beliefs, and assumptions, and you explain it to yourself in a particular way. For example, you interpret the unexpected fire drill as evidence yet again of your assistant principal's obliviousness to how hard a teacher's job is. (Surely if he'd ever taught first grade he'd know that Friday after lunch is not the time for a drill. Probably he was supposed to do this drill earlier, and he has to check it off his list by the end of the week.) You interpret the event as evidence of your assistant principal's incompetence and lack of respect.

Physical response. The event and your interpretation result in a physical response in your body. Your thoughts about your assistant principal's lack of respect produce stress hormones that make your heart race, your throat constrict, and your hands tremble.

Urge to act. Almost simultaneous to the physical response, you feel an urge to do something. You may or may not act on this impulse, but it's useful to notice what you feel compelled to do in those first moments. As you fume over your assistant principal's incompetence and disrespect, you might start composing mental e-mails to your principal expressing your frustration.

Figure 9.1: The Cycle of an Emotion

CYCLE OF AN EMOTION

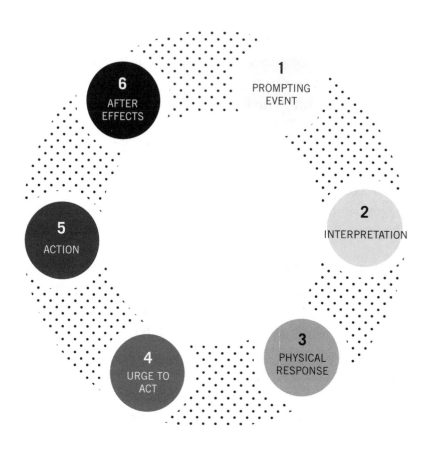

From *The Art of Coaching Workbook: Tools to Make Every Conversation Count* by Elena Aguilar. Copyright © 2021 by Elena Aguilar. Reproduced by permission.

Action. Then there's what you actually do. You may or may not feel as though you're in control of your behavior at this point. As you're herding your students out the door, grabbing your class list and emergency supply backpack, you might yell at someone, slam a door, or shoot a dirty look at your assistant principal when he asks for your attendance list. Later you might send off that angry e-mail or just reach for a bag of cookies.

Aftereffects. Finally, we think about how the emotions you are experiencing in any emotional cycle can send ripples outward, affecting other emotions, thoughts, and behaviors, and your body. The aftereffects themselves can serve as a prompting event that sets off another emotion cycle. For example, your anger at your assistant principal can lead to a cycle of anxiety about your job more generally. The aftereffects might include feeling physically exhausted or having regrets about how you behaved.

Remarkably, this six-part cycle is the universal structure of all emotional experiences. When you can identify the parts of the cycle, you can intervene in your own experience, and you can coach a client to intervene in their experience of an emotion. You'll gain a much deeper understanding of this concept if you explore it through your own experiences.

Reflecting on an Emotion Cycle

Identify a recent unpleasant emotional experience that you want to reflect on. In a couple sentences, describe what happened:

1. Prompting event: What event triggered this cycle? This is the who, what, when, and where.

2. Interpretation: How did you interpret the event? This is the why.

3. Physical response: What happened in your body?

4. Urge to act: What did you want to do?

5. Action: What did you actually do? What did you say? Be specific.

6. Aftereffects: What was the consequence of what happened and how you responded?

Reflect

Where in your cycle do you think you could most easily make a change and steer your experience in a different direction?

Look at how you interpreted the event—stage 2. What other ways are there to see the situation? How might a different way to interpret the situation shift your emotional experience?

For Further Learning

→ Read *Onward: Cultivating Emotional Resilience in Educators* and *The Onward Workbook*.

→ Enroll in an online or virtual course on coaching emotions and coaching for resilience (information at http://www.brightmorningteam.com).

Using the Supportive Approach

Do this activity to gain a deeper understanding of how to use the supportive approach and of the language that reflects it.

Now that you've got a solid understanding of emotions, let's explore how facilitative coaching helps someone explore and process their emotions. In *The Art of Coaching* (pp. 171–172), you can read about the supportive approach. As a reminder, supportive coaching helps to:

- provide confirmation;
- offer encouragement;
- maintain focus and motivation;
- build self-esteem and self-confidence;
- highlight moments of success and progress toward goals; and
- encourage risk-taking.

Being supportive is not about fluffy words and pats on the back but rather about communicating authentic empathy. When you coach using a supportive approach, you might recall the concept of strengths-based coaching that we explored in this workbook in Chapter 5. There's an intersection here between these two thinking tools: strengths-based coaching can help us be specific when we're taking a supportive approach. When we understand and recognize our client's strengths, we'll be more authentic and precise when we're using a supportive coaching approach. We'll also be able to guide our client to remember and reanchor in their own strengths if we're thinking through a strengths-based framework.

Tips and Reminders

- When using a supportive approach, we'll likely offer thoughts and reactions more than we'll ask questions.
- Active and reflective listening is really useful and appropriate when you intend to take a supportive approach.
- Be authentic and specific if you offer praise.
- Be mindful of your nonverbal cues and how those can also communicate empathy. Consider key nonverbal moves to communicate your care.

Practice

What follows are some scenarios we hope will resonate with you. For each one, craft a response that reflects the supportive approach. Use your imagination and add details if you want. Also consider the key nonverbal moves you can make to demonstrate your empathy and care. Start with an example to guide you.

Example Scenario

A teacher is slumped on his desk when you walk in. He says, "That's it. I had the worst day ever." He hands you a note on which a student has drawn a cruel caricature of the teacher and has written some very unkind words.

A supportive response: Oh, man. Yeah, this probably qualifies as your worst day ever. What do you need from me right now? How can I help?

Key nonverbal move: Sit down quickly, at the teacher's level, next to them (not across from them).

Your Turn

Scenario 1

A teacher is looking over midterm grades. He says, "I'm so frustrated. We worked on these standards for weeks, and only 62% of students mastered them."

A supportive response:

Key nonverbal move:

Scenario 2

A teacher says, "My principal only gives me critical feedback. Yesterday morning, she poked her head in my room, and in front of my students, she said, 'Don't be late with today's attendance.' And that was it! I feel like I can't do anything right in her eyes."

A supportive response:

Key nonverbal move:

Scenario 3

A teacher tells you that he's interested in becoming the department chair next year but that he's not sure he has enough experience. "Also, it seems like Mr. Green is a likely candidate since he's already on many committees."

A supportive response:

Key nonverbal move:

Scenario 4

You walk in to meet with a teacher just as a parent is leaving the classroom. The parent slams the door on the way out, saying, "You'll be hearing from me again!" The teacher's eyes are welling with tears as she tells you that she's not sure what she did wrong.

A supportive response:

Key nonverbal move:

Summarize Your Learnings

What feels easy for you about using the supportive approach? Why?

What feels hard for you about using the supportive approach? Why?

Make Plans to Use the Supportive Approach

Identify an upcoming coaching conversation in which you might be able to use this approach—perhaps with a client you know is having a hard time or with a client with whom you usually don't engage in this way. Script a few words you could say or ask that would emerge from the supportive approach. Do this here or in your coaching notebook for that client.

Using the Cathartic Approach

Do this activity to gain a deeper understanding of how to use the cathartic approach and of the language that reflects it.

In *The Art of Coaching* (pp. 166–168), you can read about the cathartic approach. As a reminder, cathartic coaching helps a client to process and release emotions.

When using the cathartic approach, it's likely that we'll ask probing questions, questions that are wide open and expansive, and sometimes we'll offer what can sound like a supportive response, followed by a question. It's always important for a coach to pay attention to a client's nonverbal cues. But especially when we coach around emotions and use cathartic approaches, we want to hone in to how a client communicates through their body language. This will give us feedback about how our coaching is being received.

Tips and Reminders

- Active and reflective listening is also really helpful when taking the cathartic approach.
- If a discussion of emotions might feel new or out of the ordinary for your client, it can be helpful to ask for permission to discuss feelings.
- It can be helpful to name your observations of a client's nonverbal communication as a way to help them bring their own awareness to their emotions.

Practice

What follows are some scenarios that we hope will resonate for you. For each one, craft a response that reflects the cathartic approach. Use your imagination and add details if you want. Start with an example to guide you.

Example Scenario

A teacher is disappointed in how the unit launch went. He's slumped over on his desk, resting his cheek in his hand as he says the following: "The kids just seemed bored the whole time. Carlos threw out the popsicle stick model he'd created at the end of class. I thought they'd love that. I worked so hard on this lesson and now I just feel like I should scrap the plans for the rest of the unit and just stick to the boring lessons in the curriculum guide."

> A cathartic response: I'm sorry to hear this and your body language is suggesting that you're feeling really down. I think it would be helpful if we unpack some of the emotions you're experiencing. How does that sound if we start there?

Your Turn

Scenario 1

It's September and a teacher reviews the standardized test results from last year. "This is heartbreaking," they say. "On all of the assessments I did throughout the year it seemed like they were mastering the standards, and I am devastated by these results. I don't want the kids to see these, and I don't want my name published in the paper as someone who is failing our kids. Plus, I don't even know how our superintendent will respond. What am I supposed to do?"

A cathartic response:

Scenario 2

The new teacher you're coaching seems unusually quiet and withdrawn today. She responds to your questions with one or two words. And then she starts crying and she tells you that her favorite student cursed at her today. "I know I should have a tougher skin and not take an 11-year-old's words so harshly," she says.

A cathartic response:

Scenario 3

The teacher you're supposed to coach keeps avoiding you and won't return your e-mails or texts. You run into him in the hallway, and he says, "I feel like you're just going to be another person who tells me everything I'm doing wrong. I have so much work to do, and I don't have time for one more meeting. It's nothing personal; I just don't want coaching."

A cathartic response:

Scenario 4

The teacher you are coaching hasn't followed through on any of the things she said she was going to do last time you met. When you ask why those things didn't happen, the teacher says, "I feel like you're not coaching me. Like you just give me lists of things to do. That's not what I thought coaching would be. And I'm not sure I agree with the things you're telling me to do anyway."

A cathartic response:

Summarize Your Learnings

What feels easy for you about using the cathartic approach? Why?

What feels hard for you about using the cathartic approach? Why?

Make Plans to Use the Cathartic Approach

Identify an upcoming coaching conversation in which you might be able to use this approach. Script a few things you could say or ask that would emerge from the cathartic approach. Do this here or in your coaching notebook for that client.

Using the Catalytic Approach

Do this activity to gain a deeper understanding of how to use the catalytic approach and of the language that reflects it.

In *The Art of Coaching* (pp. 169–171), you can read about the catalytic approach. As a reminder, catalytic coaching helps to guide a client to:

- reflect on feelings;
- prompt self-discovery and problem-solving; and
- take responsibility for past and future actions.

As the name suggests, when we take the catalytic approach we're trying to speed up the rate of change. We do this through asking questions that have a spark to them. Sometimes our questions can feel like they are *confrontational* (see the confrontational approach in Chapter 11), but when we ask questions from the catalytic approach our intention must be to *facilitate* someone else's thinking rather than direct it.

Tips and Reminders

- When using the catalytic approach, it's likely that we'll ask a lot of probing questions.
- Sometimes we might throw in a clarifying question or two—if the intention is to help the client, themselves, get clear on what is happening.
- Your tone of voice and body language might be a little more assertive or bold when using the catalytic approach, but always communicate care and kindness.

Practice

Following are some scenarios that we hope will resonate with you. For each one, craft a response that reflects the catalytic approach. Use your imagination and add details if you want. Use the following example to guide you.

Your Turn

Scenario 1

A new teacher is anxious about Back-to-School night. "I'm just afraid that parents will think I look too young to be teaching high school."

A catalytic response:

Scenario 2

The semester is ending, and a teacher is frustrated that he hasn't been on top of grading. "I am going to be spending all weekend reading journal assignments and essays that they turned in a month ago. I've been teaching for 5 years, and I don't know why I keep letting this happen!"

A catalytic response:

Scenario 3

It's the end of the year and a new teacher is feeling proud of having finished strong. "Everyone says the first year is so hard, and there were rough moments, but it was also great!" he says. "I'm so excited for next year!"

A catalytic response:

Scenario 4

A teacher who has taught fifth grade for many years is moved into a second-grade position because of declining enrollment. She's understanding of the reason but nervous about teaching a grade she's never taught. "People think I'm a good teacher," she says, "but what if now they see that I'm not! I mean, teaching second grade is a whole different thing!"

A catalytic response:

Summarize Your Learnings

What feels easy for you about using the catalytic approach? Why?

What feels hard for you about using the catalytic approach? Why?

Make Plans to Use the Catalytic Approach

Identify an upcoming coaching conversation in which you might be able to use this approach. Script a few things you could say or ask that would emerge from the catalytic approach. Do this here or in your coaching notebook for that client.

Practicing Facilitative Coaching Approaches

Do this activity to bring together your learning about the facilitative coaching stance and to hone your understanding of when to use one approach or another.

After you have a good sense of how to use the cathartic, catalytic, and supportive approaches, then you need to consider when to use one approach or the other or how to sequence your responses. Although there are some general suggestions for when to use one approach or another, it takes practice with these approaches for you to see the impact they can have, and to hone your decision-making skills. Let's practice first, and then you'll be ready to consider our suggestions.

Instructions

For each of the scenarios that follow, craft one response from each of the three approaches that we've explored in this chapter. Then imagine how your client might receive your question or statement. To activate your imagination, try putting yourself in your client's shoes. Finally, after you've reflected on the impact that each approach might have, determine which approach you'd use or start with. Read the following example to better understand this activity.

Example Scenario

The new teacher you are coaching is preparing for her end-of-year evaluation with her principal. She's really nervous, as she's had very little feedback from her principal, and she finds him to be reserved and formal. She's also worried about a parent complaint that she got in the middle of the year. But she's feeling positive about the growth that her students made and about the learning community that she's built in her classroom. "I just don't know what he is going to focus on or what he wants to see. I feel like I'm going to be walking in blind and I really want to teach here next year."

A supportive response: What you're feeling right now is normal. The end-of-year evaluation is nerve-wracking for many teachers.

How this response might be received: The teacher could feel validated. It's always nice to hear that you are normal!

A cathartic response: I'm hearing a lot of emotions in what you're sharing. How about if we start by unpacking those a bit?

How this response might be received: I think this new teacher might appreciate an opportunity to recognize and name all of these emotions.

A catalytic response: So how do you want your principal to experience you in this meeting? What do you want him to say about you afterward when he's debriefing with the assistant principal?

How this response might be received: The teacher could feel energized and empowered. I think I would have appreciated this question.

Where to start: I think because this is a new teacher, I'd start with the cathartic response. I think if the teacher was able to name her own emotions, she'd feel more grounded. Depending on what she says in response, I might use the supportive approach if she seems like she's not accepting of her emotions. And I'd probably want to use the catalytic approach at some point in the conversation because that would help her feel more in control in this conversation.

Scenario 1

You've been coaching a teacher to implement the new instructional methods that your district has adopted. You've just observed him trying to use these new strategies. He delivered only half of the lesson plan, and that half didn't go very well. When you sit down to talk with him, he says, "I was opposed to adopting these methods. I don't think they're what our kids need. You saw what happened—I couldn't get through the lesson! We need to stick with the basics. Or just stick with something. Every year our district adopts the latest fad and we never make any growth."

A supportive response:

How this response might be received:

A cathartic response:

How this response might be received:

A catalytic response:

How this response might be received:

Which one to pick:

Scenario 2

It's early November, and the new teacher you coach walks into your office with tears in her eyes. "I just can't do this," she says. "I never feel like I've done enough, I work all weekend, I have no social life, and I can't sleep because I'm worried about everything I have to do. I lost my room keys today, and when I had to ask the custodian to let me in he gave me a lecture about security and keeping track of my stuff. And then the office assistant called me and berated me for turning in my attendance late. And then just when I thought I could get through the day, Cristy peed in her pants—again—and the worst part was how all the other kids reacted. I have worked so hard to create a safe and kind classroom and they were so mean to her. I really don't think I will make it through this year."

A supportive response:

How this response might be received:

A cathartic response:

How this response might be received:

A catalytic response:

How this response might be received:

Which one to pick:

Scenario 3

You've been coaching a teacher who is in the middle of his sixth year in the classroom. Students and parents love him, and he's respected by his colleagues. He tells you that he's interested in being a mentor next year but that he's not sure if he'd be good at it. "Maybe I'm still too young to be a mentor," he says. "Or maybe I'm not mentor material. I am not the most organized person, and I don't think I have great stories of wisdom or advice to give. My kids don't get the highest scores on tests and stuff. People say I'm a good listener, but maybe a mentor has to be someone who's super successful in everything."

A supportive response:

How this response might be received:

A cathartic response:

How this response might be received:

A catalytic response:

How this response might be received:

Which one to pick:

Scenario 4

You've been analyzing office referral data with a teacher you coach because the principal has given her feedback saying that she sends too many kids to the office. The teacher points out that the majority of her referrals are because a child failed to follow directions or was disrespectful. "We have to hold high standards for behavior," she says. When you ask her to give you examples of disrespect, she gets upset. "I feel like I constantly get mixed messages. Our principal comes into my class and tells me that too many kids are talking out of turn and that I'm lowering expectations for students and not holding them accountable. And then I'm told that I'm sending too many kids to the office. No one tells me how to get Alex to stop talking or how to get Joaquin to stay in his seat for 10 minutes. I'd like to see what someone else can do with these kids."

A supportive response:

How this response might be received:

A cathartic response:

How this response might be received:

A catalytic response:

How this response might be received:

Which one to pick:

When to Use One Approach or Another

Do this activity to refine your understanding of which coaching approach to use in different situations.

When coaches first learn about these different approaches, they can feel excited by the options, but they can also feel overwhelmed. We've been there: A client says something, and our minds spin as we wonder, *Should I offer a supportive response? Or would it be better for me to ask a cathartic question? Or should I first ask a clarifying question or two? What's the right thing?*

Here are three questions to consider asking yourself to decide what kind of response to offer in a conversation.

1. **How is your client feeling?** First, consider your client's level of emotional distress. If it's high, you probably need to begin with a supportive response. When someone is in the grips of an intense emotion, they don't have the cognitive wherewithal to process probing questions. You need to first help them come back into a place where they can access their thinking abilities, and often a supportive approach paves the way.

2. **Might it be helpful for them to recognize and name the emotions they're experiencing?** The answer to this question is just about always yes. We rarely get to process emotions at work, and it's usually empowering and helpful. You'll find that some clients will be more receptive to cathartic questions than others. This feedback will help you adjust for that specific person and will help you figure out how often to take a cathartic approach. For clients who don't seem receptive to your cathartic questions, that doesn't mean that you shouldn't ever ask them—it just means you are more selective about when you take the cathartic approach. The cathartic approach helps someone process their fears, frustrations, embarrassment, guilt, apathy, and other unpleasant emotions—as well as feelings of joy, satisfaction, fulfillment, and anticipation.

3. **Do they have the emotional and cognitive capacity to make a decision?** The catalytic approach is powerful—it's probably the approach that Elena uses most often—so we encourage you to get skilled at using it. Catalytic questions invite a client to take responsibility for their actions, to make a decision, or to take ownership over who they are being. To truly benefit from catalytic questions, clients need to first feel fairly clearheaded.

As you might be figuring out, sometimes the question to ask is not *which facilitative approach* to take but rather how to sequence our responses to our client. It's likely that if you follow the sequence of supportive, cathartic, and catalytic, your coaching will have an impact. Although your thinking will evolve on this as you grow as a coach, know that there is no right thing to say. What's critical is that you pay attention to the impact of your words on your client. How does your client respond? Does your response help them reconnect with their own capacity and agency? Remember that the goal of any coaching conversation is greater agency and increased capacity—that clients feel more empowered and able to do something that they weren't able to do before you met. There can be many paths to empowerment and capacity, but as long as you're seeing and hearing evidence that your coaching is leading in those directions you're going down a worthwhile path.

Now it's your turn to apply these ideas. Recall a coaching conversation that didn't go as well as you wish it had.

Can you remember what your client said just before things began to feel like they weren't going well? Write down what your client said:

What was your response? Write that down here:

Now consider the facilitative coaching approaches you've learned about in this chapter. Imagine that you can travel back in time and imagine what you would have said. Perhaps you would have used various sentence stems from the cathartic approach, or perhaps you would have sequenced the facilitative responses you used differently. Write down what you could have said, and, again, imagine how your client might have received those questions or statements.

Attending to Your Own Emotions

Do this activity to take care of yourself if—or when—you get overwhelmed.

Coaches can get easily overwhelmed by the weight of coaching others. Many of us are empathetic, and with all that's on our plates feeling stressed and overwhelmed is not a rare experience.

When we ask educators how they're feeling, the most common phrases we hear are, "I'm so tired," "I'm overwhelmed," and "I'm so stressed." What's really interesting is that *tired*, *overwhelmed*, and *stressed* aren't emotions per se. They signify an *emotional state*, meaning they emerge out of emotions. (*Fine, moody*, and *numb* are also emotional states.) As you read in Chapter 7, emotions can be grouped into eight categories: fear, anger, sadness, shame, jealousy, disgust, happiness, and love. The state of being overwhelmed usually crosses unpleasant core emotional families, so a first step when we feel overwhelmed is to identify which emotions are a part of the overwhelm.

When emotional overwhelm stems from an obvious single factor, the underlying emotion can be fairly straightforward to identify as, for example, grief or fear. Yet it is also possible to surface the emotions when the source of the overwhelm appears to be "out there." If your overwhelm sounds like, "I just have so much to do and think about and not enough time," it can be helpful to explore what emotions might be lurking under the surface.

Often when we pause and interrogate our own emotions, we are surprised—and relieved—by the answers we find. What am I *afraid* will happen if some of these things don't get done? What *shame* am I avoiding by being rigid in my priorities right now? Who or what do I get to stay *angry* at by claiming I don't have enough time? Ouch! It can sting a little to acknowledge that we are ultimately responsible for our feeling of overwhelm, but after the initial shock it is also tremendously empowering.

Flag this page and come back to it when overwhelm creeps in.

1. *Describe it.* Look at a list of core emotions (see Chapter 7) and identify those that are part of your overwhelm. You can also explore these emotions metaphorically. If your overwhelm was a color, what would it be? What shades? What textures?

2. *Sense into it.* Can you locate the overwhelm in your body? What are the physical sensations associated with it? Are there places of contraction or numbness? Is it warm or cool? Still or active? Close your eyes and sense your overwhelm. Write down what you notice.

3. *Intensify and release.* One way to bring movement back into physical sensations is to practice briefly intensifying them and then releasing. Maybe you notice a tensing in the shoulders. Squeeze them a little tighter for a few seconds and then release. Experiment with doing this around a few sensations that you noted before and record your observations.

4. *Recall previous experiences.* Remember a time when your overwhelm was just as intense. What helped you ease back into calm and presence? Maybe your overwhelm lessened naturally with time. That's okay. It's helpful to remember that all emotions have a natural life cycle. What in the past has helped?

5. *Identify one tiny next step.* By this point, you may already be noticing the overwhelm softening and a greater sense of empowerment. What actions feel possible from this state? What is one small, doable step you can take to reconnect with your own agency in this situation?

Of course, you can also use these strategies with your clients when they feel overwhelmed. But it's important to check in with yourself now and then on how you're feeling.

Wrapping Up the Facilitative Stance

Do this activity to help you remember the facilitative approaches and identify what was most important for you in this chapter.

When we observe coaches, one of the biggest problems we see is that coaches can get stuck on asking one kind of question. We'll talk more about this in Chapter 14, but we'll notice that all of their questions are of one variety (general probing, or supportive, or instructive). The most effective coaches intentionally draw on a wide set of approaches. And when we debrief with them after, they are explicit about which approaches they used and why. We know you want to be an effective coach, so one of the first steps is to remember what's in your coaching toolbox. So how will you remember what's in this chapter? How will you remember what constitutes a catalytic question? How will you remember why to use a cathartic approach?

We know that if we can create simple visual images for new concepts, our brain is more likely to remember them. So now, in the boxes on the next page, create a simple visual that represents each facilitative approach. And yes, we've added a new metaphor—the umbrella! You can think about facilitative coaching as the umbrella below which the supportive, cathartic, and catalytic approaches are found. This might be a good page to photograph or copy and then include in your coaching notebook to help you remember these options.

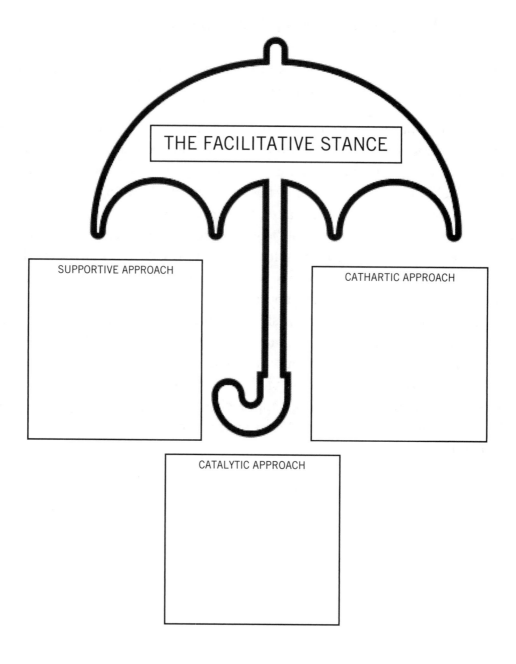

THE FACILITATIVE STANCE

SUPPORTIVE APPROACH

CATHARTIC APPROACH

CATALYTIC APPROACH

From *The Art of Coaching Workbook: Tools to Make Every Conversation Count* by Elena Aguilar. Copyright © 2021 by Elena Aguilar. Reproduced by permission.

CHAPTER 10

Exploring Facilitative Coaching Activities

Sometimes when we're coaching, we can incorporate an activity to guide a client into deeper reflection on their behaviors, beliefs, and ways of being. Many of these activities are a sequence of facilitative questions—so you might be wondering where the action is! We consider them to be *activities* because they are composed of a series of reflective prompts that need to be used in the sequence in which they're organized here and that can be used with anyone. In this chapter you'll find some of our favorite coaching activities and prompts—the ones that best exemplify Transformational Coaching and that can have the most profound impact.

Coaching Around Core Values

Do this activity to learn how to use the core values in coaching.

In Chapter 1, we asked you to identify and reflect on your core values. Similarly, we always ask new clients to do this activity, usually during the first meeting, as it helps us understand a tremendous amount about who someone is and how they aspire to be in the world.

After engaging a client in the same process that you went through in Chapter 1, we follow up with a bunch of questions. To be clear, we usually don't ask all of these in the same conversation. We'll pick and choose depending on what the client responds to. The follow up questions can include:

- What did it feel like to go through the elimination process?
- Where do you think your core values came from? Which experiences or people in your life contributed to this value being so important for you?
- Do you think your core values were different 5–10 years ago? Why or why not?
- What's something you've done recently that has reflected one of your core values?
- Can you recall a time when you did something that conflicted with one of your core values? What happened? What might have played a role in making it hard for you to uphold a core value?
- Which of your values feels easiest for you to uphold on a daily basis at work?
- Given that our values are often aspirational, which of your core values feels hardest to regularly embody?

Knowing your client's core values and understanding something about the significance of those values can be like seeing their guiding stars. Our core values are like our guiding stars, fixed in the sky even when we can't see them. When you know your client's core values and you understand the significance of those values, you can orient your coaching to navigate by those values. Your client has determined where they want to go and who they want to be. Transformational Coaching is a journey you take your client on to help your client live their life and accomplish work in alignment with their values.

Elena always writes her client's core values on the first page of her coaching notebook. In Figure 10.1 you'll see what that looks like. You'll also see that on that first page of her notebook she jots down the client's Myers-Briggs type (see Chapter 1) because she finds that invaluable in coaching.

Figure 10.1: Elena's Coaching Notebook

When Elena prepares to meet with a client, she glances at this first page to remind herself of who they want to be, and she keeps the client's values at the forefront of her mind when she's in conversation. When a client expresses confusion or uncertainty about a decision they need to make, Elena often references one of their core values, asking a question like, "If you were going to make this decision based on a commitment to your core value of _____, what would you do?"

Often, reminding our clients of their core values is like clearing the clouds in their thinking, revealing the values to navigate by. Often this is all it takes to help clients know what to do. When a client is distressed about something, you might hear in their narrative that one of their core values was violated—either by someone else or by something they did. In those moments, you can say something like, "I know that kindness is one of your core values. It sounds like your [or their] actions may not have been demonstrating that value. Do you think that's contributing to your distress?"

You can also reference a client's core values to help them recognize their growth and success. Whether a lesson goes well or flops, you can ask a teacher to reflect on how they stayed true to their values. That can help a teacher reframe what might have felt like a challenge (*"We never finish the lesson!"*) through a strengths-based, core values-aligned perspective. If a teacher values process, community, and depth over breadth, she might overplan lessons and never finish them.

Finally, at the end of a school year, you can ask clients to reflect on their growth through the perspective of alignment to values. This can sound like:

- Can you share three instances this year when you intentionally acted on a core value?
- When did you make a decision that was based in one of your core values?
- Which value felt easiest to demonstrate this year and why?

When we act from our core values we feel good because we are acting with integrity. When we act with integrity, we feel authentic. And this authenticity is so important: We ache to be our true selves—and to have those true selves be accepted. Coaching around and toward core values is a powerful way to cultivate resilience and to help a client feel anchored in their truest self.

Practice

Practice using core values in three different scenarios.

Support a Client in Hard Times

Your client (a teacher) has three core values: family, responsibility, high expectations.

Scenario: The teacher is distressed because a student's mother met with the principal and complained that the teacher is too strict.

Which of the teacher's core values might be most relevant to the situation?

How does considering the teacher's values help you understand their distress?

What might you say to help the client make the connection between her distress and her core values?

Support a Client to See Strengths

Your client (a teacher) has three core values: justice, collaboration, joy.

Scenario: The teacher has been working on increasing student engagement and building strong relationships with students whose backgrounds are different from his. It's the end of the first semester and the teacher is reflecting on his growth in these areas. He's disappointed by benchmark assessment results and is questioning whether he's been focused on the wrong things.

What could you ask him that would help him connect his core values to his reflection on the first semester?

How might he reflect on his growth through the lens of his core values?

How could you help him reflect on the benchmark assessments through the lens of his values?

Consider a Client You Are Currently Working With

Your client's three core values (if you haven't had a values discussion with them, you can try to identify their values):

From *The Art of Coaching Workbook: Tools to Make Every Conversation Count* by Elena Aguilar. Copyright © 2021 by Elena Aguilar. Reproduced by permission.

How could engaging with the client about values move your work forward with them?

What might you say in your next meeting to engage with the client about their values and move your work forward with them?

The Legacy Question

Do this activity to guide a client to name their own vision and goals for themselves.

Many educators feel disempowered. They feel like people in offices far away make decisions about what they can say and do with their students without seeking input from those who know best what it takes to teach children. They feel like factors outside of their immediate control, including poverty and structural racism and other forms of injustice, play a determining role in outcomes for their students. New teachers can feel overwhelmed by the demands of the profession. Veteran teachers can feel disconnected from what brought them into the profession. It's hard to stay anchored to a vision in the transactional environment that characterizes most schools. It's no wonder that turnover and burnout is as high as it is.

The legacy question is in Elena's basic coaching toolkit. She leads clients through this reflective process when they're distressed as a way to create a catalytic experience. But she also asks her clients these questions when they're thriving—as a way to propel them onward in their learning. The legacy question is considered a facilitative activity because it guides a client toward their own insights, vision, and definition of success.

Your Turn

The best way to understand the impact of this activity is for you to do a part of it. Call to mind a student you teach, a teacher you coach, a colleague, or someone on your staff. This person should be struggling in some way, and they should be someone you care about but with whom you're not feeling very effective (as a teacher, coach, friend, or supervisor).

Write down their name or initials:

What do you appreciate about this person? What are their strengths? And what are they struggling with?

Now, imagine it's 10 years in the future and you haven't heard from this person in a decade. They get in touch and send you a message sharing their memories of you. What do you hope they will say? Write down the message exactly as you'd receive it, in their voice.

For you to fulfill your hopes for how they'll remember you, what are the implications for what you do or say to this person now? If you're thinking about a student, what does your hope for how they'll remember you imply in terms of how you teach this student? If you're thinking about a coaching client, what does your hope imply for what you'll say in your next meeting with them?

How did it feel to engage in this reflection?

Of course, this exercise works best when you coach someone through it in person. On the page, in a book, there are some limitations because we can't ask you follow-up questions or nudge you along in places that could be helpful. However, we expect you've done enough to understand the impact this process can have. Now read through the cloze script for a detailed description of how you could engage a teacher in this activity.

A Cloze Script for the Legacy Question

COACH: I want to ask you to call to mind a student who is struggling, a student in whom you see some potential, and that you care about. [Pause] Can you tell me about that student? What's their name? What do you appreciate about them? What are they struggling with?

Allow the client to describe the student. If necessary, ask clarifying and probing questions to elicit the student's strengths and positive attributes. Be sure that the client's empathy for the student is activated.

COACH: Okay, _____ [client's name], I want you to imagine something. I want you to imagine that it's _____ years [as many years until the student graduates from high school] from now, and you get an e-mail from _____ [student's name]. [Pause] And _____ [student] says,

"I don't know if you'll remember me, _____ [teacher's name], but you were my _____ [grade or subject] teacher. And I'm graduating from high school next month, and I wanted to invite you. I know you're probably super busy and maybe you have bad memories of me, but I'd be honored if you were there."

[Pause]

And you're not sure if you can go, but at the last minute you decide to go, and when you get there you end up sitting right behind _____ [his/her/their] family. When _____ [student's name] crosses the stage, looking so mature in that cap and gown, and when _____ [he/she/they] looks at _____ [his/her/their] family, they're cheering and screaming _____ [student's] name, _____ [student's name] also sees you. And a huge smile spreads across _____ [his/her/their] face. [PAUSE FOR 5–10 SECONDS]

Now, when _____ [student] goes back to _____ [his/her/their] seat, and after the ceremony is over, what do you want _____ [him/her/them] to say to their friends about you? About how _____ [he/she/they] remembers you as their _____ [grade or subject] teacher? [Pause for 2 seconds] *How do you want to be remembered?*

We anticipate that reading the cloze script gives you an idea of the impact this could have on a teacher. You can download this cloze script from our website, http://www .brightmorningteam.com, and tuck it into your coaching notebook so that you have the prompts handy.

For Further Learning

→ Read Chapter 10 of *Coaching for Equity* for an example of how Elena uses this in a conversation.

Questions to Elicit Symbolic Thinking

Do this activity to learn another way to help a client think about who they want to be in the classroom.

Sometimes when Elena thinks of her work as a coach, she sees herself as an owl or an eagle, high above a landscape, with a wide perspective and vast ability to see. It hasn't always been this way, and she hasn't always been able to use this metaphor. But using this metaphor now is a powerful reminder about how she wants to be.

Using symbolic thinking and metaphor helps us access our subconscious and our deeper commitments. In this facilitative exercise, you invite your client to identify a symbol for or representation of who they are being as an educator—that symbol could be an animal, bird or mythical creature, a weather pattern (the doldrums? A tornado?) or form of water (a pond or waterfall?), a fruit or plant, another object found in nature, or shape or texture.

Some people are strong symbolic thinkers, and these questions will be generative and offer insight. Other people are more concrete thinkers, and these questions may not be helpful. As you get to know your client, listen to whether they draw on metaphor and symbolism when they talk or to explain their thinking. This will be a good cue for you to offer them prompts like those that follow.

The Questions

- What kind of [e.g., animal, weather pattern, symbol] are you being in the classroom?
- What's possible if you're that _____?
- How does this reflection help you think about yourself and your work?

Follow-Up Questions

If the symbolism isn't empowering or doesn't have potential to have a positive impact on others, then ask:

- What kind _____ do you want to be in the classroom?
- What would you have to do to be that _____?
- How does this reflection help you think about yourself and your work?

After you ask the first question, then you want to guide your client in exploring the impact of being the way they've identified. Is that who or what they want to be? If not, what do they want to be? And what needs to happen so that they can be that animal, weather pattern, bird, or plant that they want to be?

Your Turn

What kind of animal, weather pattern, or symbol are you being as a coach?

What's possible if you're that _____?

Optional:

What kind of _____ do you want to be as a coach?

What would you have to do to be that _____?

How does this reflection help you think about yourself and your work?

Elena Reflects

If I'd been asked these questions in my first (very difficult) year coaching, and if I was being honest, I would have answered in the following way:

What kind of animal, weather pattern, or symbol are you being as a coach?

I think that as a coach I'm being a hyena. I'm circling around the teachers I perceive as being weak, waiting for them to fall so that I can eat their bones. I feel angry at them.

From *The Art of Coaching Workbook: Tools to Make Every Conversation Count* by Elena Aguilar. Copyright © 2021 by Elena Aguilar. Reproduced by permission.

What's possible if you're that way?

No one wants to work with a hyena. Teachers aren't going to be open and vulnerable with me if they perceive me as wanting to eat them.

What kind of animal do you want to be as a coach?

I'd like to be an owl, or an eagle. A bird that sees everything going on from above. I don't want to be a predator, just to be clear, but I think of those birds as having a broad perspective and being wise and intentional about how they use their energy. Or maybe I'd want to be like a wolf in Yellowstone—an animal that has a positive influence on the whole ecosystem. Not one that destroys.

What would you have to do to be an owl, an eagle, or a wolf in Yellowstone?

I clearly need to explore the anger I'm feeling at teachers. I need to figure out why I don't feel like I can partner with them. Why I feel adversarial toward them. I think I need to better understand the role that others expect me to play, and I need to decide whether I want to play that role, or want to find another ecosystem to work in.

How does this reflection help you think about yourself and your work?

I didn't realize I felt this angry or that I thought about teachers as being prey. I think that's because I feel so on edge at this school. I feel like I have to be on the defensive or I'll be eaten. This helps me recognize that there's a lot of toxicity here. And at the same time, I want to shift my way of being. This isn't who I want to be. I feel embarrassed that I'm being this way. I don't feel like I'm showing up in a way that's aligned to my values. This is painful to recognize, but also helps me understand why I've felt so much conflict.

Using Visualization and Guided Imagery

This activity will illustrate visualization techniques and prepare you to use them with clients.

Transformation is a journey *toward*, not a journey *away*. A clear and compelling vision of the future we want to create is necessary to transform the ways of being, thinking, and doing that have led to our present circumstances. Visualization and guided imagery help clients crystallize a vision that will pull them into the fullest expression of their potential.

Here's what this might look like.

Mental Rehearsal Visualization

A teacher says, "This year, I'm really trying to increase student engagement." The coach invites the teacher to imagine herself in a lesson where students are highly engaged. What are students doing? How are they seated? What are they working on? What is the teacher doing during the lesson? How does she feel?

Ideal State Visualization

A new principal wants to strengthen her rapport with staff. The coach guides her through a visualization of a positive interaction with a staff member, in which the principal embodies every quality she aspires to have. As they debrief the experience, the principal identifies several actions she can take to realize her vision.

Practice

For each of the following scenarios, identify a visualization exercise that could be helpful. What questions might you ask?

Scenario	Visualization exercise	Questions I could ask
Example: Teacher struggling with an annoying student	*The student 15 years later, talking to a friend about their experience with the teacher*	*What do you hope will be true for [student] in 15 years?* *What do you hope [student] will say about you?*
Teacher not sure whether they want to keep teaching		
Teacher whose perfectionism is making planning hard		
Department chair wanting to run more focused meetings		

Note: See also *The Art of Coaching* (p. 178).

Now pick one of these scenarios and script the visualization exercise you might take the person through. The purpose of doing this is to build confidence guiding a client in the moment, when you likely will not have a script. As you write, try to script language you might actually use.

Practice reading aloud what you wrote. How comfortable would you feel saying this? What would help you feel more comfortable using this technique?

Using the Body to Access and Shift Emotions

This activity will develop your practice of noticing and naming physical sensations to access and shift strong emotions.

Our emotional experience has its roots in our body. Try this quick experiment. Tighten your jaw. Tense your neck and raise your shoulders slightly. Tighten your abdominal muscles. Take a few quick, shallow breaths. How do you feel?

Most people who shape their body in this way will feel a corresponding shift in their emotional state, however subtle. Perhaps you felt more anxious, scared, or tense. Now try this: Lift your shoulders as high as possible, then allow them to fall. Do this again. Soften the belly area. Release your jaw. Take three long, slow, expansive breaths. Now how do you feel?

Many will feel a greater sense of calm, perhaps more focus. You may feel less reactive. This happens because our thoughts, emotions, and physical sensations are inextricably linked. The connection among those parts of ourselves offers two implications for our work:

- Tuning into one aspect of our present experience can give us insights into others. For example, noticing tension in our jaw can clue us in to tense thoughts or an underlying mood of anger.
- Adjustments made in one aspect can shift our experience in others. For example, focusing on softening the jaw muscles can similarly soften our thoughts and anger.

Laurelin Reflects

I was recently coaching a leader who is preparing to make a major shift in his life. It was the start of the conversation, and he was rapidly downloading several updates since our last conversation. As he spoke, I noticed my breath becoming shallow, my stomach tightening, and a slight tingling along my arms. Because I have a practice of cultivating body awareness, I noticed these sensations and recognized them as nervousness.

When my client paused, I said, "I'm noticing as you speak that I'm beginning to feel nervous. Instinctively, I'm wanting to back away right now. I'm curious whether that has any significance." My client stared at me, incredulous. "Wow," he said. "That is exactly how I'm feeling, and I hadn't even recognized it. I need to have a conversation with _____ about this change, and I've just been dreading it. I keep finding excuses not to do it. But if I'm honest, preparing for that conversation really would be the most helpful thing to talk about today." And we did.

By the end of our time, my client knew who he wanted to be in his upcoming conversation and was grounded in his values and priorities. As he summarized his takeaways, I reflected to him that I was feeling centered and relaxed in my body. "Me, too," he said. "It's like a weight has come off my shoulders that I wasn't even aware I was carrying. I'm actually excited now to share with _____ what I've been planning."

We often talk about coaching being an instinctual process. This doesn't mean, however, that our instinct materializes from thin air. Rather, instinct is the result of listening deeply to all that is available to us—our clients' words, their nonverbal cues, the emotional current of the conversation, and our own physical responses. The body is a crucial tool to leverage our full wisdom as coaches.

Body awareness can be tremendously helpful in supporting clients to access and shift the strong emotions that can help or hinder meaningful action. Unfortunately, many of us have been conditioned to keep our awareness in our heads, tuning out all but the most intense body sensations. In reality, however, the body is constantly sending signals that provide insights into our health, emotions, relationships, and physical environment.

To harness our bodily wisdom, we need to develop a vocabulary of physical sensation. Building your own bodily awareness and vocabulary of sensation is a prerequisite to supporting clients to do the same.

Try this practice:

1. Assume a comfortable seated position and take a few slow breaths. Many find it helpful to close the eyes when learning to tune into the body.
2. Allow your awareness to drop down into the chest area. Name any sensation there:

   - Is it warm or cool?
   - Relaxed or tense?
   - Alive or numb?
   - Still or in motion?
   - Heavy or light?

3. Allow your awareness to drop into the belly. Name sensations there. "My belly is warm and heavy."
4. Gradually scan outward, down the legs, into the feet. Naming sensations along the way. Repeat out the arms and into the hands.
5. Bring your awareness back to the breath. What is the background mood in your body right now?

From *The Art of Coaching Workbook: Tools to Make Every Conversation Count* by Elena Aguilar. Copyright © 2021 by Elena Aguilar. Reproduced by permission.

Once you have noticed and named physical sensations, you may want to explore shifting those sensations. Often the emotions we need to attend to are unpleasant ones. Here are two ways to experiment when you sense a strong difficult emotion and its corresponding physical sensations in the body:

Dial up the intensity of the physical sensation. If you notice tension in one part of your body, tighten just a little more. Hold for two to three breaths, and then release.

Take three deep breaths and imagine the breath going into the part of the body where you notice tension, inflating it like a large balloon.

Try one or both of these techniques, and then check back in with the emotion. How has it shifted? It is sometimes helpful to repeat these exercises for full effect.

We recommend doing practices like these several times a day. They don't take long. With time, you will notice increasingly subtle sensations in the body. Those sensations can be a valuable source of insight during coaching.

Because body awareness is new to many coaches, we encourage you to spend a good while exploring this for yourself before you engage clients in these activities. But when you feel ready and you suspect your client might be open—go ahead and try! Start simple and guide them to take deep breaths into a part of their body where they notice tension or invite them to share what they notice about how their body feels. Always follow your client's cues, and if they're into this, go further.

When Finding Strengths Is Challenging

Do this activity when you're not sure how to help your client see their own strengths and maybe you're also struggling to see their strengths.

In Chapter 7, we introduced the concept of strengths-based coaching. When we focus on strengths, our conversations can be supportive, cathartic, and catalytic. But to focus on strengths, we need to be able to see strengths. Sometimes seeing strengths is easy, but what if you are struggling to see any of your client's strengths? Or what if your client has trouble naming their own strengths?

Sometimes it's hard to see strengths—even when a client has many. Maybe your client values humility and is not forthcoming about their strengths. Maybe your client is experiencing a difficult moment and is focused on everything that's wrong in their lives. How can we draw out clients' strengths so that we and they can see them more clearly?

It's important to note that we find strengths by mirroring what we see back to the client so that they recognize their strengths. Coaches refrain from stepping into a place of judgment or evaluation as much as possible—and naming strengths is a form of judgment. We want to be careful about doing that, in part because we don't want our clients relying on us to point out their strengths. It's also far more impactful when you see your own strengths.

Here are three facilitative strategies you can use to help a client see their own strengths:

1. *Tell stories.* We are usually the heroes of our own stories. Inviting clients to share stories of triumph and connection allows them to showcase their strengths indirectly. For example:

   - When was the last time you felt really proud?
   - Tell me about someone who has helped you become the person you are today.

2. *Give credit.* When something goes well for your client, explore how *they* contributed to that outcome. For example:

   - How might things have turned out differently if you hadn't been involved?
   - I noticed the conversation in the group really shifted when you said _____.

3. *Find the positive.* We've all experienced that one piece of criticism that drowns out twenty compliments. Help your client tune in to the praise and affirmation they get from others. For example:

   - _____ [Name of student] really seemed to connect with today's lesson. Why do you think that is?
   - What do you think your colleagues appreciate most about working with you?

Read the following transcript to see how to put these three moves to use in working with a client. What strengths surface in the course of the conversation? Are they strengths of the head, hands, or heart? As you read, code what the coach says with a 1, 2, or 3, according to which of the facilitative strategies the coach uses.

CLIENT: Hi, come on in. I'm just finishing up.

COACH: Thanks. What's that you're working on?

CLIENT: Oh, this? [*laughs*] So my French 2 students have been learning expressions for the weather. As their end-of-unit project, they had to draw up a 5-day forecast and video record a weather report for the news. I'm just doing a little editing to put the France logo on them and make them look a bit more professional. I told them I'd put together a private YouTube channel so they could see each other's videos.

COACH: Wow! You know how to do all that? I had no idea our French teacher was also a video editor! What do your kids think about all this?

CLIENT: Oh, they think it's a hoot. A lot of them really ham it up during the videos, wear funny ties and all that.

COACH: [*smiling*] And what do they think of you going the extra mile to do this for them?

CLIENT: Well, this is the second year I've done this. In my end-of-year survey, several of my kids last year mentioned this as one of their favorite projects. Some of them still jokingly announce the weather to me when we cross in the hall. "Hey, Monsieur! *Il pleut aujourd'hui!*"

COACH: It sounds like you've really found a way to tap into this generation's love of multimedia to make their study of French stick.

CLIENT: Yeah, I just try to keep it interesting.

COACH: I hear that. So are we digging back into proficiency grading today?

CLIENT: Yeah, that sounds right. Like we talked about last time, this has been a gradual transition over the past 2 years. On the whole, it's been a really positive shift, both for me as a teacher and, I think, for the kids.

COACH: How so?

CLIENT: Well, I really see them getting into the assignments more. Thinking more expansively in terms of what kids know and can do rather than on whether they demonstrate something at the exact moment I'm looking for it, it's reconnected me with that creativity I had in my first few years as a teacher. I feel less beholden to the activities in the book, and I'm thinking more about, you know, how a French speaker would actually use this vocabulary or this grammar construct.

COACH: I can hear your willingness to stay flexible and creative in your approach. And what impact are you noticing on kids?

CLIENT: Well, I think they're thinking that way, too. Not like, "I have to learn this because Monsieur Andrade said I did," but "I want to learn this so I can actually talk to someone someday." A lot more kids this year took me up on the pen pal offer I made at the beginning of the year—even though they were just starting their study of French—and they've stuck with it more than in past years.

COACH: I'm sure their pen pals appreciate that!

CLIENT: Oh, for sure. I got an e-mail a month ago from the teacher in Fort-de-France, whose class we're paired up with. She said they've never worked with such a responsive class. In the past, things have usually tapered off after the initial excitement of the first month or two. The fact that my kids keep writing and that her students see how much they're improving, is motivating them to want to write more. Some kids are even talking about wanting to meet in person one day.

COACH: It sounds like your flexibility and creativity is really adding to how much students value what they're learning. And not just your kids, but students all the way in Martinique! This new emphasis on proficiency, rather than grades for grades' sake, is drawing out the best in them.

CLIENT: [*Smiles shyly*] I hadn't thought of it like that, but I suppose that's right.

COACH: So what's on your mind regarding your first years?

CLIENT: Right. So. . .

Think about a client or colleague you are having a hard time working with right now, someone whose gifts aren't immediately obvious to you. Write two questions or prompts you could use for each move to draw out that person's strengths. Practice saying these aloud and refine them until you feel comfortable saying them.

Tell Stories

1.

2.

Give Credit

1.

2.

Find the Positive

1.

2.

Did I Make a Mistake Becoming a Coach?

Do this activity when you're feeling uncertain about whether you want to be a coach.

We're including this activity in the chapter on facilitative coaching activities because it's one you can engage in yourself—or one you can modify and invite a client to do. We all have moments of self-doubt when we question our choices, be those to teach or become a coach. Since you became a coach, have you ever found yourself in one of these moments?

- A client asks you a question to which you have no good response, and you find yourself rambling just to fill the silence.
- In the middle of a coaching conversation, a client starts sobbing. You feel overwhelmed by this display of emotion.
- You're trying to be facilitative, but you feel the conversation is going nowhere and are bursting to tell the client what to do.
- You observe a teacher and find yourself thinking, *I miss teaching! I miss being with kids! And I could teach this lesson so much better. I'd probably have a great impact on students if I went back to the classroom.*

We've all been there. Though it can help to get external validation in these moments of doubt, no one knows you better than yourself. In rough spots, you have the potential to tell yourself exactly what you need to hear. So what do you need to hear?

In the following space, write a brief letter to your coach self that affirms your strengths and value. Flag this page so you can easily find it when you're feeling down. Use one of the following prompts if it's helpful, or start wherever you'd like. Experiment with different tones—playful, heartfelt, tough love. What do you most need to hear?

- I am so glad you are a coach! I particularly love how you _____.
- And you're constantly learning! Since you started coaching, I've seen you _____.
- Don't forget that amazing moment when you _____.
- You are a beacon of courage and compassion, like that time when you _____.
- You are contributing to the transformation of schools by _____.
- One concrete way that the experience of kids has improved through your work is _____.
- Remember why you got into this role. You coach so that _____. And I believe in you.

Dear _____,

With love and gratitude,

CHAPTER 11

Practicing Directive Coaching Conversations

As we explained early in this book, we can categorize our coaching moves as either facilitative or directive. There aren't hard and fast rules about what makes coaching facilitative or directive: Lots of the things we say and do fall into both categories at the same time. But thinking about intent and impact can help us group our coaching moves and make informed decisions about how we want to coach.

As a reminder, when you take a facilitative stance in coaching, you guide someone with a light touch to find their own insights, understandings, and behaviors. When you take a directive stance in coaching, you're applying a bit more pressure, a firmer nudge, toward new behaviors, beliefs, and ways of being. A Transformational Coach uses both facilitative and directive coaching strategies.

We're guessing that you're familiar with directive coaching as it's (unfortunately) far too common in schools and organizations. Directive coaching is often premised on an assumption that the coach is an expert who knows best and that the coach's role is to *get* someone to do something. This kind of coaching has a limited impact.

However, it's possible to be directive and have a transformative impact. A Transformational Coach may have expertise that can (and should) be shared, and this can be done in a way that honors who the client is and what they know. We group directive coaching into three approaches: prescriptive, informative, and confrontational. In this chapter, we'll provide a dip into these three approaches. But because they are probably familiar to you, we don't go into them in depth.

Using the Confrontational Approach

Do this activity to gain a deeper understanding of how to use the confrontational approach and of the language that reflects it.

Now that you've got a solid understanding of mental models, let's explore how directive coaching helps someone explore and process their beliefs. In *The Art of Coaching* (pp. 202–203), you can read about the confrontational approach. As a reminder, confrontational coaching helps to (1) raise awareness; (2) challenge the client's assumptions; (3) stimulate awareness of behavior, beliefs, and ways of being; (4) see the consequences of an action; and (5) boost the client's confidence by affirming success.

The word *confrontation* makes a lot of us uncomfortable because we associate this word with conflict. Perhaps it's easier to think of confrontation in this context as a way of interrupting thoughts. When you coach using a confrontational approach, you help your client deconstruct unhelpful mental models and shift their beliefs. A coach is poised to use this stance because they build a close relationship with their client; they don't supervise their client; and coaching conversations are confidential, which creates greater psychological safety for the client. Confrontational coaching can lead to new behaviors and ways of being that contribute to your client's transformation and ultimately that contribute to the success and well-being of students.

Tips and Reminders

- When using a confrontational approach, we ask clients to explore their assumptions and reasoning and to see situations from different perspectives.
- We can use the confrontational approach when we guide clients down the Ladder of Inference (see Chapter 3) and present data they don't notice.
- We ask questions that invite perspective taking such as, "Would you be willing to explore _____?"
- We are calm and confident, and we draw on our reserves of courage so we can interrupt beliefs and ways of being that don't serve students.

Practice

What follows are some scenarios that we hope will resonate with you. For each one, craft a response that reflects the confrontational approach. Use your imagination and add details if you want.

Your Turn

Scenario 1

A middle school teacher is designing a lesson for a racially and linguistically diverse classroom and she is thinking about how to support students to meet the school's goals. She says, "These kids can't do this level of work. They were 2 years behind when they got here. How are we supposed to make up for that?"

A confrontational response:

Scenario 2

A teacher leader is feeling burned out after the first semester of school because she is on a dysfunctional leadership team. She says, "No one appreciates or values me. I feel like everyone is out to get me all the time. I am going to resign from the leadership team next week."

A confrontational response:

Scenario 3

A veteran teacher who tends to be hard on himself designed an elaborate lesson that fully engaged his class, except for one student who claimed that the lesson was boring and a waste of time. This teacher says, "I put so much time into this lesson, but it turns out it was a waste of time."

A confrontational response:

Scenario 4

You and the principal observe an experienced teacher. His first comment after you walk out of the teacher's classroom is, "I don't know why that teacher bothers so much. Those students aren't going to college anyway."

A confrontational response:

Summarize Your Learnings

What feels easy for you about using the confrontational approach? Why?

What feels hard for you about using the confrontational approach? Why?

Make Plans to Use the Confrontational Approach

Identify an upcoming coaching conversation in which you might be able to use this approach—perhaps with a client you know is telling rut stories or thinking with problematic mental models or with a client with whom you usually don't engage in this way. Script a few words you could say or ask that would emerge from the confrontational approach. Do this here or in your coaching notebook for that client.

Using the Informative Approach

Do this activity to gain a deeper understanding of how to use the informative approach and of the language that reflects it.

In *The Art of Coaching* (pp. 203–204), you can read about the informative approach. As a reminder, informative coaching helps guide a client to:

- use resources and tools they may not have identified on their own; and
- have a thinking partner (their coach) as they determine their next actions.

When using the informative approach, it's likely that we'll ask concrete questions, present options for our client to consider, and offer resources, tools, and explanations to offer greater context. Most of our stems will be more declarative rather than rooted in questions (e.g. "There's a useful book on that topic by _____" or "An effective strategy to teach is _____").

Most coaches play this role at some point with their clients. But there are dangers with this approach—namely, that it's grossly overused—and the coach needs to be careful of when and how they use this approach. When using the informative approach, consider a gradual release into independence so that your client doesn't become overreliant on you as their source of expertise.

Tips and Reminders

- Offer a selection of resources and guide the client to make decisions. This can sound like, "Some teachers do this. . . and others do that. . . What do you think would work best for your students?"
- Use this approach in conjunction with facilitative approaches so your client stays at the center of their own learning.

Practice

What follows are some scenarios we hope will resonate for you. For each one, craft a response that reflects the informative approach. Use your imagination and add details if you want. Start with an example to guide you.

> **Example Scenario**
>
> A first-year leader is 1 month into her job as assistant principal at a school she's brand-new to. She is expected to lead the first staff meeting of the year. Very little is documented about how meetings are run at this school, and she is not sure if she needs to draw on previous meeting structures or can design her own. She says to her coach, "Could you just tell me how I should design this meeting?"
>
> An informative response: Can you think of any staff members who have been here for a while who might be able to tell you more about how meetings have been run in the past? Perhaps you can reach out to others to get their suggestions. What do you think of trying that?

Your Turn

Scenario 1

A teacher has been assigned to teach a class that a veteran teacher (who just retired) used to teach. She was handed a single sheet of paper with a one-paragraph overview of the course. She asks you, "What am I supposed to do with just this?"

An informative response:

Scenario 2

Your client's school is devoting its professional development to culturally responsive teaching, which is new to your client. Your client has been asked to implement culturally responsive strategies into his lesson and asks you, "Which strategies do you think I should use? Which are the best ones?"

An informative response:

Scenario 3

The district uses their own teacher evaluation rubric and your client is new to the district and to the teacher evaluation process. She says, "How do I find more information about what to expect?"

An informative response:

Scenario 4

A new school leader has just received feedback that he comes across as too wishy washy in his supervisory conversations. He shares, "I want to learn more about how to be an effective manager who communicates well."

An informative response:

Summarize Your Learnings

What feels easy for you about using the informative approach? Why?

What feels hard for you about using the informative approach? Why?

Make Plans to Use the Informative Approach

Identify an upcoming coaching conversation in which you might be able to use this approach. Script a few things you could say or ask that would emerge from the informative approach. Do this here or in your coaching notebook for that client.

Using the Prescriptive Approach

Do this activity to gain a deeper understanding of how to use the prescriptive approach and of the language that reflects it.

In *The Art of Coaching* (p. 205), you can read about the prescriptive approach. As a reminder, prescriptive coaching helps to guide a client to:

- act on guidance from the coach;
- understand the ethical and sometimes legal issues that need to be addressed with immediacy; and
- shift behaviors more quickly.

Transformational Coaches should rarely use the prescriptive approach and should do so with caution. It's appropriate to use when a coach sees or hears something that merits a direct response because of legal, safety, or ethical guidelines that need to be followed. The prescriptive stance also may involve advice giving, but only when the client is open to hearing it; you will need to ask permission from your client to give advice. When a client can't direct their own learning, you can also use this stance.

Tips and Reminders

- Use this approach when legal, ethical, or safety issues are at play.
- Use with caution.
- If your client responds to your advice with a lot of "yes, but" responses, they are not open to hearing what you have to offer.

Practice

What follows are some scenarios we hope will resonate with you. For each one, craft a response that reflects the prescriptive approach. Use your imagination and add details if you want. Start with an example to guide you.

Your client is a Black woman in her early 20s who is a new elementary music specialist. She is introverted and often needs time to process information before speaking. After a recent staff meeting, your client shared that a White male teacher in his 60s asked her what she thought about the school's new approach to arts instruction. When your client failed to offer a response right away, the White male teacher said, "I always thought Black people were more boisterous and loud. You're so quiet." He then laughed and followed up with, "I'm only kidding. You know that, right?"

A prescriptive response: You need to report this to our principal. That's a microaggression that can lead to more offensive commentary unless this issue is addressed. Do you need any support setting up a time to meet with our principal?

Your Turn

Scenario 1

A teacher keeps confusing two of her Latina students, calling each by the wrong name. The teacher says in front of the class, "I'm just going to give you each a nickname."

A prescriptive response:

Scenario 2

Your client is on an improvement plan and keeps neglecting to share their lesson plans with their supervisor. They say to you, "I'm just so forgetful and busy, but I promise I'll submit my plans tomorrow." This pattern has occurred for 3 weeks.

A prescriptive response:

Scenario 3

A leader you coach often forgets about your weekly meeting time. This seems to reflect a broader pattern of struggling with time management and organization.

A prescriptive response:

Scenario 4

A new teacher you're working with comes to your meetings overwhelmed by everything they need to do. When you ask your client what they would most like to talk about, they start crying and say, "I just don't know."

A prescriptive response:

Summarize Your Learnings

What feels easy for you about using the prescriptive approach? Why?

What feels hard for you about using the prescriptive approach? Why?

Make Plans to Use the Prescriptive Approach

Although we find that most coaches overuse the prescriptive approach, we've also observed instances when a coach could have used the prescriptive approach but felt that they weren't *supposed to*. Can you think of a time or two when a prescriptive approach might have been the right thing to try? Jot down your reflections about when you might want to use this approach in general or with a specific client.

Identifying Limited Mental Models

A skilled Transformational Coach is always listening to how someone thinks. How they think is what they believe. What they believe becomes what they do. We live inside the thoughts we develop, the beliefs we hold, the stories we spin. Our stories can be empowering and affirming, or they can be limiting and destructive. We have choice about the stories we tell and the beliefs we hold.

The beliefs we hold can feel comforting to us—they're familiar and we know how to operate within them. When our beliefs are challenged, we can get defensive. A Transformational Coach's role is to help someone recognize the stories they are living in, see the impact that living in those stories has for the client and the people in their lives (including their students), and then decide if they want to continue holding those beliefs. Often, to do this we need to take a confrontational stance. But before we get to how we interrupt mental models, we need to learn to hear them. We need to hone our ability to recognize when a client is thinking and behaving inside of a limited mental model.

In *The Art of Coaching*, these mental models are called *river and rut stories*. In the language of psychology, rut stories are called *cognitive distortions* (read more about these in *Onward: Cultivating Emotional Resilience in Educators*). Whether we call them *rut stories, limited mental models, problematic beliefs,* or *cognitive distortions,* a Transformational Coach needs to recognize when a client is expressing them.

Elena has found that in schools and organizations the five most commonly expressed limited mental models are those in Table 11.1. As you read these, consider whether you hear these expressed in your school or organization or whether you express them. You might put a star by those that you hear most often in your workplace and that you express.

Reflect

Which of these mental models have you expressed at some time in your career? What have you said, or thought, that reflects this mental model?

What were you feeling when you were holding that mental model? Which emotions were present for you?

Table 11.1: The Most Common Limited Mental Models

Mental model	Description	Sounds like. . .
Black-and-white thinking	Things are either right or wrong, good or bad, all or nothing. With either-or thinking, there is no gray area or middle ground.	"You can't rely on admin for anything. Every time I make a request, it's turned down."
Overgeneralizing	Conclusions are made based on one fact, event, or situation.	"My principal never tells me anything I'm doing right!"
Personalizing	People blame themselves or others for things that they had no control over; they express a victim consciousness. Their emotional distress has to do with *who they are* and who other people are.	"This must be my fault somehow."
Unrealistic expectations	Feeling adamant about how things should be and what people should do. When things don't go as expected, people blame themselves and others.	"I should. . ." "He should. . ." "They should. . ."
Jumping to conclusions	Making negative assumptions without evidence or with only a little bit of information.	"She didn't make eye contact with me when we passed each other in the hall. I must be in trouble."

Practice

Read the statements in the first column and decide which of the most common limited mental models you hear. Note your assessment in the second column, and in the third column provide your rationale: What makes you categorize it in this way? In the last two rows, write down something you've heard in school lately that you suspect reflects a limited mental model and then analyze it. We've done the first one as an example.

The Most Common Limited Mental Models

Black-and-white thinking
Overgeneralizing
Personalizing
Unrealistic expectations
Jumping to conclusions

What you hear	Limited mental model expressed	What makes you think it's this mental model?
I understand that they are only 5 years old, but they should know better. Who acts that way at school? Where would they learn that behavior?	*This could be unrealistic expectations.*	*I think the statement, "They should know better," reflects expectations and the statements about their behavior.*
I worked so hard on that lesson and incorporated your feedback. I prepared all the materials days ahead of time. And I still failed—my slides were out of order. I can't believe our principal observed that lesson. I can't face him in the meeting today.		
I'm not a perfectionist. I just have high standards. I won't accept anything but the best from myself—or my students.		

What you hear	Limited mental model expressed	What makes you think it's this mental model?
I have such bad luck. Nothing ever goes my way. I can't believe my assignment is being changed a week before school. Every year something happens that makes me feel like I start the year on a bad foot.		
Last year we had a disagreement about Back-to-School Night. I'm sure she won't want to work with me on committee again.		
I just got an e-mail from our principal, and she's asking me to meet today after school. She doesn't say why but I'm guessing it has to do with my student's father that she met with yesterday. I can't do anything right in her eyes. All I get is a constant stream of negative, critical feedback. She's relentless. I wish she'd just come out and tell me that she wants to fire me.		
The district is trying a new teacher evaluation system this year. They're probably trying to appear responsive to feedback, but I'm sure they're just looking for a way to speed up the process to get rid of teachers.		

What you hear	Limited mental model expressed	What makes you think it's this mental model?
Something you've heard		
Something you've heard		

If you did this activity and talked about it with someone else, you'd probably find that they have different classifications of these statements. That's because some of them could be both personalizing and jumping to conclusions, or you could interpret them differently. The skill is to develop an ability to hear when someone might be expressing one and then to explore your assessment through your follow-up questions.

Other common limited mental models that we hear in schools and organizations include:

- **Catastrophizing:** Thinking everything has gone wrong or will go wrong, for example, "This will be a disaster."
- **Disqualifying the positive:** Ignoring or explaining away any positive fact or experience or rationalizing that something good doesn't count, for example, "Today was a fluke; tomorrow they'll be out of control again."
- **Magnifying or minimizing**: Giving something more credit or importance than it deserves or doing the opposite and giving it less credit than it calls for; knowing how someone else feels about you, for example, "I can just tell she doesn't like me; she never looks at me during our team meetings."

Using Confrontational Coaching to Interrupt Limited Mental Models

You can use different strategies to interrupt a limited mental model, including cathartic, catalytic, and confrontational approaches. Often, at the root of the limited mental model are emotions that need to be recognized, honored, unpacked, attended to, processed, and released. This can be done through cathartic and catalytic approaches, and sometimes it can also be done through a confrontational approach. Finally, you can use all three approaches in the same conversation. Sometimes to undo a knot like a limited mental model, you need to apply a number of strategies.

How you decide which approach to use has to do with the trust you've built with your client and your understanding of what works with them. That can take time to figure out, so try all three approaches and pay attention to the impact of your coaching. Here's an example of how you can respond to a limited mental model through different approaches.

Example

Client says. . .	Coach's response
I worked so hard on that lesson and incorporated your feedback. I prepared all the materials days ahead of time. And I still failed—my slides were all out of order and the animations didn't play and I forgot to include a key activity. I can't believe our principal observed that lesson. I can't face him in the meeting today.	Hears an *unrealistic expectations* mental model
	Cathartic • I'm hearing you express some strong emotions. Can you identify the feelings that are coming up for you? • It sounds like you had a hard day. How could I be most helpful to you right now? • You have high expectations for yourself. What comes up for you when you don't meet them?
	Catalytic • What are you hearing yourself express? • Is there any other way to see what happened?

Client says. . .	Coach's response
	Confrontational
	• I know you worked so hard on that lesson. What are you believing about yourself right now? [Listen to response] If that's what you believe, what is possible for you?
	• It sounds like you're holding unrealistic expectations for yourself. Having slides out of order isn't a big deal. Would you be willing to unpack what you're feeling and thinking?
	• This isn't the first time I've heard you express expectations for yourself that sound unattainable. I'm guessing you've noticed this tendency in yourself. What's the impact on yourself, and your students, of holding unrealistic expectations?
	• What if you didn't believe that you'd failed in teaching this lesson just because your slides were out of order? Who would you be if you didn't believe this?
	• You're holding unrealistic expectations for yourself again. We've both noticed this tendency in your thinking before. What do you get by thinking this way?

Your Turn

In the next example, generate the cathartic and catalytic responses you'd offer (see the coaching sentence stems in Chapter 7). Then read the suggestions for the confrontational response and put a star by the one you'd feel most comfortable using.

Client says. . .	Coach's response
Every year the district tells us that they've adopted this or that new program or model or shiny thing and that it'll be the answer to all of our problems. And of course, 6 months into implementation, they decide to go in another direction. I am so sick of dealing with this. I can never trust a word out of our superintendent's mouth—it's just one false promise after another. And in the end, when things don't go right, they always blame the teachers.	Hears *black-and-white* thinking and *personalization (feeling victimized)*.
	Cathartic
	Catalytic
	Confrontational • It sounds like you've reached a point of frustration. What do you intend to do about it? • When people use the words *every, always,* and *never,* it's a clue that they're engaging in what's called black-and-white thinking. Does that resonate, or do you ever notice yourself thinking in an either-or, all-or-nothing way? [Listen to response] What do you think are the limitations to thinking in this way? What's within your sphere of influence or control when you operate within this mental model?

Client says. . .	Coach's response
	• I'm hearing two things: black-and-white thinking and that you feel you're always a victim—that you're powerless under the whims of the district. If that's the way you think about working in this district, do you want to consider exploring other job or career possibilities? I'm willing to help you think through those. • I'm hearing your frustration and pain. I also hear that you're feeling disempowered. One way to feel more agency or power is to shift your mindset or your mental model. If you want my support to do that, let me know.

Now, it's your turn to create responses from all three coaching approaches.

Here are a few tips for using the confrontational approach which you may have noticed in the previous examples:

- Name the mental model you're hearing—and invite your client to respond to your observation.
- Name what your client is thinking through a limited mental model and ask your client to choose whether to continue operating within it, or to explore other ways of thinking.
- Give your client *choice*—to disagree with you, to push back, and to decide whether they want to interrogate their feeling. Most people who experience limited mental models are feeling some level of disempowerment.

In this situation, read what the client has said, and then determine your responses.

Client says. . .	Coach's response
I just got an e-mail from our principal, and she's asking me to meet today after school. She doesn't say why, but I'm guessing it has to do with my student's father that she met with yesterday. I can't do anything right in her eyes. All I get is a constant stream of negative, critical feedback. She's relentless. I wish she'd just come out and tell me that she wants to fire me.	Hears:
	Cathartic
	Catalytic
	Confrontational

Now, recall something that a client has said recently that you now understand reflected a limited mental model. Or you could recall something you've said at some time in your career which has reflected a limited mental model. (Be honest: We've all done this!) If you can't think of anything, then make something up.

Client says. . .	Coach's response
	Hears:
	Cathartic
	Catalytic
	Confrontational

Interrupting limited mental models is not always easy. You may experience what feels like resistance from your client. Sometimes this happens when our relationship with our client isn't strong enough yet, or sometimes it happens when a client can't hear what you are trying to say. In that case, don't push. We've had clients come back after we tried to challenge a limited mental model and say something like, "A few weeks ago, you said you thought I was catastrophizing. I thought about it and I can see how I have that tendency."

Shifting limited mental models is a key skill for a Transformational Coach, and fortunately doing so becomes easier with practice. Next time you're in a coaching conversation and you hear a client express what you think might be a limited mental model, jot down their words and then come back to this section to reflect on what kind of mental model it might be and to generate possible responses. There have been many times when after reflecting on a statement made by a client, we've started a subsequent coaching conversation saying something like, "Last time we met, you said _____. If it's okay, I'm hoping we can go back to that and unpack it a bit. What do you think?" (And yes, this is being directive!)

Shifting Out of Victimhood

This activity will help you understand and interrupt limited mental models.

Once we've learned to pick up on the mental models that hold clients back, we can draw on strategies to guide or direct them out of those mental models. You could think about the process of helping someone shift out of unhelpful mental models as being a facilitative coaching process—which would be valid. You can also think about guiding this process from a *confrontational approach* if you are, perhaps, a little more insistent that your client engages in this reflection. Remember that your client will be unlikely to be responsive to your nudge if they don't trust you.

As described in Chapter 11 of *The Art of Coaching,* unhelpful mental models include common rut stories such as an "I'm the victim here" story; the "Oh well, I did my best" story; and the "It's not possible" story. Each of these stories has its roots in what's called *victim consciousness,* which is expressed through statements such as, "I have no control here. This is happening *to* me."

Dr. Stephen Karpman developed a model of the dynamics of human interaction when victimhood is at play. He identifies three roles in this drama triangle:

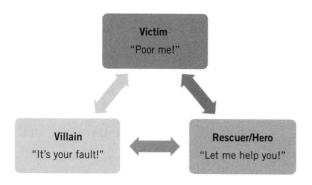

Have you ever had any of the following thoughts?

- "Can't we all get along?"
- "They're doing it wrong."
- "You're not giving me enough time!"

These three statements represent the hero, villain, and victim roles (in that order). Although they seem true, they ultimately represent a disempowering story. Instead we could ask:

- "How might conflict help to deepen this relationship?
- "What am I not seeing that's leading them to act this way?"
- "How can I manage my time to get to the things that really matter?"

Let's look at how one coach helped his client recognize the victim consciousness that he was operating in. This coach had previously introduced Karpman's drama triangle to his client.

CLIENT: I'm so fed up with standardized tests. It's such an artificial assessment of student learning. Preparing for them and administering them takes weeks of valuable instruction time. I wish the district would just call them off this year!

COACH: I hear your frustration! Sometimes anger is a wake-up call to act. Are these feelings you want to act on?

CLIENT: What can I do? They're mandated by the state.

COACH: Let's pull out the drama triangle. [Pulls out a graphic] As you look at this, what insights do you get into how you're thinking about state testing?

CLIENT: So, the villains are the tests—and probably the Department of Education and the school district for mandating them. And maybe my principal is also a villain, though I'm also hoping she'll be a hero and stand up to the district. I suppose that puts me in the victim role. Or, more to the point, my students are the victims. I don't see how we have any power to change the testing requirements.

COACH: Great reflections. What feelings are coming up for you right now about this issue?

CLIENT: I'm mad, that's for sure. [Pauses] And I think I'm also a little sad. The school year is flying by so quickly and there's so much more I want to share with my students. [Pauses again] I'm jealous of teachers in private schools who don't have to deal with these requirements. And I'm scared that my kids may not be ready, or that doing poorly on the test will only reinforce the belief some of them have that they're not smart.

COACH: That's a complex array of feelings, all understandable. How is villainizing the tests and the school system protecting you?

CLIENT: I suppose. . . Ouch. I suppose it lets me feel like if these things *do* happen, if we don't get to everything, or if my students do poorly, that it won't be my fault.

COACH: I can certainly understand wanting that! That's the allure of the drama triangle—from the victim role, we get to be blame-free. And what are the unintended consequences of viewing you and your students as victims in this situation?

CLIENT: That's a tough one. If I'm honest, it's keeping me from considering what might be possible. It's allowing me to be less invested in preparing my students for the test, which might mean they do worse when the time comes. And blaming others is keeping me from taking responsibility for how I go about preparing for my students the test.

COACH: That's a powerful insight. So what experience do you want to create for your students around testing this year?

The secret to shifting out of victim consciousness lies in viewing ourselves and others as inherently creative and resourceful. This experience isn't happening to me—I am actively (co)creating this experience. Of course, this is easier said than done. It helps to have the following questions in our coaching notebook to ask our client or to use for self-reflection:

- Do I see myself as the victim, the villain, or the hero (or some combination) in this situation? How does seeing myself in this way allow me to avoid responsibility for something?
- How might _____ [another person in the situation] view my role?
- What are the unintended consequences of my story? What is it costing me or others?
- What feelings haven't I fully felt yet?
- How might this situation help me learn and grow?
- If I accept that I am whole, creative, and resourceful, how would I see the situation? What would I do?

There is one context in which we don't use this framework: when working with clients whose lives have been shaped by systemic oppression due to their skin color, religion, gender identity, or other identity markers. When a client's "stuckness" is rooted in systemic inequity or implicit bias, asking them to unpack their own victimhood is not only counterproductive but also insulting and perpetuates the oppression they're already experiencing. In these cases, we turn to other resources like the lens of systemic oppression, the spheres of control, and strategies for dealing with strong emotions.

Practice

Think back to a situation at work within the last couple of years that felt unfair. Jot down a few phrases or words to remind you of that situation.

Who or what was the villain in the situation? Who or what did you want to be the hero?

How did seeing yourself as the victim allow you to avoid responsibility for something?

What feelings did you need to feel, or do you still need to feel, about that situation?

How was that situation ultimately an opportunity for you to learn?

How, if at all, have your feelings about the situation shifted in exploring these questions?

Practicing Directive Coaching Approaches

Do this activity to bring together your learning about directive coaching stances and to hone your understanding of when to use one approach or another.

After you have a good sense of how to use the confrontational, informative, and prescriptive approaches, then you need to consider when to use one approach or the other. Sometimes it may be more obvious when to use one approach over another, and at other points you may still be weighing whether to be informative, prescriptive, or confrontational in your stance. It takes practice with these approaches for you to see the impact they can have and to hone your decision-making skills.

Instructions

For each of the scenarios that follow, craft one response from each of the three approaches that we've explored in this chapter. Then imagine how your client might receive your question or statement. To activate your imagination, try putting yourself in your client's shoes. Finally, after you've reflected on the impact that each approach might have, determine which approach you'd use or start with. Read the following example to better understand this activity.

Example Scenario

The second-year teacher you are working with is committed to understanding her students and to developing positive relationships with them. Recently, when you were observing a lesson, you heard a student share that instead of being referred to by the pronoun "he," the student wants the teacher and class to use "they/them." The teacher responded by saying, "But it's right before the Christmas holiday. Maybe we can start using they/them after we get back from break. This way it's less confusing for all of us."

A confrontational response: I know you're committed to developing positive relationships with your students, but it seems like you were prioritizing your own comfort. What sort of effect do you think your comment had on your student?

How this response might be received: The teacher may feel initially defensive, but if there is strong relational trust between the coach and the client, it could be impactful. The teacher might also be grateful to the coach for speaking so directly—given that she's holding a commitment to relationships.

An informative response: Most students who change their pronouns are affirming their true identities. I know you are doing your best to validate your students for who they are, and the article "Respecting pronouns in the classroom" may be a good place to start.

> *How this response might be received:* This teacher may appreciate the resource so she can better understand what is happening for her student. Maybe she just has a knowledge gap around gender identity.

A prescriptive response: Would it be okay if I shared some feedback about how that landed for me and how I can imagine it might have felt for the student?

> *How this response might be received:* This teacher, if she is open to learning and growing, and if there's enough trust between the teacher and coach, could appreciate the direct feedback.

Where to start: I think that because this teacher is eager to develop positive relationships with students, I would start with the prescriptive approach. The prescriptive approach addresses behaviors with more immediacy, which ultimately can ensure that less harm is caused to the students in this teacher's class. I would want my client to understand how a comment like that can sound dismissive and hurtful. I may also take an informative approach and provide resources on pronouns and gender identity so that she could better understand her students. Finally, I might use the Ladder of Inference to help my client deconstruct their underlying beliefs. It can be powerful to dig into the roots of our assumptions to see their origins.

Scenario 1

You are working with a teacher who describes herself as disorganized and always behind on things. When you've observed her, you have noticed that she frequently doesn't have materials for her lessons at hand. You've also seen her scrambling to finish grades, rushing to department meetings, and apologizing to your principal for not responding to her e-mails. You had set up an observation of another teacher, and you and your client were going to visit his classroom, but your client forgot and never showed up. When you met, she said, "I'm so sorry. I can't help it. I'm just this way."

A confrontational response:

How this response might be received:

An informative response:

How this response might be received:

A prescriptive response:

How this response might be received:

Which one to pick:

Scenario 2

It's springtime, and the teacher you're coaching knows that the time between spring break and the end of May can be one of the most challenging times in the school year. He struggles with classroom culture, and to control his class he has begun to use a points system to reward and punish his students when they misbehave. During your most recent class observation you heard the teacher begin the class by saying sarcastically, "Let's see how many of you lose points today. Anyone want to make a bet?"

A confrontational response:

How this response might be received:

An informative response:

How this response might be received:

A prescriptive response:

How this response might be received:

Which one to pick:

Scenario 3

You are working with a teacher who has been in the classroom for 10 years and is considering applying for an administrative credential. They recently shared, "If I were leading this school, here's what I would do," which was followed by comments about how they would shape up the teaching faculty by firing underperforming teachers and taking a stricter stance towards professionalism. "This school needs to remember its traditional roots, and I would hold our current teachers to a higher standard. Their way of approaching teaching and learning is a joke. Times have changed, but that doesn't mean what's best for kids has to change."

A confrontational response:

How this response might be received:

An informative response:

How this response might be received:

A prescriptive response:

How this response might be received:

Which one to pick:

Scenario 4

You are reviewing last spring's test scores with a teacher who works with a majority of English learners. This teacher is defensive about the data because she feels like her students' limited English proficiency causes the students to underperform on state tests. She feels protective of her students and wants to make sure they feel seen, cared for, and valued. She also believes she is the only one in the school who truly understands her students and knows how to teach them best. She sees the data as meaningless and defends her role as the one teacher who can teach her students.

A confrontational response:

How this response might be received:

An informative response:

How this response might be received:

A prescriptive response:

How this response might be received:

Which one to pick:

Wrapping Up the Directive Stance

Do this activity to help you remember the directive approaches and identify what was most important for you in this chapter.

Just like you did at the end of Chapter 9, we want you to reflect on how you'll remember what's in this chapter. How will you remember what constitutes a prescriptive question? How will you remember why to use an informative approach? How will you remember the power of using confrontational coaching?

In the boxes that follow, create a simple visual that represents each directive approach. This might be a good page to photograph or copy and then include in your coaching notebook to help you remember these options.

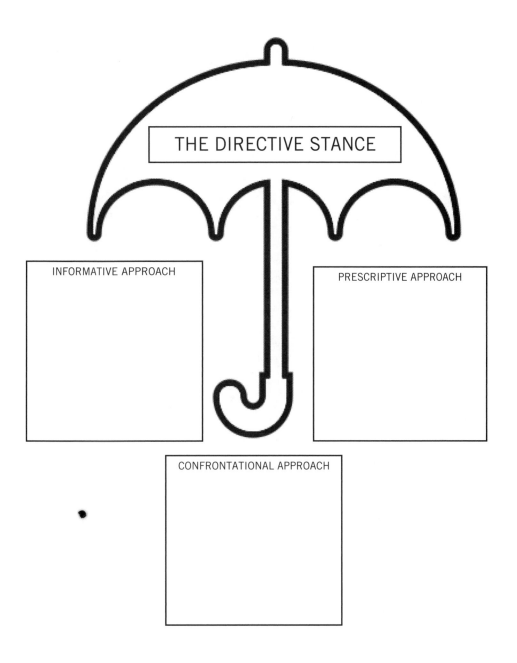

THE DIRECTIVE STANCE

INFORMATIVE APPROACH

PRESCRIPTIVE APPROACH

CONFRONTATIONAL APPROACH

From *The Art of Coaching Workbook: Tools to Make Every Conversation Count* by Elena Aguilar. Copyright © 2021 by Elena Aguilar. Reproduced by permission.

CHAPTER 12

Exploring Directive Coaching Activities

The activities we'll talk about in this chapter—including conducting classroom observations, talking about data, analyzing student work—are likely to be familiar to you. In most places, these activities define what a coach does. We're hoping to continue to expand your thinking about how to do these activities and to describe what it's like to do them as a Transformational Coach. When we observe a classroom or look at student work, we pay close attention to how a teacher's beliefs manifest and to their way of being. We look for a teacher's strengths and their potential and possibility—which *always* exists. We activate our courage, curiosity, and compassion, and we remember that learners require psychological safety.

In this chapter, we provide you with many examples of what it sounds like to engage in these directive coaching activities. We want you to see how we incorporate facilitative coaching strategies into the conversations. As you read these, we encourage you to think about what's similar to the way you already coach and what's different.

Conversations About Data

Do this activity to refine your skills in talking about data.

Conversations about data are meaningful entry points for you and your client to recognize the impact of their beliefs, behaviors, and ways of being on the people they serve. These conversations can be painful, challenging, generative, and inspiring. They can often lead to significant breakthroughs when clients are able to analyze and reflect on data and use those learnings to shift their practice.

Data Analysis as a Vulnerable Process

While coaching conversations on their own can invite vulnerability, looking at data adds another layer of vulnerability for you and your client. The conversations that center on data can be ones that empower or disempower. Take a moment to reflect on the first times you were observed or asked to look at student performance data.

What was that experience like for you?

How did that experience shape your views on data?

These reflections may allow you to build empathy as you work with your clients to analyze student achievement data, observation notes, surveys, or other data sources.

Five Considerations for Conversations About Data

The following considerations can be used in directive and facilitative conversations about data.

Provide Time for Individual Analysis and Reflection
Before you meet to discuss the data, both you and the client review the data. These questions can guide your reflection:

- What do I notice? What patterns can I find? What are the top two or three patterns I see?

From The Art of Coaching Workbook: Tools to Make Every Conversation Count *by Elena Aguilar. Copyright © 2021 by Elena Aguilar. Reproduced by permission.*

- What do I interpret about what I notice? What conclusions can I draw from these patterns?
- What does this data indicate about impact (on students, colleagues, relevant constituents)?
- How are these conclusions connected to teacher-client goals?
- What are the implications of these conclusions for students?

Develop Questions Based on Your Analysis and Reflection

Your client may have much to offer about their interpretations of the data. And depending on their conclusions, they may feel overwhelmed or not know where to begin. Be prepared with questions to guide your client to see the impact of this data on their work, goals, students. Questions can include:

- If you were to come up with a headline based on this data, what would it be?
- Let's consider one specific student as we examine this data. What does it tell us about the impact on this one student?

Create Space for Emotions

In conversations about data, both pleasant and unpleasant emotions may surface for your client. Acknowledge these and invite your client to identify the emotions that are emerging. Emotions that arise in data conversations are often connected to a teacher or leader's identity, sense of self, and the impact they hope to have on those they serve. In moments where difficult emotions arise, support your client to step back from the data and see it as one component of a much larger portrait of the work they are doing. "Right-sizing" the data—helping your client see how this data fits into a broader picture—can support your client to make actionable changes that feel manageable.

Let the Client Lead

As with all coaching conversations, empower your client to share their conclusions first—don't lead with, "Here's what I noticed." If or when they ask for your interpretations, make sure that your client has shared as fully as possible. Some clients may feel stuck, so you may need to walk through the data together. If a client seems closed off to discussing data or doesn't see some of the patterns that are emerging, you may need to be more directive.

From *The Art of Coaching Workbook: Tools to Make Every Conversation Count* by Elena Aguilar. Copyright © 2021 by Elena Aguilar. Reproduced by permission.

Develop Action Steps Linked to a Client's Goals

As you discuss next steps based on the data analysis, revisit the client's goals to determine where this data fits in. Make sure these action steps are time bound so you and your client can determine when to collect follow-up data to compare with what you've just collected.

A Conversation About Data

Before you and your client discuss a data set, you may first want to surface your client's beliefs and attitudes about data. Read the following excerpt from a conversation about data between a coach and a second-year teacher. Underline questions that focus on beliefs and put a star next to questions you might consider using in your conversations.

COACH: Padma, before I do my first observation, I thought it would be helpful if we could have a conversation about data and your views about it, just so we're on the same page about how we'll use it in our work together.

PADMA: Sure, that sounds good. But when you say data, it sounds so clinical. What do you mean?

COACH: Yes, when I think about data in this case, I think about the tangible sources of information that give a teacher insight into their work: student work samples, school demographic information, anecdotes that you hear from parents, classroom observation notes, and video excerpts of your teaching. Any of these examples would be considered a data source we would use to talk about your practice and growth.

PADMA: Okay, that makes sense.

COACH: But before we get into any of that, I'm wondering if I could learn more about you and your beliefs and experiences with data. Would you be willing to talk about that?

PADMA: Sure.

COACH: I know you're in your second year now, and I imagine you already have a lot of data to work with. I'm curious about what data represents for you.

PADMA: I've never thought about what it represents. It's just examples of things I do or how I teach. But now that you're asking, I guess the most direct representations of me are the videos of my teaching, from my certification program, and the observation notes my mentor took last year. And those were scary. So I guess when I think about what data represents based on those sources, it's like it's showing who I am.

COACH: Tell me more about "it's showing who I am."

PADMA: I'm often so focused on what my students are doing and so if we were to talk about student work samples, I'd say, "Oh, that's a representation of that student." Of if we were talking about school demographics, I'd say, "Oh, that's information about our school population." But if we talk about classroom observation data or videos, I think about me. And I feel exposed.

COACH: When you say "exposed," what are you feeling?

PADMA: I'm not sure, but I feel like someone can see me fully—all my mistakes and what I sound and look like—and I feel like people can see all of that and that makes me feel. . . maybe a little worried or embarrassed.

COACH: Thank you for sharing that. I'd like to come back to emotions in just a moment. First, I'd like to note that when I asked you about what data represented for you, you focused only on class observations, when other adults are observing you, rather than data sources in general and what all of it represents. What do you make of that?

PADMA: I guess because you'll be observing me soon, I have more anxiety than I thought. Like if we talked about student work or tests or even reports I've written for my students, I think I feel less exposed, but in this conversation the data I feel most worried about is the observation data.

COACH: I'd like to explore some of the beliefs you're holding about yourself when you're looking at classroom observation notes or videos. Sound okay?

PADMA: Yes, I guess. But what do you mean?

COACH: Well, when you watch a video of yourself teach, or when you read a transcript of classroom observation notes, what do you think about?

PADMA: I think about all the things I'm doing wrong. I can see my mistakes, and then I'm thinking about if I'm really doing a good job.

COACH: I want to acknowledge your vulnerability in sharing this. It can be hard to say these things out loud. I also wonder, what do you believe about yourself as a teacher?

PADMA: I believe that this is what I'm meant to do. I believe I'm doing the right thing for kids.

COACH: How do you compare that belief to the thoughts you have when reviewing observation data?

PADMA: I guess it doesn't match up. I do feel like I'm a confident teacher, but then I doubt myself when other people watch me. Like I'm only good when no one's watching.

COACH: Whoa. That's a big insight! I want to challenge that thinking a little bit if that's okay. Feel free to challenge me back.

PADMA: Okay.

COACH: Aren't your students watching you every day?

PADMA: Yes, they do. But they're not so critical.

COACH: What do they say about you as a teacher?

PADMA: I get good feedback from students. And their families are happy, too. They do well on their exams and quizzes, and they say my classes are engaging because I make learning interesting. Their families often thank me for being so caring, too. I work really hard to meet their needs.

COACH: I can hear that commitment and your deep care. So what makes an adult observing you or a video recording different?

PADMA: I guess I doubt myself.

COACH: Yes, that's really common for newer teachers. So for our upcoming observation, I first want to share that you'll be determining what I look for, so hopefully that will allow you to feel more empowered.

PADMA: [nods]

COACH: What could you tell yourself during my observation that is more aligned with what students and families say rather than your self-doubt?

PADMA: I don't know. Do you have any suggestions?

COACH: Sometimes it's helpful to remind yourself of the positive comments you've heard or received. Or pick a mantra to repeat.

PADMA: I like the positive comments. I got a very nice letter from one of my students last year, and I keep it in a folder on my desk.

COACH: How might you use that letter in this case?

PADMA: I could read it before the observation. I think it will be a good reminder of the impact I can have.

COACH: How do you feel now when you think about being observed? Are there other supports you need?

PADMA: I'm glad I get to determine what you look for. I like the idea of reading this student's letter. I guess I'm still afraid, though, but feel better.

COACH: I'd like to make one more recommendation if you're willing to hear it.

PADMA: Go ahead.

COACH: I'd like to repeat back something you said earlier in this conversation: "I believe that this is what I'm meant to do. I believe I'm doing the right thing for kids." How might you remember that before the class observation?

From *The Art of Coaching Workbook: Tools to Make Every Conversation Count* by Elena Aguilar. Copyright © 2021 by Elena Aguilar. Reproduced by permission.

PADMA: I'm going to write that down. I need to look at that every day. Thanks.
COACH: Do you have what you need for now?
PADMA: I do, thank you.

Reflect

What, if anything, surprised you in what the coach said in this conversation?

What did you notice about how the coach used facilitative and directive strategies?

Far too many times in recent history, data has been used as a weapon to destroy teachers. How do you want to use data in coaching? Write down your commitment or sketch an image or symbol to represent how you want to use data.

Do this activity to expand your understanding of how to do observations and to help you figure out which tools might be most useful.

We consider observations to be a directive coaching activity because the coach is seeing and hearing what's going on through their perspective—all of the data that's recorded is filtered through their observation. This is different from what would be captured on video, which would be far more facilitative activity. This isn't a bad thing—it's just a thing. And it's worth noting. That said, the follow-up conversation with the client can be facilitative.

We hold that a Transformational Coach must have permission to observe a client. There's far too much risk to your relationship and the trust you're building to just walk into a class and observe a teacher. And so, the first step in setting up an observation is to discuss the observation with your client, describe what the process will encompass, and get their input in what you'll focus on in your observation. Ideally, what you'll focus on is connected to the teacher's goals or inquiry question. If a teacher is focusing on developing positive relationships with students, you could focus on the teacher's nonverbal communication. If the teacher is focused on ensuring that all students are engaged in activities, you could focus on evidence of student engagement. If the teacher is focused on incorporating strategies to meet the needs of English learners, you could pay attention to how often and at which points those strategies are included.

There are times when it's useful to observe an entire lesson, and it can also be very useful to observe 15–20 minutes of a lesson. Decide with your client which portion of the lesson you'll observe. Also determine when you'll debrief the lesson together. As soon as you leave the classroom, your client is going to wonder what you thought. We encourage you to debrief as soon as possible, although we also know you'll need some time to reflect on the observation and prepare for that follow-up conversation.

Now you need a way to document observations. You'll see an example of the simple tool we use in Table 12.1. You can easily create your own table like this, or download a blank one from our website, http://www.brightmorningteam.com.

Tips for Classroom Observations

- Record your observations in 5-minute increments, identifying teacher words and actions and student words and actions. If you know names of students, use their initials. If you don't, use "s." or "st." to identify students.

Table 12.1: Classroom Observation Tool

Teacher: Charles			Grade level: 11
Observed by: Lori Cohen			Subject: Statistics
Focus: How teacher fosters independence (through gradual release) and students find solutions to the problems.			

Timestamp	Teacher words and actions	Student words and actions	Coach questions and thoughts
10:05	C writes warm-up on the board: A company manufactures juice boxes. . .		
	C continues to write warm-up on the board.	St. are talking informally about their weekends.	
	C says, "Let's get started, guys." Class quiets down and looks at the warm-up.		
	C still writing on the board.	Class focuses on the screen.	
10:10	C writes, "The Test Bomb" on the board along with "What is Big Data? Why does it matter?" on the other board.		
	"I'm looking for an answer from everybody on this."		
	C interacts with st. about their seating and ensuring they're on task.	St. in back shares that they were focused, "I'm doing my work."	
		There's some quiet talk among the students (not discernable)	
	C goes to write on the other board: The Central Limit Theorem. "What's going on here?"		

(Continued)

From *The Art of Coaching Workbook: Tools to Make Every Conversation Count* by Elena Aguilar. Copyright © 2021 by Elena Aguilar. Reproduced by permission.

Timestamp	Teacher words and actions	Student words and actions	Coach questions and thoughts
10:15	C asks st. to compare their answers with their peers.		
	C, "If there's not someone next to you, slide down."	One student slides near her friend. They smile at each other and ask whose book they want to use.	
	"We're going pause, answer a question and continue. . . Can someone show us what the picture look like?" St. asks a question, C responds, "Yes, and more. . . You're all going to want to look at this [as st. writes on the board.] This is different from what we've done so far."	One student goes to write on the board while the teacher talks and continues to give instruction.	
10:20	St. writing on the board. C asks about questions about the picture. St. shares about the scale. C writes on the board, "not drawn to scale."	St. shares they were unsure about what they were asked to do and explains where he may have made a mistake.	
	Teacher asks st. to think about what the corrective step might be.	St. draws a new picture.	
	C looks at individual st. work and validates st. answer. "If this were a test answer, this is the kind we're looking for."	St. explains her rationale.	

- Consider including a row at the end for your questions and thoughts, but do not share these notes with your client; this final section can be helpful so you don't forget your on-the-spot questions and reflections from the lesson.
- Review your notes after the observation and make sure they're clear. You might want to share your notes with your client before you meet, so they can reflect on them, or you might review them together.

From *The Art of Coaching Workbook: Tools to Make Every Conversation Count* by Elena Aguilar. Copyright © 2021 by Elena Aguilar. Reproduced by permission.

Practice

We want to give you a taste of what it can look like to gather classroom observation data and to think about how you'd use it in a conversation. Review the classroom observation data in Table 12.1. In the notes, column 1 contains teacher words and actions, and column 2 contains student words and actions. Column 3 is not shared with the client but can be used to write questions and thoughts that come up during the observation.

Synopsis: Charles is a high school math teacher who has been teaching all levels of high school mathematics for 10 years. His professional goals this year focus on shifting away from being teacher-directed. This lesson is from an 11th-grade statistics course, and there are 24 students in the class. Charles is employing a gradual release model to help foster student independence. He has asked the coach to note the times when he shifts responsibility from teacher- to student-directed teaching and actions.

As you review the notes from this observation, (1) highlight anything that stands out to you; and (2) jot down questions or thoughts in the third column.

Reflect

What strengths would you celebrate in this teacher?

What would you ask this teacher when you meet to debrief this observation?

Do this activity to reflect on another way to capture observations.

When you are observing leaders, whether for a meeting or for an entire day, it can be helpful to have a tool to document the range of interactions they have over the course of their day. Similar to the classroom observation tool, you will want to agree on what you're observing for and when you'll conduct this observation. Throughout your time observing, write down the leader's words and actions along with the people with whom they're interacting. Use the third column in each section to identify any reflections or impressions you have so you don't lose these insights as the observation continues. (This practice is especially useful for daylong observations.) You can download a copy of the leader observation tool from our website, http://www.brightmorningteam.com.

Practice

Review the following leader observation synopsis and sample notes. In the notes, column 1 contains leader words and actions, and column 2 contains constituent (e.g., staff) words and actions. Column 3 is not shared with the client but can be used to write coach questions and thoughts that come up during the observation.

Synopsis: Ian Landers is a middle school principal in his 35th year in his career and his 20th year at his site. This year the district has asked all site-level leaders to shift their discipline practices to restorative circles, and Ian is struggling with the transition. He and his administrative team are discussing a recent incident in which a Southeast Asian student called a White student the N-word and how to approach next steps.

As you review this sample, (1) code the observation notes for what stands out to you; and (2) write down any of your own questions or thoughts in the third column.

Name of leader: Ian Landers (IL), Principal of Uhuru Middle School
Date: December 16, 2019

Context	Leader's words and actions	Constituent (students, colleagues, staff, families) words and actions	Coach's questions and thoughts
What kind of interaction is this? With whom (e.g., meeting, one-on-one conversation)? Quick huddle with IL, assistant principal (AP), and dean of equity (DE)	8:00 IL, sits down with AP and DE at a small round table. "We need to talk about that incident that happened last week [Southeast Asian student called a White student the N-word] and what we're going to do. I've met with the dean of students, and she is working with the student who used the N-word, and she is working with both students and families around this language. We have a translator who speaks Laotian, so we can ensure communication is happening. We're not set up for restorative practices yet, but we're talking about approaches that could work best here. I want us to think about how to handle this and how to educate our teachers. I also am concerned about our Black students, and how this incident is having an impact on them." IL sighs.	AP and DE nod. DE is writing notes in their notebook. AP has laptop open. DE nods: "I'm already hearing ripple effects in the community. It's bad. I'm thinking we might need to include more professional development with our teachers on classroom curriculum and the role of language. I'm worried about the science and math departments, though, as not all teachers in those departments are willing to take time to have these conversations." AP: "We need to figure out where we want our focus to be. We have four different professional learning initiatives on the table, including our effective culturally responsive teaching rubric. Can we align on something that makes the most sense? I see why this issue is important, but there is just so much to tackle." AP and DE both have laptops open. AP types a few times.	

Context	Leader's words and actions	Constituent (students, colleagues, staff, families) words and actions	Coach's questions and thoughts
	8:10 "Yes, I have a lot to think about here. I am going to call an admin staff meeting for Tuesday afternoon. The time of the year, along with our need for alignment, means we need to act fast. This is urgent, and we need to be on the same page so people see that we're doing something about this. I'll ask R [assistant] to send everyone a calendar invite."		

Reflect

What strengths would you celebrate in this leader?

What would you ask this leader when you meet to debrief this observation?

Teacher-Student Interaction Tool

Do this activity to understand how to use one of our favorite tools for capturing data in the classroom and to learn about how to debrief this data.

This is one of Elena's key tools in her coaching toolbox and one that's essential to use when coaching for equity. Similar to the classroom observation tool, the teacher–student interaction tool can be used as a directive or a facilitative activity. While the coach is documenting the teacher's interactions with students, the conversation about this data source can include facilitative and directive approaches.

You'll best understand this tool if you read an example of the data that a coach collected, and then a transcript of the follow-up conversation—which is what we'll guide you through doing.

You can easily create this tool or download a blank template from our website, http://www.brightmorningteam.com.

How to Use This Tool

If you tell the teacher you're going to look specifically at the quality of interactions, then the data will be skewed. However, you also need to make sure you aren't violating their trust. You need to make sure your relationship is strong enough and that they trust you enough to allow you to gather data on their relationships with students.

You might say something like this: "Thank you for being open to having me observe your classroom. I have a variety of tools that I use to understand the different dynamics in your room, and it'll take me three to five observations to use them all. Afterward, I'd like to share what I've learned with you and show you the tools and data. Would that be okay?"

You'll get the most useful data if you use this tool three to five times for 15–20 minutes each time, but if you only use it once it'll also be insightful.

In this process, the coach is asked to make a number of assessments. First, to identify student's racial and gender identities. Ideally, the coach would know how the students themselves identify and wouldn't make an assumption about their identities. However, sometimes this isn't possible, so the coach is invited to make assumptions based on how the students present. As the coach gets to know students, and as the coach encourages the teacher to have the students self-identify, the coach's observations can be revised or refined.

The coach is also asked to determine whether an interaction is positive, negative, or neutral. This is subjective and is dependent on a number of factors including tone of voice, pitch and volume, and body language. Ultimately, it can be beneficial for the coach to make an assessment. Remember, the goal of gathering data is never to have a stocked arsenal of weapons with which to tear a teacher down. The goal is to have something to talk about that might help the client come to deeper insights and understanding that could benefit students.

Practice

Read the teacher–student interaction data presented in Table 12.2.

Table 12.2: Teacher–Student Interaction Tool: Example

Teacher Mr. G	Subject/period Science/5th	Date and time May 11, 2019 12:37–1:00 p.m.	Total number of students 24
Number of female students: 16 **Racial breakdown:** African American: 3 Latinx: 12 Asian: 1	**Number of male students:** 8 **Racial breakdown:** African American: 3 Latinx: 4 Asian: 1		**Number of gender nonbinary students:** 0 **Racial breakdown:**

Interaction	Time	Positive	Negative	Neutral	Gender	Ethnicity	Notes
1	12:37			X	F	AA	Whatever's in your mouth, just get rid of it.
2	12:38			X	F	L	B, you're going home.
3	12:39	X			F	L	Bye. Have a great weekend.
4	12:39	X			M	AA	Thank you, have a seat.

From *The Art of Coaching Workbook: Tools to Make Every Conversation Count* by Elena Aguilar. Copyright © 2021 by Elena Aguilar. Reproduced by permission.

Interaction	Time	Positive	Negative	Neutral	Gender	Ethnicity	Notes
5	12:40			X	M	AA	Pass the papers.
6	12:41			X	F	L	Put pencil down, J.
7	12:42			X	F	AA	5, 4, 3, 2, 1 (redirect).
8	12:45	X			F	AA	G, go ahead.
9	12:46			X	F	AA	Yes, okay.
10	12:47	X			M	A	Please read, D.
11	12:48			X	M	AA	Come in quickly, please.
12	12:48	X			F	AA	Go ahead, S. Excellent.
13	12:48	X			F	AA	D, thank you.
14	12:49			X	M	AA	Into back table, please.
15	12:49			X	M	A	D, yes?
16	12:50			X	M	AA	Please, keep going.
17	12:50		X?		F	AA	D (redirect—"if that happens again you're going to go in the book").
18	12:51			X	M	AA	L, do you have a question?
19	12:52	X			F	AA	Yes, please, G.
20	12:52	X			F	AA	Good suggestion.
21	12:52	X			F	L	Please, ask your question.
22	12:53	X			M	A	Yes, D, yes.
23	12:53			X	F	AA	Yes, S.
24	12:54			X	F	AA	Yes, D.
25	12:55			X	M	AA	L?
26	12:55		X?		F	AA	G (redirect).
28	12:57			X	F	AA	G, attention here.
29	12:59	X			F	AA	Excellent, D.
TOTAL							

Tally up the totals.

	Total number of positive interactions	Total number of negative interactions	Total number of neutral interactions
African American males			
African American females			
Latinx males			
Latinx females			
Asian males			
Asian females			

Reflect

What do you notice in this data?

What surprised you?

What feels good to see? What's affirming?

Is there anything that raises questions for you?

What do you want to know more about? Is there anything you want more data on?

Is there anything you think your client might want work on, based on this data?

Are there any patterns? What was the flow of the interactions—were the negatives interspersed? Were they clumped together? Were the negatives due to teacher words, tone, or nonverbal communication?

When you debrief this data with your clients, you can ask any of the questions that you just reflected on. Those are all great facilitative questions. Now we want you to read a snippet of the conversation that the coach had with Mr. G, the teacher in the example provided in Table 12.2.

As you read this transcript, code it according to the stance the coach takes: Mark an "F" in the margin where the coach is facilitative and a "D" where the coach is directive.

COACH:	Yesterday I shared the teacher–student interaction tracker with you. Did you have a chance to review it in advance of today's meeting?
MR. G:	Yes, I reviewed it this morning so my observations would be fresh on my mind. I'm ready to talk about what's here. But I'll admit, I feel nervous.
COACH:	That's understandable. I want to remind you that these conversations are confidential, and I'm here to support your learning in this process.
MR. G:	Thanks, yes, I'm glad this is confidential.
COACH:	So first, what do you notice about this data? Let's talk about what's here before interpreting the data.
MR. G:	The majority of interactions in the class are with African American students, even though there are only six. There were only 2 negative interactions, 11 positive ones, and 16 neutral ones. Though Latinx students comprise the majority of the class, I had only four interactions with them.
COACH:	What else do you notice?
MR. G:	Many of the interactions are about redirecting or encouraging—when I ask students to do something to get their attention back or when I encourage them to keep going or ask a question. Most of my interactions are neutral, 11 were positive, and only 2 were negative, which I guess is good.

COACH:	What surprised you about this data?
MR. G:	Definitely the few interactions with my Latinx students. I have 12 Latinx female students, 4 of whom I interacted with, only 1 of which was encouraging—I encouraged Lety to ask her question. I didn't interact with my male Latinx students at all. If anything, I seem to draw all my attention to my African American students, and most of that is redirecting my students ("Put your pencil down;" "Whatever is in your mouth, get rid of it"). I know I give them more attention in general. I do have a series of positive interactions with my African American students, and most of those positive interactions are encouraging questions and positive behaviors. I focus a lot on D.
COACH:	What do you make of what you indicated about your African American students?
MR. G:	D (female) is an incredible student. Active, eager, engaged. She's outgoing and takes risks, too. Her photosynthesis project was really powerful. D (male) has a lot of energy, and he's always going to other lab tables while he's supposed to be in his own group. I want to make sure he is on task, and I'm working hard not to be punitive when redirecting students, particularly my African American students. Our school discipline data is not good, so I'm working hard to be more encouraging, or at least neutral. I think since that last staff meeting, though, when we reviewed discipline data, I may be overcompensating with my African American students.
COACH:	That's a good observation, and something I'd like us to come back to. I'm taking notes on your observations so we can work through these in our conversations together. Anything else you notice?
MR. G:	That's what stands out the most to me.
COACH:	What feels good to see in this data?
MR. G:	I can be an encouraging teacher, and it seems I really want to support my students. But. . .
COACH:	Go on. . .
MR. G:	I know I should feel more affirmed by this data—that it's not wholly negative, that I am encouraging students to ask questions, that I'm validating their responses. But I also feel kind of defeated when I look at what's here.
COACH:	Say more about that.
MR. G:	I'm really surprised by how little I notice my Latinx students. My males!
COACH:	You shared that you are feeling defeated based on the data related to your Latinx students. What other emotions are coming up for you?

From *The Art of Coaching Workbook: Tools to Make Every Conversation Count* by Elena Aguilar. Copyright © 2021 by Elena Aguilar. Reproduced by permission.

MR. G: Sadness. Embarrassment.

COACH: Say more about that.

MR. G: I just feel like I'm failing a good portion of the students in my class. My Latinx males are quieter, and the more outgoing students definitely get my attention. But just because they're quiet doesn't mean I can't have interactions with them.

COACH: Sometimes when we look at data and see something that surprises us, it can be really challenging, particularly in relation to race. We may experience difficult emotions, especially when we have new awareness about something. I want to acknowledge that the emotions you expressed—sadness, embarrassment—are completely normal, and these emotions indicate to me that you care deeply about meeting the needs of your students. What comes up as I share this with you?

MR. G: Yes, that's absolutely true. I care so much about my students, and I want to ensure they all feel supported by me. While I don't feel like neutral interactions are bad, and while I'm happy about the few negative interactions, I wish I was doing more to encourage all my students. It doesn't feel good.

COACH: You are allowed to feel and express these emotions, and I'd like to encourage you to do so. I also want to note that once you are aware of something, you can do something about it. Similar to what you shared earlier about your African American students, I want to note your comment about your Latinx males, as I imagine we'll want to talk more about this topic as well. For now, I want to ask, what do you imagine you might do with this new awareness? Let's imagine some possibilities so we have some action steps to draw from.

MR. G: This tool was helpful for me to see some major blind spots I'm having, and I think I need to see myself interacting with students more. Even though I hate video, I know you have been encouraging me to video myself more. I think now would be a good time to do so. I want to learn more about how common these interactions are. Am I doing this all the time?

COACH: What else do you imagine doing with this new awareness?

MR. G: I think I want to use this tool as I watch myself, so I can track these interactions as well. There's so much to learn. It's painful, but necessary, too. I want to see if being aware helps me make some changes.

COACH: I want to acknowledge the vulnerability and courage you're showing in this conversation. It's hard to do that. Yes, being more aware certainly will help.

	When would you imagine videoing yourself? Would you want me to be part of that class, or no?
MR. G:	I'm feeling pretty vulnerable still, so I think I want to video a class on my own and use the interaction tool. I can share the video with you after the class, and maybe you can use the tool, too.
COACH:	Those sound like great next steps. Next time, would you be willing to pick up with your two observations about your African American students and Latinx males?
MR. G:	Yes, I think I need more support there.
COACH:	Yes, we can talk about it. For now, I'd like to suggest that you to write a reflection based on the data and on this conversation so we can discuss it next time. Reflect on what it's like to have this awareness of your interactions and what the implications have been for your students. I will follow up with an e-mail outlining these questions as well.
MR. G:	Thank you.

Reflect

What do you notice about the coach's ways of being in this conversation?

What do you notice about how the teacher shows up in this conversation?

What do you perceive about the relationship between the coach and teacher? What are those perceptions based on?

What are two important takeaways for you from this conversation?

This activity will prepare you to design a rich video-based learning experience for your client.

Consider using video if:

- a client wants to gather another data set;
- a client wants to deepen their reflective capacity;
- a client has been working on a goal area for a while and isn't seeing improvement;
- a client insists that everything is "just fine" when it clearly isn't; or
- your assessment of a client's practice is dramatically different from their self-assessment.

We'll now take you through three steps to use video as a tool for learning.

Step 1: Get Your Client Bought Into the Value of Video-Based Learning

Before you ask your client to capture video, assess your own comfort with being recorded and watching recordings of yourself with others. Any reservations you have will subtly influence how you discuss the use of video with clients.

Be honest with yourself: Watching yourself on video is (check all that apply)

- ☐ Exciting
- ☐ Scary
- ☐ Uncomfortable
- ☐ Intriguing
- ☐ Terrifying
- ☐ Illuminating
- ☐ Boring
- ☐ Unfathomable
- ☐ Pleasant
- ☐ Unpleasant
- ☐ Humbling
- ☐ Helpful

Now pick three adjectives from this list (to add your own) that you hope your clients will use to describe their experience using video. What do you hope their experience will be? Write them here:

Here are a couple examples of how you can introduce using video with teachers:

- It can be helpful to capture some video of you teaching as we start our work together. Watching the video together is different from me observing while you teach, since if I observe when we debrief we're relying on memory and in-the-moment interpretations. Watching a recording together of you teaching will help me understand how you see your classroom. We can also use it to figure out your goals for this year. The recording process won't be intrusive, and you'll be the only one with the video file. Does this sound like something you'd be open to trying?
- We've been working on shifting the cognitive load to students for a few months now, and I'm really starting to see a change in the kinds of questions you ask and how students respond. You mentioned that you're still struggling with your 5th period class. I'm wondering if it might be helpful to get some video footage to see if we can pick up on dynamics that may be influencing the effectiveness of strategies? The video will let us start at the bottom of the Ladder of Inference. This might lead us to different actions. What do you think?

This activity is a very easy one to modify if you coach a client who is teaching on a video platform—perhaps because a pandemic has hit or because their school uses blended learning and they offer online courses.

In both cases, the use of video is framed as an opportunity for both the teacher and the coach to learn. The video is an opportunity for shared inquiry, not evaluation. Furthermore, the emphasis is on video providing a more objective set of data about what's happening in the teacher's class. Finally, the teacher is given the choice about whether to engage in this process.

Step 2: Create a Useful Recording

Here are some tips for maximizing the potential for learning from video.

- *Be clear on purpose.* Discuss what you each hope to learn from the video. It can be helpful to design a set of questions or a quick observation guide to use when watching the video later.
- *Strategize about setting.* Discuss what would be most helpful to record. What time of day? What part of the lesson? All students or some in particular? Is there any potential interference the coach should be aware of (e.g., a loud air conditioner)?
- *Prepare students.* For the recording to be as unobtrusive as possible, the teacher should acknowledge the recording for students. She might say something like, "You may notice Ms. Elena is with us today. She'll be recording part of our lesson for my own professional development. No one will watch this recording but the two of us. So that I can learn as much as possible from this, I'd be grateful if you'd all just ignore her and behave as you normally would." After the first five minutes, most students—and even the teacher—forget that they are being recorded.
- *Check sound quality.* Most coaches record the teacher and the students, perhaps focusing on the teacher during direct instruction and students during group work. The coach should be in a position where it is easy to capture audio, including student voice, and may want to use a microphone. (If you record on a smartphone, inexpensive microphones are available to improve sound quality.)

Step 3: Learn from the Video and Identify Next Steps

In his book on video-based professional learning, instructional coach Jim Knight notes,

In our research, we have found that it is best that [the coach and teacher] watch the video separately because that way (a) the teacher watches the video without concern for what someone else thinks; (b) the teacher can watch the video at his own pace, stopping and starting whenever he wishes; and (c) coach and teacher can engage in more meaningful conversations when they have both watched the video ahead of time and don't have to divide their attention between the video and their colleague. (Focus on Teaching, p. 48)

If you and the teacher agreed on a set of viewing questions or an observation guide during the planning stages, make sure you both have this available during your independent viewing. People tend to be hard on themselves, so remember to have both of you watch for and write down things you like in the video.

When you come together to discuss the video, the goal is usually to identify what went well and to decide on one or two specific adjustments the teacher would like to experiment with as a result of what they saw. Begin by acknowledging the strengths evident in the video. Then turn to the viewing questions or observation guides and of course, now's the time to use all of your Transformational Coaching strategies. The mind the gap framework might help you identify the learning need to help your client reach their goals. Strengths-based coaching (and head, heart, hands) can remind you of your client's positive attributes. Using facilitative and directive coaching strategies will ensure that this is a meaningful, helpful conversation.

One last thing: You will be more convincing in encouraging teachers to record themselves if you have used video yourself as a teacher or are using it to improve as a coach. Your clients will be more open to being recorded when they're teaching if you also ask to record your coaching conversations so that you can improve as a coach.

Plan

Identify a client to whom you'd like to propose recording video. What will you say to them to introduce the idea and get them bought into it?

Imagine you are now going to record video of this client (they said yes!). Consider the criteria described in step 2. What equipment will you use? Where will you position yourself? How will you ensure a quality video without being intrusive? Mentally walk through the experience, then write your plan in the following space.

Write down five questions to use in the debrief with this teacher. These can be questions that you can offer regardless of what you capture on video—so do this now!

Finally, go and make plans to do this! When will you talk to your client about using video?

Analyzing Student Work

Do this activity to learn how to analyze student work with a teacher.

Looking at student work can reveal a lot about the impact a teacher is having and how to meet students' needs. We suggest using a four-phase protocol to analyze work with teachers:

1. Set context and identify goals.
2. Make predictions.
3. Make observational assessments.
4. Draw inferences and conclusions.

We'll talk you through these phases and offer you examples of what it sounds like to coach in this phase. As you read the examples, underline phrases that you might want to use.

Phase 1: Set Context and Identify Goals

- Ask your client to select a piece (or a few pieces) of student work.
- Invite your client to determine a goal for looking at student work, something that will help gain greater insight into their students, teaching, or anything related to their goals.

Example

COACH: Dorian, I'm excited to talk with you about some of your student work so we can gain greater insight into what they need. Do you have something in mind you'd like to look at together?

DORIAN: Yes, I'd like to review these document-based question paragraphs I've asked my students to write. They're new to historical analysis and primary sources, and they're just learning how to select evidence that matches their topic sentences.

COACH: What are you hoping for as we look at their work?

DORIAN: There's two things I want to look for:

- Were students able to select a piece of evidence that matched their topic sentence?
- Were students able to write an interpretation in support of their evidence? In other words, does the interpretation match the evidence itself?

COACH: How will those insights be helpful to you?

DORIAN: They'll help me determine whether the way I scaffolded the lesson was effective.

Phase 2: Make Predictions

Before looking at the student work, invite your clients to respond to these questions:

- What might we *expect to see*?
- What might we *expect to learn?*

Example

COACH: What might we expect to see as we look at these examples?

DORIAN: We might expect to see that almost every student will have (1) the main idea in the first sentence, their topic sentence; (2) one quote from one of the three primary sources they received (i.e., a letter, a newspaper clipping, or a paragraph from a memoir); and (3) and an interpretation of their quote with the phrase "this piece of evidence, letter, newspaper, or paragraph illustrates. . ."

COACH: What else?

DORIAN: I chose a few examples from different students: one of my stronger students, one student who is meeting expectations, and one who is falling below expectations. But I did lots of checks for understanding this week, and the third student I identified (the one falling below expectations) showed their understanding through our practice sessions. I am hoping to see if that practice transferred into this paragraph.

COACH: So I'm hearing that you expect us to see the three things you identified [repeats those three items], and we're looking for evidence of transfer from the lessons you taught to this paragraph.

DORIAN: Yes.

COACH: What might we expect to learn from looking at these paragraphs?

DORIAN: That I scaffolded and differentiated instruction well enough to meet a diverse range of students. These samples are reflective of that range.

Phase 3: Make Observational Assessments

Look at the student work together and make observational comments:

- What do students *actually* present?
- What *facts or patterns* do we notice?

From The Art of Coaching Workbook: Tools to Make Every Conversation Count *by Elena Aguilar. Copyright © 2021 by Elena Aguilar. Reproduced by permission.*

Sentence stems could include

- One fact I notice is _____.
- A trend I think I see is _____.
- I can quantify that by saying _____.
- I notice that _____.

Example

COACH:	For this first round of review, we'll focus on only what we can observe. We won't make meaning of our observations just yet. And we'll try to identify as many things that we can observe. For example, I might say, "I notice that Xavier has a topic sentence." How does that sound?
DORIAN:	Great.
COACH:	Because we're looking at three different paragraphs, we'll spend about two minutes on observations of each paragraph. I can document what you observe.
DORIAN:	Sounds good.
COACH:	Okay, what do you notice in Xavier's paragraph?
DORIAN:	I notice a topic sentence. I notice he uses evidence from the newspaper article. I notice he uses the phrase, "This newspaper clipping illustrates. . ." I notice he attempts an analysis.
COACH:	When you say attempt, how do you know that?
DORIAN:	Because he paraphrases the quote rather than explaining what the quote means.
COACH:	Okay. What else do you notice?
[This process continues with the next two student work samples.]	
COACH:	What facts or patterns do we notice?
DORIAN:	Each student used the newspaper clipping. Each student had a clear topic sentence, and that they all looked similar. Two students interpreted the quote, and one paraphrased the quote.

Phase 4: Draw Inferences and Conclusions

After all observational comments are made, discuss inferences and conclusions:

- What *hunches* do we have about causes for what we observe?
- *Why* are we getting the results we are?

Sentence stems could include

- This pattern or trend might be because _____.
- Maybe we're not seeing _____ because _____.
- A reason for this result could be _____.

Then ask:

- So what? And now what?

Example

COACH: What conclusions can you draw from your observations?

DORIAN: It seems students really understood topic sentences, and the similarities in their sentences I think were a result of a lot of modeling. We looked at one example a lot and students seemed to mirror that example.

COACH: What else?

DORIAN: They all chose the newspaper clipping as their piece of evidence.

COACH: What do you make of that?

DORIAN: Among the three primary sources, it was the most compelling for students. It's also the one we used in class to model. Jakayla, my strongest student, used this newspaper clipping in our whole-class model, and I think because I validated Jakayla's use of the clipping and quote, students latched onto that as a source they would want to use.

COACH: What other conclusions can you draw?

DORIAN: Two out of the three students here were able to interpret their quotes, but Xavier wasn't. He paraphrased.

COACH: What do you make of that?

DORIAN: Xavier struggles with the difference between summary or paraphrasing and interpretation. Or at least in this example he does. I don't think he was able to transfer his skills yet because he may need more practice.

COACH: I'm going to put a star next to that point for us to come back to. How are you feeling so far about what you're noticing and concluding?

DORIAN: I'm feeling good about my scaffolds to get students to this point. I wonder about the influence Jakayla has over her classmates. Students really pay attention to what she says and does, and I validate her a lot, too. I wonder about the challenge level of the other two primary sources. Perhaps they were too challenging or perhaps I didn't do enough in class to unpack them. And I also wonder how many students had patterns like Xavier's: They paraphrased the quote rather than interpreted the quote.

COACH:	We have a lot of directions we can go in. What would you like to focus on most?
DORIAN:	I think I'd like to look at more student samples to see what patterns we can notice in student interpretation. That feels like the area that may have more variety in response.
COACH:	Let's do that for now. What has been most helpful so far?
DORIAN:	I like how we're not necessarily judging the work but observing it. It's helping me take a step back from the work a bit.
COACH:	Where could I be more helpful?
DORIAN:	Let's look at those other examples. I'm really curious about students' interpretation skills.

Reflect

How does this process for reflecting on student work compare and contrast to how you've coached teachers on looking at student work? Or how does this process compare to how you were coached on looking at student work when you were a teacher?

What might be challenging about using this process for looking at student work? Why?

Call to mind a teacher you're coaching with whom you'd like to look at student work, but you're uncertain about whether they'd be receptive to doing so. How do you think this teacher would react if you were to use this four-step process? What can you anticipate about how they'd engage in the process?

Thinking about that same teacher, how do you think their behaviors, beliefs, and ways of being might shift if you were to look at student work together?

What could you say to this teacher to help them be open to looking at student work together?

What's holding you back from inviting them to look at student work together?

What are your next steps to look at student work with this teacher? Determine them and then decide when you'll take these steps by, and then do them!

Using a Gradual Release Model and Scaffolding Learning

This activity will help you identify your client's strengths, gaps, and growth areas and scaffold their learning using a gradual release model.

Developing a plan for gradual release here is a good way to understand the model. As we guide you through your plan using the following instructions and tool, consider a client you are working with now or someone you've worked with recently. A sample of this tool can be found on p. 405.

Step 1: Identify Your Client's Strengths, Gaps, and Growth Areas

The graphic in Figure 12.1 represents your client's zone of proximal development (ZPD). The first bubble represents where your client is most autonomous—where they demonstrate the greatest comfort and competence in their knowledge and skills. The middle bubble is where you will devote your time and energy in identifying your client's gaps and growth areas; the better you know your client, their strengths and skills, the better you will be able to identify the types of learning activities that fall within their ZPD—their optimal learning zone. The outermost bubble represents areas that are outside your client's optimal learning, where the gaps and growth are significant; they will need to accomplish what is in their optimal learning zone before they can work in those areas.

Figure 12.1: Client Learning Zones

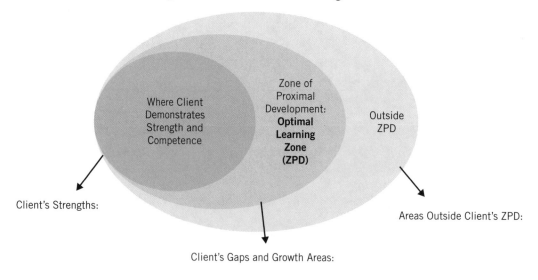

From *The Art of Coaching Workbook: Tools to Make Every Conversation Count* by Elena Aguilar. Copyright © 2021 by Elena Aguilar. Reproduced by permission.

Use the space provided after Figure 12.1 to list your client's strengths and gaps so you can home in on the specifics of their optimal learning zone.

Step 2: Generate a List of High-Leverage Activities Within Your Client's ZPD and Aligned to Their SMARTE Goals

a. Review your client's SMARTE goals and list them here. Keeping these goals in the forefront of your mind will help you design learning to meet these goals.

b. If you and your client brainstormed a list of high-leverage activities to support them in meeting their goals, include those here. Based on how well you know your client, you also may be able to generate your own list or add new items. Which activities will help your client best meet their goals and close their gaps? List as many as you can think of in the space provided.

Step 3: Go Back Through the List You Generated and Assess Your Client's Capacity to Implement Them

Put a star next to activities you believe will best contribute to your client's growth.

Step 4: Design and Scaffold Learning Using a Gradual Release Model

Just as you might scaffold independent student work in a classroom, you will create opportunities for your client to demonstrate their learning and growth independently, moving from more coach-directed work to your client's independent demonstration of learning. The following graphic is one possible way for you to think about scaffolding your client's learning. Complete this scaffold for each of your client's SMARTE goals.

Client's SMARTE goal:

Figure 12.2: Scaffolded Learning Plan

Coach Directed	Coach–Client Directed	Client Directed

Coach-directed activities: What do I need to research, create, share, and model for my client so they can build knowledge, skill, and capacity in this area?

Coach-client activities and conversations: What will my client and I do together so my client can build knowledge, skill, and capacity in this area?

Client independent practice and integration: What will my client be able to do on their own? How will they demonstrate their knowledge, skill, and capacity in this area?

Coach-directed activities: What do I need to research, create, share, and model for my client so they can build knowledge, skill, and capacity in this area?

Coach-client activities and conversations: What will my client and I do together so my client can build knowledge, skill, and capacity in this area?

Client independent practice and integration: What will my client be able to do on their own? How will they demonstrate their knowledge, skill, and capacity in this area?

Figure 12.3 is a sample for what this process might look like.

Figure 12.3: Sample Gradual Release Plan

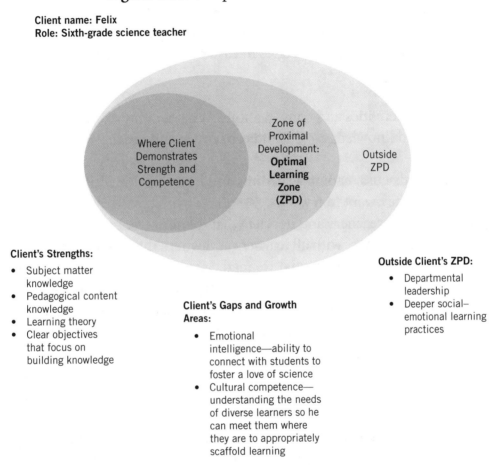

Client name: Felix
Role: Sixth-grade science teacher

Client's Strengths:
- Subject matter knowledge
- Pedagogical content knowledge
- Learning theory
- Clear objectives that focus on building knowledge

Client's Gaps and Growth Areas:
- Emotional intelligence—ability to connect with students to foster a love of science
- Cultural competence— understanding the needs of diverse learners so he can meet them where they are to appropriately scaffold learning

Outside Client's ZPD:
- Departmental leadership
- Deeper social–emotional learning practices

Client's SMARTE goal: to foster students' love of science through differentiating instruction to meet the needs of all learners by meeting them where they are and using brain-based, culturally responsive techniques to building stronger relationships and support students' capacity to grow.

Figure 12.4: Coach Directed Activities

Coach Directed	Coach–Client Directed	Client Directed

Coach-directed activities: What do I need to research, create, share, and model for my client so they can build knowledge, skill, and capacity in this area?

- ☐ Identify select readings about culturally responsive teaching and brain-based practices for us to read and review together.
- ☐ Plan co-observations of peer science teachers who are skilled in these areas.
- ☐ Begin a list of possible strategies in case my client isn't able to identify them on their own.

Coach-client activities and conversations: What will my client and I do together so my client can build knowledge, skill, and capacity in this area?

- ☐ Read and discuss reading selections and have client identify the brain-based strategies they want to try.
- ☐ Observe peer teachers and debrief what we notice. Identify places where teacher was able to connect with all learners and where they were using brain-based techniques that aligned with what we read. Make a list of possible activities to try.
- ☐ Plan an observation where the client is trying a specific strategy and co-design formative assessments to measure student impact (survey questions and in-class activities); debrief observation and review student work together.

Client independent practice and integration: What will my client be able to do on their own? How will they demonstrate their knowledge, skill, and capacity in this area?

- ☐ Client designs a lesson on their own using brain-based culturally responsive strategies; client also designs formative assessment tools to measure impact.
- ☐ Client invites me in for an observation or videos their lesson so we can see this in practice.
- ☐ Client considers brain-based culturally responsive practices and formative assessments for all their lessons.

Practice

Step 1: Identify your client's strengths and gaps and growth areas.

Step 2: Generate a list of high-leverage activities within your client's zone of proximal development (ZPD) and aligned to their SMARTE goals

a. Review your client's SMARTE goals and list them here.

b. If you and your client brainstormed a list of high-leverage activities to support them in meeting their goals, include those here. Which activities will help your client best meet their goals and close their gaps? List as many as you can think of in the space provided.

Step 3: Go back through the list you generated and assess your client's capacity to implement them. Put a star (*) next to activities you believe will best contribute to your client's growth.

Step 4: Design and scaffold learning using a gradual release model. Complete this scaffold for each of your client's SMARTE goals:

Client's SMARTE goal:

Coach-directed activities: What do I need to research, create, share, and model for my client so they can build knowledge, skill, and capacity in this area?

Coach-client activities and conversations: What will my client and I do together so my client can build knowledge, skill, and capacity in this area?

Client independent practice and integration: What will my client be able to do on their own? How will they demonstrate their knowledge, skill, and capacity in this area?

CHAPTER 13

Transformational Technical Tips

In this chapter, we'll consider some technical tricks of the coaching trade, but through the lens of Transformational Coaching. Which means, they may not feel very technical!

The systems we establish—organizational structures, calendars, plans, schedules, planning, communications, and note-taking tools—create the conditions for Transformational Coaching. The following questions guide us to modify what might seem technical into something transformational:

- What organizational structures, systems, processes, and tools set us up to coach?
- How do we prioritize time and space to establish meaningful coaching relationships?
- How can we bring humanity to creating structures and systems that honor process and mistake making, include multiple ways of sharing information, allow for relationships to be central to the work, and ultimately serve the social, emotional, and academic needs of all students?

An Internal Systems Check

Before we can dive in, let's see what you already know, what you feel most comfortable with, where your growth edges are, and what you hope to learn as you complete the activities in this chapter. Take a few moments to fill out this inventory.

Statement	Your reflection 5 = strongly agree 3 = neutral 1 = strongly disagree
I have well-designed systems for my coaching work, and I am set up so I have everything I need for each coaching conversation.	
I use a series of planning questions and tools to prepare for my coaching conversations.	
I use note-taking templates and tools or I have a clear system for note-taking during a coaching conversation.	
I have a series of tools and questions for reflection, and I take time after each conversation for reflection.	
I know myself (my values, habits, ways of being) and how that self-knowledge has an impact on how I set up my coaching work.	
I am proactive in my organizational habits (e.g., planning, calendaring) and take pride in these habits.	
I am easily able to adapt my coaching to virtual environments.	

Based on your rankings, identify patterns you notice. Where did you score the highest? The lowest? Where do you want to focus your learning?

Planning for a Coaching Conversation

Do this activity to develop planning habits that will transform your coaching conversations.

A tremendous amount of the success of any conversation lies in the planning and preparation. The following conversation planning tool, used in conjunction with the conversation note-taking tool and reflection tool, will lead you through a powerful planning, conversation, and reflection process that allows your mind, heart, body, and spirit to be fully present for your client and make every conversation count. This planner will work for any kind of coaching conversation, whether you are a newer coach or a deeply experienced coach. As you come to know these tools, you will find there are times you want to use all three in conjunction to support a conversation; at other times you will use one of them on its own.

This coaching conversation planning tool addresses the two essential questions:

1. Where does my client need to go?
2. Who do I need to be?

Practice

Select someone you are currently coaching and practice using this template to prepare for a conversation. You don't need to address all these questions; they are meant to inspire your thinking as you consider your client and their context. You can download this template from our website, http://www.brightmorningteam.com.

Table 13.1: Coaching Conversation Planning Tool

Question or topic	Responses and coach's notes
Focus	
What kind of conversation will we be having? ☐ General coaching conversation ☐ An introductory conversation ☐ A goals conversation ☐ A conversation about beliefs ☐ A conversation about equity* ☐ Other: _____	

* When considering that coaching allows us to develop the tools, skills, knowledge, and capacity to support all our students, then all coaching conversations are conversations about equity, yet there are times when you need to specifically focus on issues of equity.

(Continued)

From *The Art of Coaching Workbook: Tools to Make Every Conversation Count* by Elena Aguilar. Copyright © 2021 by Elena Aguilar. Reproduced by permission.

Table 13.1: (Continued)

Question or topic	Responses and coach's notes
Where does my client need to go?	
• Where did our last coaching conversation end, and what do I need to come back to with my client? • Was there anything I said I'd check in on next time? • Is there any data I gathered from our last conversation (observation notes, feedback, student work and voices) that would be important to address in this conversation?	
Where does my client need to go—goals and intentions	
• What are the goals for this coaching • conversation? How might my goals align with my client's goals? • What are my intentions for this meeting? • What do I want my client to think and feel by the end of it? • Where will there be opportunities to make this space more equitable? How might I do so?	
Where does my client need to go—knowledge of the client	
• What are my client's strengths? Gaps? How could I leverage their strengths to support their areas for growth? How could I help them see their own strengths and assets? • What do I know about my client's identity markers (e.g., race, class, gender identity) and how they impact who they are and how they show up in their work? What do I want to be curious about?	

Table 13.1: (Continued)

Question or topic	Responses and coach's notes
• What might my client's disposition be? • What do I anticipate might be happening with my client or might be challenging? • How can I make this conversation matter to my client? What do they care about that I can connect this conversation to? • What questions can I ask to support my client in understanding the beliefs or mental models they may be holding? • What else might I ask?	
Where does my client need to go—knowledge of the context	
• What information do I know and need to know about the school population (students, staff, families) that will inform my coaching? • How are the identities of students being affirmed, valued, and represented throughout the school and in the classroom? • How does my client acknowledge, respond to, and affirm the backgrounds and identities of all students to create engaging, accessible, inclusive school and classroom environments? • How are students engaged in rigorous, meaningful learning, and are they mastering the content? How do I know? • What values are being upheld and prioritized in the school and classroom spaces?	
Who do I need to be—coaching approaches	
• What stances might I take to support my client? • Can I anticipate that my client might want to engage in any coaching activities? Which ones might I suggest and use?	

(Continued)

Table 13.1: (Continued)

Question or topic	Responses and coach's notes
• How might I support my client in exploring beliefs, behaviors, and ways of being? • Do I anticipate my client will need to release emotions? What works for them to process emotions? • Are there any materials (articles or tools) that I might gather and bring with me?	
Who do I need to be—attending to self	
• Who do I need to be in this conversation? Who does my client need me to be? How do I need to show up? • How might I activate empathy, curiosity, and compassion for my client? What will help me stay in these dispositions? • What triggers do I need to be aware of? How will I manage those triggers? • How will I prepare myself to be fully present for this conversation?	

Reflect

Which parts of filling out this planner felt easiest for you? Why?

Which parts of filling out this planner felt most challenging? Why?

What would you revise or change from this planning tool for your own conversation planning?

Preparing Yourself for a Coaching Conversation

Do this activity to reflect on how you prepare your way of being for a coaching conversation.

A large part of what will make a coaching session successful is your disposition—how you show up to the conversation. When coaches are calm, grounded, open, and present to support their client, they create the conditions for their client to learn. The following activity invites you to identify what practices work best for you to prepare yourself to show up fully to your coaching. After completing this activity, consider creating a list of these grounding practices somewhere in your notes where only you can see them.

Some examples to get you thinking:

- Meditating
- Listening to music you love
- Taking a walk
- Stretching
- Writing an intention (How do you hope to show up to the conversation?)
- Saying mantras
- Talking with a trusted colleague as a sounding board

What do you do to get grounded and present in your work? What routines or rituals do you have? List them here.

How do you take stock of your mood before a coaching session? What strategies might you use to shift your disposition to be ready for coaching?

What gets in the way of you being fully present for a coaching conversation? What can you say to yourself or do in the moment to be fully present for your coaching?

From Planning to Practice: The Coaching Conversation

Do this activity to learn a simple structure to use for a coaching conversation.

Just as a planning template offers you structure to think about where your client is and who you need to be in a coaching conversation, an effective coaching conversation offers a structure to think in the moment and to work with your client toward growth. The following is a template you can use to give form to a conversation. It offers both a structure for the conversation itself and a way to take notes on the conversation. We've created a structure for note-taking because of the key roles it plays in Transformational Coaching: note-taking gives us a way to observe and think inside the conversation and offers us an opportunity for reflection following it. We call this our conversation-shaping tool.

Review the components of a coaching conversation in Table 13.2. You may want to use your planning guide from the previous pages to either role-play a conversation or use this template and your planner for an upcoming conversation.

Table 13.2: Conversation-Shaping Tool

Time	Conversation components	Conversation transcript
5 min.	*Check in and chat*	Make sure to set a timer for this portion so you devote enough time to the session. This portion does not need to be written down.
2–4 min.	*Check in with the client*: • "What's on your mind?" • "What do you most want to be true by the end of this conversation?	
2–4 min.	*Check in on previous commitments* "How did it go when _____?"	
30–45 min.	*The conversation* Include any questions, big ideas, or topics from your preparation work here. You may need more space to document the conversation.	
5 –7 min.	*Closing* Ask client to reflect on what they learned, how they feel, and any next steps they need to take. Ask for feedback (what was helpful, not helpful).	

Reflect

How do you document your coaching conversations? What do you typically write down?

What would you revise or add to your own conversation planner?

Reflecting on a Coaching Conversation

Do this activity to explore a new structure for reflection.

After a coaching conversation you want to know whether you supported your client in feeling more empowered and more deeply connected to their vision, values, and abilities. As clients don't always tell you this directly (although sometimes they will!), you need to create a structure that works to support your reflection.

> In *The Art of Coaching* Elena writes, "After a coaching meeting, the first thing I ask myself is whether I think my client is feeling more optimistic about what he can do. Does he feel more empowered? Did he reconnect with his vision, values, and abilities? This is sometimes a hard road to chart—optimism and self-sufficiency are challenging outcomes in our schools—and sometimes the journey is rough or painful. I don't always reach this end, but I'm always aiming for it—and when I hit it, and I know I've reached it, it's been a good day of coaching."

Identify an upcoming coaching conversation that you want to reflect on afterward. Put a note in your calendar or coaching notebook so you'll remember to come back here and use the coaching conversation reflection tool to reflect. It's fine if you don't answer all of the questions. You can download this tool from our website, http://www.bright morningteam.com.

Table 13.3: Coaching Conversation Reflection Tool

Questions	Reflections
• How did this coaching experience create meaningful change for students and my client? How did I make this conversation count?	
• What did I notice about my own coaching? About my thoughts and feelings today?	
• What kind of impact did my coaching have on my client today? How do I know?	

From The Art of Coaching Workbook: Tools to Make Every Conversation Count by Elena Aguilar. Copyright © 2021 by Elena Aguilar. Reproduced by permission.

Questions	Reflections
• When did my coaching feel effective today? What made it feel that way?	
• What was challenging for me in today's session? What made it challenging?	
• What did you notice about my own listening? About my inner dialogue?	
• What do I think was "not said" by my client today?	
• What indicators were there today that my client made progress toward their goals?	
• What are my next steps to help my client move forward?	

After you reflect on these questions, then here's one more question to reflect on: How did this process of reflection help you think and feel about your coaching conversation?

The Intersection Between Organizational Systems and Educational Equity

Do this activity to explore your values and beliefs about education, to understand dominant culture and white supremacy and its connection to the systems we create, and to identify ways you can dismantle aspects of white supremacy to make your coaching more inclusive and equitable for your clients.

You can learn a great deal about yourself as you look at how your already existing coaching behaviors may be rooted in belief systems and structures that have shaped you throughout your schooling. This reflection will enable you to shift your practices to be more inclusive and equitable for those you work with. This is true for all of us, regardless of our race or ethnicity, because we're all on a learning journey when it comes to un-learning racism and other forms of bigotry.

Read

With a highlighter or a pen in hand, read the following section about where some of our values about education come from. Identify key concepts that may have an impact on your practice as a coach and implications for students and schools.

Where Some of Our Values Come From—An Exploration Into the Dominant Culture

The United States was founded on Eurocentric principles of white supremacy, capitalism, and patriarchy. These principles have become the sometimes invisible building blocks of dominant culture and of our education system. As a consequence, a lot of the practices in our education system and professional lives are rooted in principles that, if made visible, many educators would choose to disrupt. When we start looking at the elements of our schools that have been built on this flawed foundation, we start to see evidence of the flaws everywhere—in the role of discipline in our schools and the demographics of discipline, in who holds power in our schools, in how success is defined, and in whose values and views shape the curriculum.

These basic and deeply problematic elements of our schools are directly responsible for educational inequities and opportunity gaps for populations which have not been served equitably in our schools, particularly our Black and Brown students. When we neglect to reflect on where our systems and practices come from—and the harm these practices have inflicted—we unwittingly perpetuate more harm.

Perhaps the place you work contains abundant resources and a healthy workplace culture, or perhaps your site is limited by the strictures of slim budgets, facilities in disrepair, overcrowded classrooms, and a toxic culture. Most school sites are a combination of these

---

From *The Art of Coaching Workbook: Tools to Make Every Conversation Count* by Elena Aguilar. Copyright © 2021 by Elena Aguilar. Reproduced by permission.

extremes. Though much of what happens in our workplaces can feel out of our control, the systems we create in our work as coaches—our organizational tools such as our calendars, our notes, and our reflections—are well within our spheres of control and influence and can be a critical component in creating conditions for Transformational Coaching. The systems we create also can offer some needed structure where it may otherwise not exist. Effective coaching is about creating conditions that center the client in any circumstance.

What concepts in this section do you want to remember?

What do you want to learn more about?

Reflect

Spend some time reflecting on your own values and experiences in education. This will help to expand your reflections in connection to the reading you just did. You may want to walk and think about these questions, write or draw responses in your journal, or talk with a colleague about them.

As a student in school, what did you understand as the purpose of education?

As an adult, what do you understand as the purpose of education?

When you were growing up, what were students praised for in school? What were students disciplined for? Think about a couple of students whose identities were different from yours in various ways and think about yourself.

What were you taught about what success in school looked like? Who taught you that?

What values did your school systems uphold? How did you see those values reflected in your school communities?

Which of those values did you accept or reject when you became an educator?

What does success look like for you now? What do you think success looks like for students now?

What values do you communicate to those you work with?

Revise: Change Systems Within Your Spheres Influence

How might you use your spheres of control and influence to dismantle systems that don't serve our schools and students, and, instead, create systems that are equitable, inclusive, transparent, and supportive of those you serve? Tema Okun's and Kenneth Jones' (2001) work identifies the ways white supremacy manifests in our society in both overt and insidious ways.

In the first column of Table 13.4 you'll read a description of white supremacy culture that's based on Okun and Jones' work. The middle column includes antidotes to white supremacy culture (what we can do differently). In the right-hand column you've got space to identify what you can do as a coach to be more equitable.

Table 13.4: Indicators of White Supremacy Culture

White supremacy characteristic	Antidote	What I want to do and practice in my coaching
Perfectionism: When we are perfectionists, we fail to appreciate our own good work, more often pointing out our own faults or "failures," focusing on inadequacies and mistakes rather than learning from them. Perfectionism is a harsh and constant inner critic.	Develop a learner's orientation: Presume that everyone will make mistakes and that those mistakes offer opportunities for learning. Realize that being your own worst critic does not actually improve the work, often contributes to low morale among those you work with, and does not help you or the group to realize the benefit of learning from mistakes.	
Quantity over quality: If we subscribe to the idea that what can't be measured has little value, we undervalue process and put too much emphasis on product. We can't effectively mediate a conflict between content (the agenda of the session) and process (people's need to be heard or engaged).	Explore core values: Make sure you and your client explore what matters and refer to these values in day-to-day work. Use these core values to create process or quality goals in your planning and look for ways to measure process goals. Additionally, to honor process, learn to recognize times when you need to move away from the agenda in order to address your client's underlying concerns.	

(Continued)

White supremacy characteristic	Antidote	What I want to do and practice in my coaching
Worship of the written word: When we do not value multiple ways of sharing information, those with strong documentation and writing skills are more highly valued, even in organizations where ability to relate to others in person is key to the mission.	Be flexible in communication: Take the time to analyze how people inside and outside the organization get and share information. Determine the types of documentation and communication practices that best serve your client. For any type of communication practice, make sure ideas can be clearly understood (e.g., avoid academic language, buzzwords).	
Either-or thinking and only one right way to do things: When we see things as either-or (good-bad, right-wrong, with us–against us) we believe that there is one right way to do things and that once people are introduced to the right way, they will see the light and adopt it. This way of thinking is reductive and places a priority on either the dominant view or a single view of a situation as opposed to recognizing a situation's or a process's complexity and nuance.	Accept that there are many ways to get to the same goal: Notice when you find yourself or others using either-or language and push to come up with more than two alternatives. When working with communities from cultures different from your own, never assume that, in the absence of a meaningful relationship, you or your organization knows what's best for the community. Be clear that you have some learning to do, and then do that learning.	

Setting up our internal systems is a lifelong process and will be something we attend to throughout our careers and beyond. The more attuned we are to the systems that exist within us and how our behaviors can be more equitable and inclusive, the better we will be able to support our clients and our students—and ultimately, transform schools.

For Further Learning

→ Read Coaching for Equity.

→ Enroll in a virtual Coaching for Equity learning experience (information at http://www
.brightmorningteam.com)

Designing Your Work Life: Setting Priorities

Do this activity to identify which executive functioning practices you already do, which ones you are curious to learn more about, and which ones are gaps for you so you can determine your priorities for setting up your coaching practice.

You will be better able to design your work life if you have an understanding of executive functioning. Executive functioning is an umbrella term to describe the mental processes that enable us to plan, focus attention, remember instructions, and juggle multiple tasks successfully. Like an air traffic control system for the brain, these skill sets filter out distractions, prioritize tasks, set goals, and control impulses (Center of the Developing Child, 2011; Goldstein, 2018).

Research on the developing brain indicates how our childhood experiences shape our executive functioning, which in turn shapes who we are throughout our lives. Our executive functioning affects how we achieve in school and how we regulate emotions and shape our relationships with others; it defines our capacities for leadership and decision-making and profoundly affects our overall health and well-being. Because our school systems are inherently inequitable, children have received uneven support in building their executive functioning capacities.

What research consistently tells us, however, is that our brains are dynamic and can change according to what we do and experience—this is good news, of course, for teachers and the young people they are supporting. And it's also good news for coaches. We know that the adult brain is still able to build the complex networks required for executive functioning—our clients can grow and change, and so can we.

A Self-Assessment of Executive Functioning Habits

With a pen in hand, review this list of executive functioning habits for a coach and mark each item with the following symbols:

★ = This is something I already do/think about.

? = This is something I want to learn more about.

✓ = This is a gap for me. I need to learn and grow in this area.

- *Know your professional self.* Coaches, teachers, and leaders need attend to themselves just as they attend to others. Exploring who you are, how your background and identifying markers have shaped who you have become, and what personal and professional structures work for you, will ensure the systems you create will be sustainable, equitable, and supportive for those they serve.
- *Keep a calendar.* You could also use a planner or some type of logbook where your meetings, obligations, and appointments will go, and strive to be consistent using it. Some organizations have software that everyone is required to use; others allow you to organize your time in the way that best suits you.
- *Create an organizational system that works for you to keep track of your clients, projects, and responsibilities.* Create a way to establish systems to easily track the work you're doing, such as folders, note-taking, and planning templates. Make sure whatever system you're using is easy to access.
- *Plan proactively.* Recognize that planning, reflecting, and learning are part of your role as a coach. Engaging in these proactive practices will support you in prioritizing the needs of those you serve, reduces unnecessary stress, and allows you to identify the resources you need. Schedule time in advance of your coaching sessions or meetings for planning, and make sure you set aside time as well for reflecting and learning. We know this can be hard in a busy work environment, so you may need to schedule concrete learning activities, such as interviewing a colleague, completing a reflection log, checking on progress toward goals or reading an article.
- *Schedule both work sessions and breaks.* When we think about scheduling our time, we often neglect our breaks. Author and researcher Robert Pozen (2012) suggests taking a 15-minute break for every 75 minutes of work so our brains can consolidate information and retain it better. As you look at your days and weeks, make sure you include several breaks where you take time away from your work—and from screens.
- *Think of communication as a three-step process: pre-interaction, during interaction, post-interaction.* Intentionally considering all work-related communication in these phases helps you make sure that your client will be supported.

☐ Pre: Anticipating a meeting or session allows you to create the conditions for successful communication. Consider what your client or team needs to know in advance. Send ahead reminders or material to read a couple of days in advance so people have time to prepare and process information.

☐ During: The conversation you have with your client (both spoken and non-verbal), what you write in your coaching log, notes from a conversation or session, and any action items for follow-up together comprise the heart of the communication.

☐ Post: Follow-up communication allows you to close the loop on any topics that need to be addressed or to summarize information. Sometimes post-meeting and -session communications are brief (e.g., a thank-you for attending or giving a presentation), and sometimes they further elaborate on decisions and action items.

- *Draft, pause, review, send.* Good written communication takes time—we want to ensure our message, tone, ideas, and requests are clear to our audience. Most written communication occurs in e-mails, but tone does not come across well in an e-mail, so we need to be wary of sending anything that may be charged. Sometimes we have a strong reaction to e-mail we receive, but unless it is an emergency, a rapid response may not be the best one. First, ask yourself if this communication is best as an e-mail. If you've decided to communicate electronically, start by writing a draft; then, ideally after taking a break, review your draft (by reading it aloud, if possible, or by having a trusted confidant read it). Only then, click send.

- *Set short-term, bite-sized goals.* Often the first goals we set are lofty ones. These grand goals are too broad, too many, and will take too long to accomplish to be meaningful in the shorter term. When writing these first goals, make sure you set a realistic time frame, then set some short-term goals within the larger goals. At the beginning of each week, identify one to three goals for the week (key things you hope to accomplish), and return to them at the end of the week. Reflect on what happened and why. Doing so will help you hone both your ability to set goals and your ability to meet them.

- *Celebrate successes.* Just as setting weekly goals can be a powerful ritual, creating a ritual of celebrating successes at the end of each week can shift how you experience your work. Write down these successes and share them with a colleague or trusted friend. Be as specific as you can and give yourself credit. Doing so boosts oxytocin levels in your brain, which also contributes to your overall physical and mental health.

From *The Art of Coaching Workbook: Tools to Make Every Conversation Count* by Elena Aguilar. Copyright © 2021 by Elena Aguilar. Reproduced by permission.

Setting Priorities

Which of these executive functioning habits did you identify with a ⭐? These are your strengths. Note them here.

Which of these executive functioning habits did you identify with a **?** ? Identify one area you want to learn more about and consider next steps toward that learning.

Which of these executive functioning habits did you identify with a ✓? How did these gaps align with what you know about yourself? What are one or two areas you most want to focus on?

How might you be able to fulfill your vision and mission for yourself as a coach by focusing on these priorities?

Setting Up for Virtual Coaching

When COVID-19 forced us into new ways of teaching, leading, and coaching, it also exposed our gaps in how to coach effectively in virtual spaces. Do this activity to prepare yourself for coaching virtually.

Reflect

What has it been like for you to move from in-person environments to virtual? What feelings have come up for you in this shift?

What has been different? What has been similar?

What has been your most powerful virtual experience—either as a coach or teacher? What made it powerful?

What's been challenging about coaching online?

Now, read Lori's reflection.

Lori Reflects

When I first started coaching, I only met with clients in person. When I became a school leader, though, I received my own coach, and she wanted to have meetings by phone. I was mystified. How would she know what I was thinking and feeling if she couldn't see me? How would I grow? In our first session, she led me through a guided meditation to identify my purpose as a leader. We did Enneagram work. I drew pictures and made Pinterest boards

---

From The Art of Coaching Workbook: Tools to Make Every Conversation Count by Elena Aguilar. Copyright © 2021 by Elena Aguilar. Reproduced by permission.

and created spreadsheets, and we worked together on these tools. We could be virtual yet still go deep.

When the pandemic hit and I started working virtually, I was thrust into the same position. I would have to support those I worked with from afar. As I worked with my coach to transition to my new work situation, we expanded our own definition of virtual coaching. We sometimes met onscreen and sometimes talked on the phone. While we used similar rituals in each of our sessions (we always started with a brief guided meditation), we also discovered new opportunities for coaching. Now having our sessions by phone presented an opportunity to get away from screens—sometimes I would take a walk while talking with my coach or just lie on my floor in my pajamas and talk. As we varied activities in new ways, I learned how powerful coaching on the phone could be. Virtual coaching has its limits, but it also has its possibilities.

For several years I've facilitated a professional learning community online, and participants come from all over the United States. Even in virtual formats, we still do deep work and collaboration, and the connections we made have been authentic and enduring. Since the pandemic hit, all my coaching clients have become virtual clients. While face-to-face coaching is powerful, I've witnessed the same transformation as a coach and as a client in virtual spaces as I have in person. I'm realizing I've become a big fan of virtual coaching.

Making the Most of Virtual Coaching: Identifying Opportunities and Needs

In the following Venn diagram, identify what seems to be true about coaching in person, what seems to be true about coaching in virtual formats, and where there is overlap between in-person and virtual coaching.

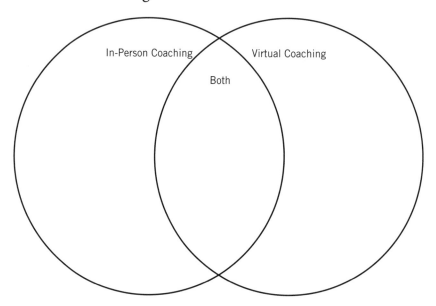

Based on what you wrote in the middle section, make a list of practices you want to continue using in your virtual coaching. Doing so may help you to see how much translates from in-person to online formats.

Based on what you wrote in the right circle, identify where you see opportunities to make the most of virtual coaching. For example, if you wrote something like, "We're on small screens" in the Venn diagram, you might write something in the following space like, "Find a way to balance screen time with phone time," or "Ask my client to choose a virtual background that most shows their mood right now." Identify as many possibilities as you can think of.

Identify what you still need to know about and learn. What questions do you have, or what do you most want to learn that will support you in virtual coaching?

Go back through your list and identify two or three priorities for your learning. Share these priorities with a colleague or with your coaching team simply create a learning plan.

If You Feel Stuck Getting Started

You may feel stuck about where to begin, or you may want more advice on what to consider when coaching virtually. As a starting place, consider the following:

- *The relationship is central.* What you co-create with your client is more important than the medium you use.
- *Make trust a priority.* The trust-building tools in previous chapters work just as well in virtual formats as they do in person.
- *Co-create learning.* Ask your client about the conditions that would be most beneficial for their learning in virtual formats.
- *Play to your strengths.* Do what you know how to do best—coach. If you want to try a couple of tools, consider the following ones to support your coaching:
  - ☐ Google Docs or Sheets: Sharing documents on your individual screens in real time is like working on the same piece of paper on a table you and your client are sitting at. Use this tool to track progress in your meetings or to co-create topics and tools in your planning sessions
  - ☐ Trello: This is a good tool for planning and prioritizing ideas.
  - ☐ Mural or Padlet: These are good for brainstorming, mind maps, and visual thinking.
  - ☐ Mood Meter: Use this for checking in on emotions.
- If you find additional tools will be an impediment to your conversations, *stick to the tools that work best for you and your client.*
- *The power is still in the planning.* While the context for coaching may differ, you still want to consider where your client needs to go and who you need to be in the conversation. You also may want to consider how to foster connection, build trust, and co-create. The following planning tool can serve as one possibility for virtual coaching.

The virtual session plan is an additional resource to use when planning for a virtual coaching conversation. It's ideal when included in your preparation and after you've planned for a coaching conversation using a tool like the one earlier in this chapter.

Virtual Session Plan	
Tech check Ensuring technology needs are met	☐ Everyone will have access to technology to engage in this meeting; I'll offer a couple of ways of engaging. ☐ I have tested the tools and prepared any documents or software in advance. ☐ I know where to go and who to reach out to if I have technology challenges. ☐ I am using tools that maximize connection, community involvement, creativity, and impact. ☐ Additional technology considerations:
Deepen connections What new or different opportunities will there be to build, foster, and create connection? Could I give my client a tour of my office or introduce them to my pet?	
Foster trust How might my client's trust in me be impacted by our phone or video connection? Is there anything additional I can do to strengthen trust?	
Co-create learning Are there any ways I can use technology or our virtual platform to enhance our learning? For example, could my client share a video of themselves teaching through this platform and we could discuss it together?	

CHAPTER 14

Planning for Ongoing Learning

Before we dig into this chapter, we want to celebrate your commitment to coaching. You've made it this far and have engaged in so many exercises, and we *know* you've already made tremendous growth as a coach! We're doing a little happy dance imagining your workbooks full of annotations, scribbled comments, stick-figure drawings, and sticky notes. We know you've noticed that your coaching conversations have improved, that you're enjoying them more, and that you're feeling like you're having a positive impact on others. We also suspect that your conversations with friends and loved ones have felt more meaningful. On the journey to becoming a Transformational Coach, we experience more authentic connection and joy with others.

We hope you're glimpsing your potential to make every conversation count. Just pause and imagine what that would feel like? What if you walked away from every coaching conversation knowing that you'd helped someone strengthen their resilience, connect to their own power, expand their beliefs, and build skills that could serve children? How would you feel if that was true? Draw a quick sketch of yourself walking away from such a coaching conversation here.

In this chapter we'll guide you in reflecting on your coaching skills and planning for further learning. While we hope you belong to a community of coaches and that you have a supervisor or coach who is committed to your growth, we're guessing that many of you are working through this book alone. We know you want to keep building your Transformational Coaching muscles, so let's explore how you can do that—in community with others, or independently.

Using the Transformational Coaching Rubric

Do this activity to reflect on your coaching abilities and create a learning plan for yourself.

We all want to do a good job. We want to feel successful and effective. But what criteria do we use to evaluate whether we're doing a good job? This question gets at the core of one of the biggest problems in coaching programs: There's often no articulation of what constitutes good coaching. When Elena was a coach in her school district, she was evaluated on a teaching evaluation rubric. This, of course, provided no useful feedback and was a time-consuming formality. And it didn't answer the question she had about what defined good coaching. Evaluation is necessary, and we believe it plays a role in helping someone develop their skills. But a useful evaluation process is based on a useful tool for measurement—a tool that's used for evaluation, for self-assessment, and to guide one's own learning.

In *The Art of Coaching* you'll find a coaching rubric in Appendix C. After that book was published, Elena developed another coaching rubric she felt was more helpful. That one is called the Transformational Coaching Rubric 2.0 (TCR 2.0), and you'll find it in Appendix A of this book. (You can also download it from our website, http://www .brightmorningteam.com.) Be warned: This rubric is massive. It takes time to process and digest. We've found it essential for goal setting and guiding our development and equally valuable as a tool for supporting other coaches in their learning.

TCR 2.0 Glossary

Domain: There are eight *domains*. These are numbered.
Indicators: Within each domain, there are *indicators*. These are identified with a letter.

How to Use the TCR 2.0

Here are some suggestions for how to understand and use this rubric. As you read the suggestions, star the ones you'd like to follow.

Phase 1: Understand the Rubric

1. Read the rubric looking for what's familiar to you. Which terms and phrases do you understand based on your reading of this workbook and *The Art of Coaching*? This step will help you see how much you've learned about Transformational Coaching.

2. Read the rubric a second time and note your questions. What's not clear? Which terms or references do you not understand?
3. Go through the rubric and highlight the five indicators that you feel are your greatest strengths.
4. Make another notation (perhaps a star) next to five indicators that you feel solid in but in which you'd like to make growth.
5. Use a different color highlighter to mark three indicators in which you'd like to improve.

Another option for steps 3–5 is to use stoplight color-coding: green for strengths; yellow for growth opportunities in familiar areas; and red for where you lack the most skill, confidence, and experience.

Phase 2: Self-Assess

After you feel familiar with this rubric (which Phase 1 should help with), do a thorough self-assessment. Go through each indicator, and as you reflect on your abilities be sure to think about (and perhaps write about) why you assessed yourself at that level. What evidence are you basing your assessment on? How do you think one of your clients would assess you?

Phase 3: Prioritize

Prioritize your learning areas. Either determine one domain or perhaps five indicators. Consider selecting areas that you feel you are already solid in, at a foundational or intermediate level, as well as some that you are foundational in. Unless we identify these learning areas and name them, we have a tendency to lean into what we are already good at. Like intention setting, naming and stating these learning areas is proven to increase our chances of following through on trying to grow in them.

Phase 4: Make a Learning Plan

As you read through the TCR 2.0, you'll likely notice that there are many activities in this workbook to support your learning. However, you might also be disappointed to find that there aren't activities to deepen your skills for some indicators. There was only so much we could fit into this book!

From *The Art of Coaching Workbook: Tools to Make Every Conversation Count* by Elena Aguilar. Copyright © 2021 by Elena Aguilar. Reproduced by permission.

You can find more resources, online courses and virtual workshops, and other offerings on our website that can help you build the skills included in the TCR 2.0. We also hope that you've got colleagues with whom you can practice—because the only way to become advanced is by practicing with others.

How will you build your skills and knowledge in the areas you've identified? What ideas come to mind? Capture those here:

Phase 5: Determine a Timeline

The last step for now is to determine when you'll come back and reflect on your growth in these areas. It might make sense to return at the end of a semester or the school year, but what's important is to determine that date and then mark it on your calendar. Otherwise, you're likely to forget. Do that right now.

You might also consider other steps you can take, and calendar those, such as soliciting feedback from clients, audio-recording a coaching conversation, and engaging a client in a facilitative coaching activity. What else can you do right now to solidify your commitment to your own learning?

For Further Learning

→ Enroll in a Bright Morning virtual or online coaching to do a deeper dive into one domain (information at http://www.brightmorningteam.com).

Analyzing Your Coaching Conversations

Do this activity to get a snapshot of the approaches you use in coaching.

We all have our tendencies as coaches. Some of us say "hmm" a lot. Others ask lots of clarifying questions. When we start coaching, it's likely that we'll ask fewer kinds of questions, as categorized into facilitative and directive approaches. We can make significant growth in our coaching simply by heightening our awareness of what kinds of questions we ask. Doing so often leads us to ask questions with more intentionality, and to ask a wider variety of questions.

For this activity, you'll record yourself in a coaching conversation. This could be a video or an audio recording that you capture on your phone. The use of video as a tool for self-reflection is a fantastic way to identify where you are demonstrating growth and helps to illuminate where and why you struggle through an objective lens. Much like teachers who use video reflection for the first time, we are always unaware of many things that might make us less impactful and simply didn't realize it (e.g., body language, facial expressions, listening skills). Yes, it's hard to watch yourself, but it gets easier and is invaluable if you are committed to developing your coaching skills.

The following activity can be done as often as you want, or perhaps once a month or once a quarter. Even if you do this only once a year, you'll still find benefit in it. If possible, record one of your first coaching conversations and then compare it with others throughout the year. You'll have striking audio or visual evidence of how you grow as a Transformational Coach.

Instructions

1. Record a coaching conversation and transcribe it. Or get it transcribed—some inexpensive software programs can do this. Look them up. If you have access to a video conferencing tool that records, many will both record and transcribe for you. If you're meeting in person, you can easily open and record a meeting from your laptop and position it so you and your client are both captured in the recording.

2. On the transcription, highlight everything you say, and code each question or statement according to the categories in the following table. There can be some subjectivity around how to categorize questions and statements, and this isn't a precise science. Group them as best you can—or consider them "unclassifiable." A "hmm. . ." that's expressed with empathy and care could be classified as a *supportive* statement. In the end, it's your decision.
3. Tally up the different kinds of questions and statements you made, and note those numbers in Table 14.1.
4. Reflect on these questions:

   - What surprises me in this data? What made it surprising?
   - What factors contribute to my tendency in coaching? Why do I coach the way I do?
   - What shifts would I like to make in my questioning during conversations?
   - What's one commitment I can make for my next conversation based on what I saw?

Table 14.1: Coaching Conversation Snapshot

Facilitative stance	Total	Directive stance	Total
Supportive		Informative	
Cathartic		Prescriptive	
Catalytic		Confrontational	
Other			
Reflective (active listening or paraphrasing)			
Clarifying question			
Unclassifiable			

Analyzing Someone Else's Coaching Conversation

Do this activity to practice analyzing a coaching conversation.

Okay, so while you'll learn a whole lot from analyzing your own conversations, you can also learn a lot from engaging in the same process with other people's conversations. If you belong to a community of coaches, this is a super powerful practice to engage in together. Each month, for example, one person could record and transcribe a conversation and present it to the group to analyze. Another option is to share the actual recording (or a video) and analyze that.

On Episode 2 of the Bright Morning Podcast, Elena coached Kathrina. (In case you haven't checked out the podcast yet, Elena coaches real educators.) What follows is a partial transcript of that conversation—what Elena said only in the first portion of the conversation. You might prefer to listen to the conversation (you'll find the podcast anywhere that podcasts are found) and then engage in this exercise, or you can jump right into it.

Read the statement that Elena made and classify it using the following notations:

Facilitative—Supportive:	Fac Sup
Facilitative—Cathartic:	Fac Cath
Facilitative—Catalytic:	Fac Cat
Directive—Informative:	Dir Inf
Directive—Prescriptive:	Dir Pres
Directive—Confrontational:	Dir Conf
Reflective:	Ref
Clarifying question:	Clar
Unclassifiable:	Un

You'll find that some statements are hard to classify without hearing tone of voice or perhaps what Kathrina said. Make a guess or note them as unclassifiable. This isn't a hard science—it's an exercise in thinking about how we classify our coaching questions. Also, note that reading only what the coach says gives you limited information about the impact she has given that you're not reading Kathrina's responses. Even so, this exercise is useful. Try it out!

So shall we get started?
What are you nervous about?
Yeah, and I can help you with that. And if you say anything afterward, you decide, you don't want to have said, we can edit that out. So just to get clear, you're worried about possibly insulting someone or hurting someone's feelings?
Well, so like you say, it's about the issue and it's also about you.
So what's the issue? Let's jump in.
It's always all over the place. That's why it feels like an issue.
Yeah, definitely. So what feels hardest about this situation?
Hmm. All right. So let's explore this element. The people I've known the longest I have the hardest time reaching. So first, what are, what are the feelings that come up around that situation?
Yeah, that's a powerful insight. I just want to sort of stop and take that in. . . I think there might be more emotions. . .
Hmm. That's a lot of pressure to put on yourself.
If you can't figure it out with one person, then it means you're a bad leader? That you don't have potential as a leader?
So what if anything was possible? What if you didn't need to look, what if you didn't need to imagine? What if there was a buffet of possibilities in front of you and you could pick whatever you want, what would you be curious about?
I know, I can see your whole face lit up.
Right. Okay. So you'd be a coach. So let's continue to play in the imaginary world for a few minutes. There's a lot we can learn from the imaginary world.
I want you to imagine then that it's a few years down the line and you are coach. . .
I want you to imagine that you are coach and you're feeling really satisfied. And now I want you to think about the situation you're in now. . .
You've known for a longer time and you're remembering the situation and how hard that was. And you're remembering the anger you felt and the sadness. 'Cause I hear sadness and you're remembering the fear. And the voice that says, who do I think I am, which I think is a voice that sometimes comes from shame.
You're remembering all of that. What do you know, what do you understand in the future about this situation?
Say more about that. Yeah.

So I'm hearing—the conditions weren't right. Or they weren't set up, the conditions. Meaning what your role was, how you perceived your role, how others perceive your role.
Okay. So "it's not just me."
How does it feel to say that, to hear that, to have that awareness?
Yeah. I can see your eyes look like they're welling up. Yeah. So why don't you say it again?
Can I make a suggestion? Say it again and take out the word "just."
No, take *out* the word "just."
Yeah. So it's the situation. It's the conditions you talked about—systems and leadership.
What's coming up for you right now?
It is hard. And I disagree with you. I think you have been practicing self-compassion you're working on it. And when you said you tell yourself, you said you start feeling like if I can't figure this out, that I'm not a good leader. . . Just the fact that you're grappling with this, that you're raising these questions. You are practicing self-compassion. You have the awareness of the need and have the desire you're already doing it. . .
So, okay. I'm going to ask you again, sort of another imagine question. What would be possible for you in your life? If you had a lot more self-compassion, if you felt really confident in your ability to love yourself and care for yourself and be kind to yourself, what would be possible?
That's a great metaphor. . . I love that. I wonder if next time you're going into a situation where you anticipate there might be some challenging relationships, maybe at some of these, some of the people you're having some conflict with before you go in, could you close your eyes and imagine putting on that waterproof jacket?
So, what does it feel like to make that connection? 'Cause again, I can see the video. I can see your eyes.
So these are tears of relief of reconnecting with your own power.
Tell me more about what you're understanding.
I think there's so much power for you in continuing to explore that metaphor. . .

Now, tally the statements in Table 14.2

Table 14.2: Coaching Conversation Snapshot

Facilitative stance	Total	Directive stance	Total
Supportive		Informative	
Cathartic		Prescriptive	
Catalytic		Confrontational	
Other			
Reflective (active listening or paraphrasing)			
Clarifying question			
Unclassifiable			

Reflect

What, if anything, surprised you about this conversation and the distribution of coaching approaches?

What insights did you get about coaching from this exercise?

What's one thing you can take away from this activity and apply to your own coaching practice?

For Further Learning

→ Listen to additional Bright Morning podcast episodes and engage in the same analytical exercise.
→ Return to the transcript in the Introduction, "Eavesdropping on a Transformational Coaching Conversation," and code what the coach says.

From *The Art of Coaching Workbook: Tools to Make Every Conversation Count* by Elena Aguilar. Copyright © 2021 by Elena Aguilar. Reproduced by permission.

Coaching the Three Bs

Do this activity to reflect on how you can more intentionally coach toward changing, beliefs, and ways of being.

What distinguishes Transformational Coaching from other models is that we coach around what people do (their behaviors) as well as what they believe and who they are being. In Table 14.3, you'll see examples of what it sounds like to coach in these three areas—which are aligned to the three goals in any coaching conversation (to build skills, expand reflection, and strengthen resilience). Many of these questions can be used in any conversation. They can also be classified as *cathartic, confrontational, supportive, catalytic, prescriptive,* or *informative*. There's an overlap in how we classify things!

To develop your ability to integrate coaching the three Bs, try the following activities:

- Plan for an upcoming coaching conversation and intentionally craft a few questions for each of the three Bs.
- Record a coaching conversation (not the same one that you planned for) and then transcribe it and categorize your questions into these three domains. Reflect on what you notice about your patterns. Do you tend to ask more questions about behaviors? Do you begin with asking questions about behaviors and then ask questions about beliefs? Are the questions you ask about ways of being intended to be catalytic?
- Copy Table 14.3 and paperclip it to your coaching notebook. During your next coaching conversation, look at it (yes, in the middle of the conversation!) and draw a question or two from it. We think it's perfectly okay to use your resources during a coaching conversation and for your clients to see you do this. You'll be modeling the learning process.
- Create your own three columned table, with the three Bs as column headers, and add your own questions. What do you say that is intended to explore behaviors, beliefs, and ways of being?

From The Art of Coaching Workbook: Tools to Make Every Conversation Count by Elena Aguilar. Copyright © 2021 by Elena Aguilar. Reproduced by permission.

Table 14.3: Sentence Stems Aligned to the Three Bs

Behaviors *To build skills*	Beliefs *To expand reflection*	Ways of being *To strengthen resilience*
• Let's script what you'll say to introduce this concept. • What are the instructions you'll give students for this activity? • What knowledge set will students need to know to access this content? • What could you try with [student's name] to build a more positive relationship? • What are the learning objectives for this lesson? • How will you know if students met your learning targets?	• I'm curious about how you came to hold that belief. • I'm intrigued by your thoughts about _____. Tell me more. • What assumptions were you operating under? • I hear that you interpreted her behavior as meaning _____. Are there any other ways you could interpret her behavior? • If you could go back in time and do that again, what would you do differently? • I hear that was hard. What did you learn about yourself from that experience? How did that experience shift your thoughts about yourself as a teacher?	• I can hear some emotions in your voice when you describe that experience. Do you want to unpack those? • What do you think that frustration was about? • What do you think she felt in that situation? • What did you notice about how you responded to their behavior? • I hear how frustrating that was. Given what's within your sphere of influence, what could we focus our conversation on? • How do you want to be remembered? • What would you do if you had nothing to fear?

Gathering Feedback on Your Coaching

Do this activity to prepare for gathering feedback from your client.

Gathering feedback from your client about your coaching is hard. It's scary. But it is invaluable if you want to refine your coaching. You can intuit and observe the impact your coaching has on a client, but you need direct feedback as well. Don't get too anxious though—the feedback can be affirming and validating. And there's little that feels as good as hearing our client's words of appreciation.

Ideally, here's how you'd get this feedback. Every 3 months or so, your clients would receive an online survey. They'd respond to a set of questions anonymously. You'd have a supervisor, manager, or coach who would collect this feedback and summarize the open-ended feedback so that your client's identity can be preserved. They'd coach you through the data and help you determine your next steps.

If you don't have someone to gather and process survey data with, you can still send out online surveys and reflect on your own. As you'll see when you read the questions below, your clients may not be anonymous if they answer the open-ended questions. This isn't necessarily a problem—it depends on how much trust you've built. They might be completely honest with you, or they may feel as if they need to answer carefully.

Survey Questions

We suggest two categories of questions on a survey. The first asks for response based on a Likert scale (a 1–5 scale: 1 = strongly disagree, 2 = disagree, 3 = neutral, 4 = agree, 5 = strongly agree). The second set asks open-ended questions. What follows are examples of questions that can be modified to fit your context.

Questions for Scaled Responses

1. My coach is helping me improve my teaching practices.
2. My coach is helping me implement the [new curriculum, new instructional strategies, etc.].
3. My coach is helping me reach my goals.
4. It's been useful when my coach has observed me teaching.
5. My coach provides me with useful resources and materials when I ask for them.
6. My coach listens to me.

From The Art of Coaching Workbook: Tools to Make Every Conversation Count by Elena Aguilar. Copyright © 2021 by Elena Aguilar. Reproduced by permission.

7. My coach respects me.
8. My coach sees my potential.
9. I trust my coach.
10. I look forward to my meetings with my coach.

Open-Ended Questions

1. What are your coach's strengths?
2. Describe a time when you felt your coach was exceptionally helpful.
3. What else would you like from your coach? What do you wish they did more of?
4. Is there anything you'd like your coach not to do? Or to do less of?
5. Is there anything else you'd like your coach to know about your experience working together?
6. Is there any other feedback you'd like to provide your coach so that they can support you better?

Communicating with Clients About the Survey

Here are a few tips for talking about the survey with your clients:

- When you ask for feedback, emphasize that the purpose is to aid your development as a coach. This reminds them that you're a learner, too.
- Thank them for their feedback. If it's not anonymous, validate whatever they've shared (even if you didn't like it or disagreed with it). You can say something like, "I hear that you feel like I've been unresponsive when you've asked for help and I'm going to take that into consideration." Of course, you can also have a conversation with them about their feedback to gain deeper understanding.
- Make sure clients know that you received and read their feedback and that you'll act on it. There's nothing worse than offering a lot of feedback and feeling like it's being ignored. You can say, "I'm glad to hear that you trust me. That's so important to me. I also hear that you'd like me to do more frequent, but shorter observations. I can definitely do that. How about if I start next week?"

Using the Feedback

After you read your client's feedback, consider these questions:

- What do I feel good about in this feedback? What feels validating and affirming?
- What was surprising?
- What was hard to read?
- What felt true, but painful to read?
- What felt painful, but is probably not true?
- What feedback do I want to take action on?
- How does this feedback match up with my assessment of my coaching skills?
- Which areas of the Transformational Coaching Rubric does this feedback suggest I need to focus on?
- What do I want to do with this feedback?

It's probably obvious, but the reason you want to do this kind of survey every few months is that you need to see how you're developing and you need the longitudinal data. It's not that helpful to only get feedback at the end of the year, when you're closing up a coaching relationship. The purpose of feedback is to help you grow. Yes, you can grow in your next coaching relationship, but it's even more impactful if you can develop over the course of working with someone.

Reflect

What feels like the hardest part of gathering feedback?

What additional questions would you want to ask your clients on a survey?

What do you need to do to gather feedback from clients? What are your next steps?

From *The Art of Coaching Workbook: Tools to Make Every Conversation Count* by Elena Aguilar. Copyright © 2021 by Elena Aguilar. Reproduced by permission.

The Conscious Competence Ladder

Do this activity to deepen your understanding of the learning process and practice self-acceptance.

When we began coaching, we often found ourselves thinking, *Coaching is so much harder than I thought it would be.* This is a common reaction to being at the start of a learning process. When we first set out to learn something, we may not appreciate how much we need to learn. When we begin to see the breadth and depth of a new subject or skill, we can become disheartened. If you're feeling daunted by how much there is to learn about coaching—that's okay. What you're feeling is normal.

The Conscious Competence Ladder (Figure 14.1) is a framework that helps us understand four stages of learning. The theory was developed by Noel Burch in the 1970s, and the model highlights the factors that affect our thinking as we learn a new skill: consciousness (awareness) and skill level (competence). It identifies four levels that we move through as we build competence in a new skill:

- **Unconscious incompetence.** At this stage, we don't know that we don't have a skill or that we need to learn it. We are blissfully ignorant, and our confidence exceeds our abilities. Our task on this rung is to figure out what skills we need to learn because we just don't know what we don't know.
- **Conscious incompetence.** At this stage, we know we don't have the skills we're trying to acquire. We realize that others are much more competent and that they can easily do things that make us struggle. We can lose confidence at this stage or give up on our learning. This is when we most need to manage discomfort, fear, and anxiety, and to boost our confidence.
- **Conscious competence.** On this rung, we know that we have the skills we have worked to attain. As we put our knowledge and skill set into regular practice, we gain even more confidence. We still may need to concentrate when we perform these skills, but as we get more practice and experience, these activities become increasingly automatic. We need to use these skills as often as possible to move into the next stage.
- **Unconscious competence.** At this level, we don't know that we have the skills. We use our new skills effortlessly and perform tasks without conscious effort. We are confident of success. To keep growing, we need to teach these newly acquired skills to others. This deepens our understanding of the material and keeps our skills finely tuned; teaching the skills also can be rewarding. Be warned: We can go backward down the ladder if we don't regularly use our skills.

Figure 14.1: The Conscious Competence Ladder

UNCONSCIOUS
COMPETENCE

CONSCIOUS
COMPETENCE

CONSCIOUS
INCOMPETENCE

UNCONSCIOUS
INCOMPETENCE

CONSCIOUS COMPETENCE LADDER

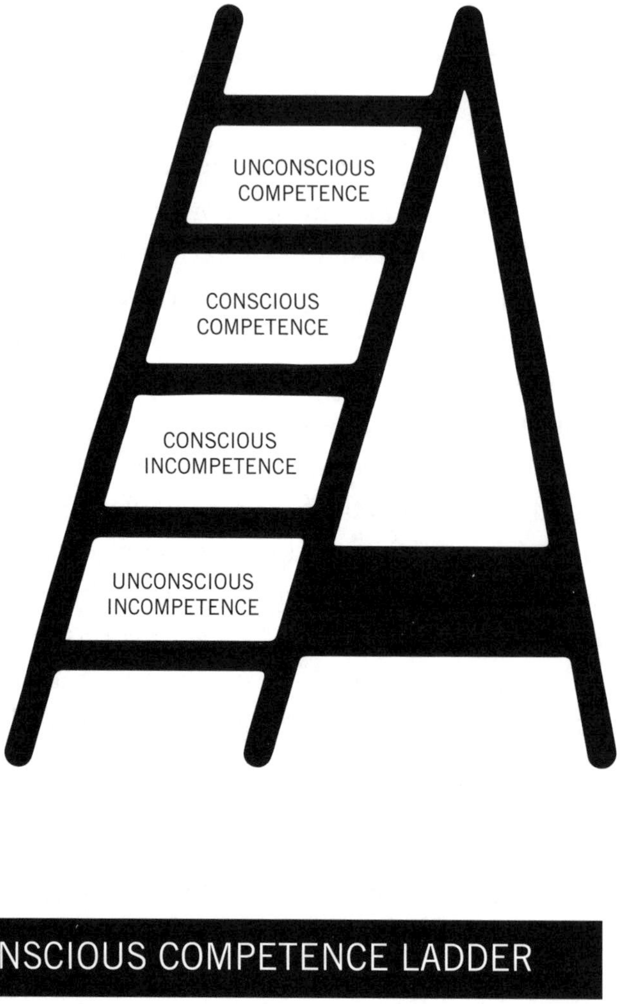

Normalizing the emotions along this learning process can help us stay motivated and manage our expectations. When you're on the *consciously incompetent* rung, reassure yourself that, even though learning a skill is difficult and frustrating, it will feel easier one day. And when you're *unconsciously competent*, remember to value the skills that you've gained and be patient with those who are still learning them.

Implications for Coaching Others

You can also use the Conscious Competence Ladder when guiding clients through a learning process. Here are some additional tips for each rung of the ladder:

- At the beginning of a process, people may not know how unskilled they are. You'll need to raise their awareness of how much there is to learn. Rubrics, exemplars, and artifacts that show the level of skill they need are useful. Give lots of positive feedback at this stage, help people see their strengths, and make sure to show clear and concrete models of high competence. Most importantly, normalize the experience of emotion at this stage.
- During the conscious incompetence stage, provide encouragement and support, and share the Conscious Competence Ladder. This helps learners understand feelings of discouragement and see that it's a phase they can move through. Use strategies to cultivate a growth mindset and keep reminding learners that they can't do whatever they're trying to do yet. *Yet* is the key word.
- At the conscious competence level, keep people focused on the skills they've learned and give them plenty of opportunities to practice those skills.
- When people become unconsciously competent, watch for complacency, offer opportunities to stay up-to-date with their skills, and invite them to teach their skills to others.

Reflect

In which coaching skills are you feeling consciously competent? (Reflective listening? Coaching behaviors? Cathartic questioning?)

What are a couple of coaching skills in which you feel consciously incompetent?

What insights does this framework give you into how you're feeling right now about your development as a coach?

Focal Person Reflection Tool

Do this activity to think deeply about one client through many thinking tools.

Select a client who you're stuck with, or uncertain how to guide them to meet their goals. Jot down their name or initials here:

Strengths-Based Coaching: Head, Heart, Hands

Area	Description and Examples
Head-based strengths	Knowledge of content, curriculum, instruction; analytical abilities and verbal skills; research-oriented, intellectually curious. This person is great at unit design, or budgeting, or creating a master schedule.
Heart-based strengths	Strong self-awareness and emotional intelligence; ability to form trusting relationships; passion, will, and commitment to a mission. This person remembers the names of students' parents, or boosts morale during hard times, or speaks up when there's tension in a team.
Hands-based strengths	The ability to get stuff done, take care of business, develop systems and structures; creative capabilities. This person organizes Back-to-School Night, or creates beautiful displays of student work, or has a very organized classroom.

What are my focal person's strengths? What are their head-based strengths, heart-based strengths, and hands-based strengths?

How could I leverage their strengths to support their areas for growth?

How could I help them see their own strengths? What kind of data could I gather and share? Would video help?

Mind the Gap

See Chapter 7 for the gaps.

I suspect my focal person might have these gaps:

Reasons I suspect they might have these gaps:

What would help me gain a deeper understanding of their gaps? Is there data I could collect? Questions I could ask them?

What are my gaps when it comes to working with this person?

Spheres of Control

See Chapter 7.

How might I use the spheres of control and influence with this person?

How might the spheres of control help me figure out where to focus my work with this person?

What kind of control and influence do I have when it comes to working with this person?

Next Steps

Which other thinking tools, or concepts in this workbook, would be helpful for me to use to better understand and serve this person? The coaching lenses? The content about emotions? What else?

What are three next steps I can take to better understand and coach my focal person? Fill in the following table.

What I'll do	When I'll do it by	Notes

CHAPTER 15

Facilitating Professional Development for Coaches

We hope that you are using the tools and exercises in this workbook with a team of coaches. Coaching is a social learning process, and it only follows that we become better coaches by developing our practice with others. We advocate for coaches to have time each week for their professional development (PD)—to carve it out or insist on having it. In this chapter, we explore how you can use this workbook and a handful of protocols to learn alongside other coaches. We illustrate this with sample plans for professional development sessions that range from 1 hour to a full day. Unlike previous chapters, this one does not include activities for you to complete. Rather, we invite you to use these resources to design PD for yourself or a group of coaches.

Protocols to Guide Your Learning

Protocols serve a number of functions in designing and facilitating learning. They help:

- use time efficiently;
- clarify expectations and agreements within the group about how the conversation will take place;
- strengthen learners' skill in collaboration and contribute to a safe learning environment; and
- balance power dynamics and personality differences to ensure more balanced participation within the group.

The point of a protocol is not to "do the protocol well" or to use a tool to control people but to have a rich conversation that will lead to new insights and expanded capacity for all learners.

We've got five protocols to share with you that we have found to be particularly effective in building coaches' skill and self-awareness.

Table 15.1: Protocols for Building Skill and Self-Awareness

Protocol	Description
Role-play protocol	Use this protocol to prepare for upcoming conversations, to practice using new coaching skills or tools, to hear how another coach might work with your client, or to experiment with different techniques to support a tricky client.
Consultancy protocol	Use this protocol to work through dilemmas that arise in your coaching and to practice using the thinking tools (e.g., mind the gap, the coaching lenses).
Artifact analysis protocol	Use this protocol with a transcript, recording, survey data, or any other artifact, when you want to see your coaching in a new light, when you feel you've stalled in your growth as a coach, or when you want to take your coaching to the next level.
Text discussion protocol	Use this protocol to discuss a text with colleagues and consider implications for your work. This could be a chapter in *The Art of Coaching*, an article, book chapter, or even a written transcript of a coaching conversation.
Being present protocols	Use these protocols to practice being fully present, a core foundational skill for Transformational Coaching. While useful anytime, it is especially helpful to practice being present at the start of a learning experience, before coaching, after intense moments, and during transitions.

In addition to these five protocols, we draw on these invaluable resources:

- Liberating structures: We especially like 1-2-4-All, 9 Whys, Heard Seen Respected, Improv Prototyping, Troika Consulting, and Wicked Questions. Available as a book or at http://www.liberatingstructures.com.
- The National School Reform Faculty: We especially like Chalk Talk, Diversity rounds, Dyads, Final Word, Four As, Making Meaning, and Three Levels of Text. See http://www.nsrfharmony.org/protocols.
- Session Lab: We especially like their Energizer activities, but this site is a treasure trove of useful and easy-to-implement protocols. See http://www.sessionlab.com/library.

Preparing for Role-Playing

Role-playing is the most powerful practice for improving your coaching. We know, it's scary and feels uncomfortable, but it will catapult your coaching skills to higher levels. Ideally, role-playing happens in trios, over the course of a couple of hours. Or, if a group of coaches convene weekly, each week a different person could be the coach.

There are a couple steps to get set up for role-playing.

Step 1

- Each person decides what scenario or situation they want to practice when they are the coach and plans for this scenario using the prompts for individual planning. Your group could agree to use prepared scenarios, like the ones on pages 474, or you could bring your own scenario that you want to practice. If you bring your own scenario, it helps if your trio members are familiar with the context in which you coach and perhaps even some of your clients. It might feel most authentic and useful for you to practice coaching Mr. T, let's say, who is an AP chemistry teacher who has been teaching for 30 years and is also a football coach. But if your colleague Janie is going to "be" him in the role-play, and she's taught kindergarten for only 2 years, it might be hard for her to really "be" Mr. T. Especially when the purpose of the role-playing is practice a coaching strategy rather than to practice a specific situation, it's more impactful to use a scripted scenario.
- Each person plans for how they'll coach.

Step 2

- The group makes decisions about what order each person will coach in and about start and stop times. Each person fills out the template.
- The group role-plays, following the protocol on page 472.

Individual Planning

Determine the scenario you want to practice when you are the coach. Then plan for your turn playing the coach.

Do you have a goal for the conversation or a direction you'd like it to go in? What do you hope will happen in the conversation?

What's one thinking tool that you'd like to keep in mind during the conversation? Options include mind the gap, the spheres of influence, and strengths-based coaching.

Which coaching stems do you want to incorporate into the conversation?

How do you want to show up, or to be, in this conversation? What do you hope to communicate in your disposition?

When you coach, what do you want feedback on? Pick one! Options include:

- ☐ Usage of reflective listening
- ☐ How much time they speak or hold silence
- ☐ Nonverbal communication
- ☐ Evidence of coaching the three Bs (behaviors, beliefs, ways of being)
- ☐ Cultivating resilience
- ☐ Coaching toward empowerment
- ☐ Balance between directive and facilitative questioning
- ☐ Other:

Group Planning

Three people are ideal for a role-play: one plays the coach, another play the client, and the third is an observer. If a group has four people, there can be two observers. When it's your turn, you are the coach.

Note that the observer will take notes and script key phrases that the coach says. They will offer feedback on the areas that the coach shares that they want feedback on. In Figure 15.1, you'll see a sample note-taking template for the observer.

Each person shares which scenario they are going to practice (if you're using a scripted one like those on p. 474–478). Then determine the order of coaching, roles, and time allocations. Each person should fill out this template so that everyone is clear on the steps and roles.

	Scenario number	Start and end time	Coach	Client	Observer
Round 1					
Round 2					
Break					
Round 3					
Round 4*					

*If your group has four people, do four rounds.

Figure 15.1: Note-Taking Template for Observer

Observer's Notes

Coach:

Scenario or situation:

Area in which the coach wants feedback:
- ☐ Usage of reflective listening
- ☐ How much time they speak or hold silence
- ☐ Nonverbal communication
- ☐ Evidence of coaching the three Bs (behaviors, beliefs, ways of being)
- ☐ Cultivating resilience
- ☐ Coaching toward empowerment
- ☐ Balance between directive and facilitative questioning
- ☐ Other:

Role-Play Protocol

This is the protocol we use most often.

Activity	Description	Time 30 min.	Time 20 min.
ROLE-PLAY PROTOCOL			
Set up	☐ Coach: Name the scenario (either a scripted scenario or one you want to practice). ☐ Coach: Tell the observer what you want feedback on. ☐ Observer: Note what the coach wants feedback on. Prepare to script. ☐ Coach: May ask the "client" to be a specific way, (i.e., "be resistant to my suggestions"). ☐ May ask the "client" to review a scripted scenario description.	3	1
Role-play	☐ Coach and client role-play. Don't stop role-playing to talk about the situation—stay in the role-play. ☐ Observer scripts what coach says and keep track of time.	12	10
Reflection	☐ Observer: review notes and prepare feedback. Remember to offer feedback based on what the coach requested. ☐ Optional: Coach and client can debrief, but not within listening distance to the observer who needs quiet concentration right now.	3	2
Debrief	☐ Observer shares observations and feedback. ☐ Client shares observations. ☐ Coach reflects on role-play.	12	7

Extension options and tips:

- If time allows, extend the time for role-playing and debriefing. There's always much more to say in the debrief section.
- Trio can switch roles and practice the same scenario again.
- If the coach wants, they can "rewind" to a specific point and can resume coaching.
- Coach can hit the pause button and can ask the observer for help if they get stuck.
- At the same time, try to push through the challenging parts of conversations and keep going.
- Remember, it's a role-play. Have fun!

Coaching Role-Play Scenarios

Here's an overview of the five scenarios we've scripted for you. On the following pages, you'll read a longer description written for the client, or teacher, in these scenarios. This might be helpful in role-playing that person.

1. The struggling new teacher: This teacher is overwhelmed by everything, dealing with common challenges for new teachers, and struggling to focus and prioritize what to work on.
2. The "Everything is great!" teacher: This teacher is stuck in routines and "how I've always done it," and doesn't want coaching—doesn't see the need for it.
3. The teacher with a deficit mindset: This teacher often uses the phrase "these kids" with a negative connotation. They talk about high expectations but instruction isn't rigorous. They come from a different background than their students.
4. Disempowered teacher: This teacher often complains about the administration and all the changes; feels unappreciated and not listened to and feels like coaching is a waste of time.
5. Emotionally distraught teacher: This is a midcareer teacher who is questioning whether or not to stay in teaching. They might be on the road to burnout or may be depressed.

Struggling New Teacher

Description

You are a first-year teacher struggling with the workload and the emotional strain of teaching. You're new to the community that you're teaching in. You feel like you're underserving your students because you're so new and struggling and you are questioning whether you should be a teacher. You've wanted to be a teacher for a long time—and although you knew it would be hard, you didn't think it would be *this* hard.

You're dealing with many common challenges—prioritizing, keeping track of assessments, report cards, other deadlines and administrative work, occasionally managing the classroom, keeping your classroom organized, and so on. You're also not seeing the results you want to be seeing from your students—it seems like they aren't learning as fast as you'd hoped and you're not sure why.

Sometimes when you talk to your coach you go all over the place—from worrying about whether you are doing right by your kids to complaining about the colleagues who talk poorly about kids. When you're asked what you want to work on in coaching, you sometimes suggest things like project-based learning, Socratic seminars, or other things you've heard about that you feel you should offer your students. Overall, you trust your coach and have a good relationship with her. She was assigned to you because you're a first-year teacher.

Your strengths are your passion for teaching, your commitment, and your enthusiasm.

Timeline

This conversation takes place in mid-November of your first year of teaching.

Notes

- The grade level and content for this teacher is up to you.
- You are welcome to "be" any way that you want—get really emotional if you want or be more withdrawn and less communicative.
- You're a bit impatient with yourself—and hard on yourself. You might have perfectionist tendencies.

The "Everything Is Great!" Teacher

Description

You've been teaching elementary school for 17 years, and you have a somewhat traditional, but high functioning classroom. You still give spelling tests on Fridays, you do a lot of textbook-based reading and teaching, and you are suspicious of all of these new strategies that teachers are using. Students are compliant, you don't deal with behavior issues, and enough students pass your class (although that's also because of how you grade—which isn't based on mastery of standards).

Sometimes you feel like you should know what others are talking about when they reference things like *sheltered instruction* or *AVID strategies*, and you feel embarrassed that you don't. You are masking a number of knowledge and skill gaps in your practice. The student population in your district has shifted in the last decade and there are small groups of English learner students now.

You don't feel like you need or want coaching. It was assigned to you because everyone in the school gets coaching at some point during the year. You're very friendly to your coach, but you don't implement the things you two talk about. You're not really interested in reflecting on your own practice. You feel uncomfortable with having the coach observe you.

Your strengths are that you have deep knowledge of the community, you have a lot of relationships with students and parents, and you have persevered through many changes in the district. You're still there. That counts. You're also organized and have developed many strong, basic routines. You could mentor new teachers—but no one has ever asked you to.

Timeline

This conversation takes place in September.

Teacher with Deficit Mindset

Description

You have been teaching for 3 years in a community that is different (racially and socio-economically) from the one you were raised in. You describe yourself as having high expectations for kids. You set big goals for student growth, and you share those with your class.

You are definitely the one doing the heavy cognitive lifting in this class—although you purport to value rigor. The tasks that students are given are low on Bloom's and Webb's depth of knowledge. There's a lot of memorization (e.g., "They just have to memorize the multiplication tables!"). The content that they explore is also often low in relevance to students, and as a result there's often low student engagement. There may be compliance but not engagement.

Your coach was assigned to work with you on incorporating strategies to support English learners. You meet every other week.

Frequently when talking with your coach, you use the phrase *these kids* coupled with some kind of deficit reference. For example, when your coach suggested that you incorporate discussion structures, you said, "Well, that might work for the kids in Ms. T's class, but these kids need much more structure. They can't handle it when I loosen up."

Your strengths are that your classroom is organized, instruction is very structured and routine, and you have developed strong routines for assessment. You also do have a value around rigor and high expectations.

Timeline

This conversation takes place in January of your third year of teaching.

Notes

- The grade level and content for this teacher is up to you. You choose what grade level/content you are teaching.

- You are a bit arrogant—or convinced that what you are doing is right. You feel that you have the answers and knowledge about what kids need. You might get irritated if I push on what you're saying.

Disempowered Teacher

Description

Every time you turn around there's something new—and now it's coaching, which is supposed to solve every problem in your school. You've been teaching for 8 years, and you've done a good job in spite of constantly changing administrations, two new superintendents, new standards, new assessments, and so on. The latest set of administrators have launched a whole slew of new programs and initiatives—in fact, they announced that your school has 12 "top priority" goals for this school year.

You feel like a victim—of unprepared and naïve administrators; of the dysfunctional district; of federal education policy. You feel like you have a lot of experience, you know what your kids need, you know what works—and you feel like your experience and expertise isn't listened to. You're not enthusiastic about coaching—it's not what your school needs (it needs to focus on student behavior, you believe). Students are out of control, admin isn't paying attention to the right things, and you have no control over what goes on. You feel powerless and are starting to feel hopeless.

Your coach is supposed to work with teachers on integrating technology and supporting English learners—the district received a grant to fund coaching in these two areas. You feel like this is a waste of time and resources.

Your strengths are that you've stuck through a lot of changes, you do care about kids—and once really loved teaching.

Timeline

This conversation takes place in October.

Notes

- The grade level and content for this teacher is up to you. You choose what grade level/content you are teaching.
- When portraying this teacher, you are welcome to "be" any way that you want—you could get really emotional if you want, or you could be more withdrawn and less communicative. You are welcome to cry or get mad at the coach.

Emotionally Distraught Teacher

Description

You are a midcareer year teacher, and you are having a really hard time. There was a fight in your classroom today, your principal gave you low ratings on your latest observation, your grade-level team is constantly bickering with each other, and you just don't think you can "do this anymore." You work all the time—you have no social life, you never exercise, you skip lunch—and you never feel like you're doing enough.

You expected your first year or two to be like this, but now in your (third, fourth, eighth...) year it just feels impossible. You are seriously thinking about whether you should quit because you also don't feel like you're doing much of anything good for kids: "A sub would probably be better for them," you say. But you also say, "I'm not a quitter."

In your classroom, you are aware that sometimes things are disorganized. You lack some basic routines and procedures. You spend a lot of time at school but aren't sure what you're doing with that time—you often don't plan lessons. You often feel unfocused and scattered.

Your strengths are that you are really passionate about teaching, you care deeply about kids, and you devote a lot of time to teaching. Your heart is in the right place, and you truly want to be a teacher.

Timeline

This conversation takes place in October.

Notes

- The grade level and content for this teacher is up to you. You choose what grade level/ content you are teaching.
- When portraying this teacher, you are welcome to "be" any way that you want—you could get really emotional if you want, or you could be more withdrawn and less communicative. You are welcome to cry or get mad at me (your coach) or anything else.

Consultancy Protocol

Why This Protocol

One of the best ways to internalize the Transformational Coaching thinking tools is in consultation with other coaches. Using the tools in a consultancy builds the mental muscles needed to use them effectively during coaching. As an added bonus, consultancies are an effective way to harness the collective wisdom of your team to support each another through the dilemmas that arise in your practice. Use this protocol to work through dilemmas that arise in your coaching and to practice using the thinking tools (e.g., mind the gap, the coaching lenses).

Minimum Requirements

Time: 30–60 minutes per person
Number of people: 3–10 people

Process

30 min.	45 min.	60 min.	WHAT	How
1	2	1	**Opening**	Facilitator reviews protocol and adjusts time as desired by presenter or as fits the group. The group may decide to spend more time on the preparation section, or in the discussion. Timing also depends on how many are in the group.
(5)	(5)	(5)	**Previous presenter report back** *(optional)*	Optional: the person who presented the previous time this group met can report on how they used the ideas generated in their consultancy.
(2)	(3)	(5)	**Presenter preparation** *(optional)*	Presenter can do a quick write or think about what they'd like to ask the group for support on. Presenter can also come prepared with something written that communicates the dilemma. If a presenter knows ahead of time that they'll be engaging in a consultancy, this stage may not be needed.

From *The Art of Coaching Workbook: Tools to Make Every Conversation Count* by Elena Aguilar. Copyright © 2021 by Elena Aguilar. Reproduced by permission.

30 min.	45 min.	60 min.	WHAT	How
5	8	9	**Presenter shares**	1. Presenter shares the dilemma—this can be verbally shared or offered in a written document. If a written description is shared, presenter can add anything they'd like before or after the group reads the document. It's appropriate for the group members to take notes about what they're hearing. 2. Presenter can ask for feedback or input in one area or key question. Asking for specific feedback or support can help a discussion stay focused and useful.
3	5	5	**Clarifying questions**	Group asks presenter clarifying questions. • Clarifying questions are yes-no or require very short answers. • Facilitator needs to interrupt if probing questions are asked and can remind the group that probing questions can be noted and raised during the discussion.
5	8	5–18	**Group reflection and preparation** Silent planning and reading time	1. The presenter can ask for the group to use a thinking tool, such as the coaching lenses (or the group may have decided to do so already). If using the lenses, the facilitator also takes a lens. 2. Facilitator restates the presenter's request for specific feedback or input on one area if this was requested. 3. Group members silently reflect on the presenter's dilemma and prepare for discussion. It's appropriate for group members to note questions and comments to contribute in the discussion. 4. In the final 2 minutes, facilitator prompts participants to write out the one big insight from their lens.

30 min.	45 min.	60 min.	WHAT	How
12	18	20	**Group fishbowl discussion**	1. Presenter moves their chair outside of the circle and can take notes if desired. 2. Facilitator reminds the group of the presenter's key question. 3. Facilitator opens this section by asking each group member briefly (in about 1 minute) to share their initial thoughts on the dilemma. A whip around allows everyone to share one initial thought. 4. Following the whip around, a less structured discussion unfolds. Group members can raise probing questions, share further insights they gained through using the thinking tools, and share other comments or reflections. 5. Facilitator needs to ensure that discussion stays focused on the presenter's dilemma and if requested, on their key question. Facilitator may also need to take action to ensure equitable participation.
1	1	1	**One minute of silence**	Group holds 1 minute of silence so that the presenter can collect their thoughts.
3	6	6	**Closing**	Presenter shares any reactions, insights, feelings about protocol or what was said; they don't need to respond to questions that were raised in the group discussion. If time permits, the group can share reflections on the experience of using the protocol.

Tips

- Designate a facilitator to manage the timed transitions through the protocol.
- The larger the group size, the more time you will need to ensure a rich conversation and balanced participation across the group.
- This protocol is particularly useful when the group incorporates a specific thinking tool during reflection and dialogue. Each person can use the entire tool, just a piece of it (e.g., if using the coaching lenses, only the lens of systems thinking), or you can

divide it among participants (e.g., each person focuses on one to two lenses). These are useful tools to try:

- ☐ The coaching lenses
- ☐ Mind the gap
- ☐ The coaching stances
- ☐ Strengths-based coaching
- ☐ The ladder of inference
- ☐ Spheres of control

- If conducting the consultancy virtually, it can be helpful to have the presenter turn off their webcam during the group discussion. If you are in person, have the presenter turn away from the group. This enables the presenter to fully experience the conversation, without needing to respond or manage their reactions. Likewise, it keeps the group tuned to one another and the dilemma, rather than engaging in dialogue with the presenter.

Artifact Analysis Protocol

Why This Protocol

Just as it is important to ground your coaching in data that you and your client collect, it is important to regularly review authentic artifacts from your coaching to illuminate habits, beliefs, and ways of being that might be limiting your effectiveness. Examining our practice with fellow coaches has the added benefit of enabling a shared understanding of effective coaching and the language to describe it. Use this protocol when you want to see your coaching in a new light, when you feel you've stalled in your growth as a coach, or when you want to take your coaching to the next level.

Minimum Requirements

Time: 30 minutes
Number of people: 1+

Before Create the artifact	*Strategize*	What is your learning goal in engaging in this analysis? Sample learning goals could include practicing a new questioning strategy, reducing your talk time in coaching, building more trusting relationships with clients, or completing the full arc of Transformational Coaching. Once you have a goal, what kind of artifacts will best support that goal? How, when, and with whom will you create the artifact? Here are four useful types of artifacts: • Video or audio recording of a coaching conversation • Transcript of a coaching conversation • Survey data from current or former clients • Observational data from another coach watching you live
	Create	Once you've strategically chosen your artifact, it's time to create it. If using audio or video, test for sound quality. If gathering survey data, have a coach colleague offer feedback on your survey before sending it out. A colleague might even collect responses on your behalf to ensure clients feel comfortable sharing honest responses. If another coach will be observing you coach, agree in advance on the observational data you'd like them to collect (e.g., stances used, coach talk time).

During Learn from the artifact	*First look*	The first time you engage with the artifact you've created is about getting acclimated with what it reveals. Seeing our practice laid bare can sometimes elicit strong emotions, judgment, and shame. It can also be a rich and powerful learning experience! Use your first look to remind yourself of your
	Second look	If working alone, we recommend written reflection at this stage. What does the artifact reveal in response to the learning goals you identified for this activity? If working with others, be sure to share your learning goals before they engage with the artifact. What strengths do they notice? What insights do they have into your goal? You might use the consultancy protocol at this stage to analyze the artifact. Or you and your colleagues might role-play something you want to practice, given what you've identified in the artifact.
After Apply your learning	*Plan*	After analyzing your artifact, write down your top three to five insights into your learning goal. Next, identify one to two steps you can take in the next 2 weeks to act on your insights. What adjustments do you want to make in your coaching? How will you hold yourself accountable to making them?
	Reflect	After 2 weeks, reflect on the impact of the adjustments you've made in your coaching. What differences do you notice in yourself? In your clients? In their impact on others? How can you continue developing your learning goal? You might decide at this point to begin the artifact analysis process all over again!

Tips

- If you prefer to work with written transcripts, several companies offer affordable, high-quality, computer-generated transcription services. We have used temi.com and been pleased with the results. Alternatively, you could do limited transcription such as scripting only the questions the coach poses.
- If your video involves filming children (e.g., while modeling part of a lesson for a teacher), be sure to check the policies in your school or district for parental consent.

Text Discussion Protocol

Why This Protocol

While Transformational Coaches rely on a solid base of skills, some concepts and frameworks can serve to deepen self-awareness and expand our ability to analyze the challenges clients bring. Use this protocol to discuss a text with colleagues and consider implications for your work. This could be a chapter in *The Art of Coaching*, an article, book chapter, or a transcript of a coaching conversation. This protocol is adapted from the "Three Levels of Text" protocol created by the National School Reform Faculty.

Minimum Requirements

Time: Up to 35 minutes + reading time
Number of people: Possible with 2, ideally 3–4 people per discussion

---

Purpose:
- ☐ To deepen understanding of a text and explore implications for participants' work.

Roles:
- ☐ Facilitator/timekeeper (who also participates).

Facilitation Tips:
- ☐ Stick to the time limits. Each round takes up to 5 minutes per person in a group.
- ☐ Emphasize the need to watch air time during the brief "group response" segment.

Process

1. Each person individually reads a text, highlighting significant passages related to the topic and identifying one section that they want to talk about.
2. Each person has a turn to speak and takes 2–3 minutes to read the passage they have selected aloud and shares:

   - How they interpret the passage or what connections they made
   - Any implications for their work

3. After one person shares, the group responds (for a total of up to 2 minutes) to what that person said.

From *The Art of Coaching Workbook: Tools to Make Every Conversation Count* by Elena Aguilar. Copyright © 2021 by Elena Aguilar. Reproduced by permission.

4. The next person shares their section, and the group responds for up to 2 minutes.
5. After each person has shared, open into an unstructured discussion about the article.

Tips

- This protocol works best for texts no longer than a typical book chapter. It is also preferable to use texts that offer some measure of interpretation or opinion.
- If using this protocol with a coaching transcript, consider using a standard form of annotation, such as those found in this workbook. You could also code for which coaching stance is being used, which learning gaps are evident, and so on.
- This protocol can also be used with podcasts, of which there are a growing number relevant to coaching (including ours at Bright Morning!). In this case, each person should transcribe up to three passages to share during discussion.

Being Present Protocols

Coaching is as much about presence as it is about knowledge or technique. We define presence as having our whole selves—thoughts, feelings, and sensations—fully tuned to the client, to our own wisdom, and to the greater good that is emerging through coaching. Presence is the antidote to distraction, judgment, fear, control, and all that can undermine our effectiveness as coaches. To summon the focus needed to stay present throughout a conversation, particularly those that challenge us, we must regularly practice presence. Use these protocols to practice being fully present, a core foundational skill for Transformational Coaching. Though it is useful anytime, it is especially helpful to practice being present at the start of a learning experience, before coaching, after intense moments, and during transitions.

Minimum Requirements

Time: 2 or more minutes
People: 1+

Process

Option 1: Connect with the Breath

- Place your feet flat on the floor and take a deep breath. Feel the floor rising up to support you. If you're seated, feel the chair doing the same.
- As you feel ready, close your eyes or take a soft focus.
- Place one hand on your stomach and the other over your chest. Take a few deep breaths.
- Notice whether you feel the breath more in the belly or in the chest. Slowly invite the breath to settle down into the belly. [Pause]
- Continue breathing and this time, at the top of your inhalation, pause for a count of 2. Slowly exhale. At the bottom of the exhalation, pause for a count of 2. Continue in this manner. [Pause]
- You can continue with this pattern, or, if you're feeling calm and ready, gradually move toward breathing in for a count of 5, holding for 5, breathing out for 5, and holding for 5. In 5, hold 5, out 5, hold 5. [Pause for 1–2 minutes]
- As you're ready, slowly bring your attention back into the room, noticing the sounds, smells, and sights around you as you open your eyes. [Pause]
- What do you notice about your experience of this present moment?

Option 2: Do a Body Scan

- Place your feet flat on the floor and take a few deep breaths.
- As you feel ready, close your eyes or take a soft focus.
- Allow your attention to sink down into the body, into the soles of your feet. Notice the sensation of your feet on the floor, in their socks or shoes. Feel their "feetness."
- Slowly allow your attention to rise, exploring each part of your body. Feel your ankles. . . your calves. . . your knees.
- Feel into the sensations of each area. Is it warm or cool? Active or still? Open or contracted?
- Slowly move up through the body. If you reach an area with no sensation, linger there. [Pause]
- When you've explored the heart area and the chest, slowly move out through the arms and into the hands, before heading to the shoulders, neck, and head. [Pause for 1–2 minutes]
- Take a moment to return to any parts of the body that would like a little extra attention. [Pause]
- As you're ready, slowly bring your attention back into the room, noticing the sounds, smells, and sights around you as you open your eyes. [Pause]
- What do you notice about your experience of this present moment?

Tips

- If using one of the scripts above, it can be helpful for one person to facilitate the exercise for others. Rotate who in your group holds this role, so you each get practice, as these exercises can also be helpful to lead with clients.

Sample 1-Hour Professional Development Sessions

Effective learning experiences include at least one of the following elements:

1. exposure to new concepts or skills
2. practice with feedback
3. reflection and meaning-making

Ideally, PD for coaches includes all three elements, for which you may need more than an hour. But if an hour is all you have, you can structure meaningful learning.

In this section, we'll show you a template that you can use to create a 1-hour PD session for each of these three learning experiences, and then we'll give you an example or two of that PD session. You might notice that the layout for the agendas differs slightly from what Elena recommends in *The Art of Coaching Teams*. Here we're offering a simplified version of what's in that book—of course, feel free to adapt this so that it includes the additional elements that Elena recommends our agendas include.

Exposure to New Concepts or Skills

In Table 15.1 you'll see a template of an hour-long PD session for a session in which you are engaging with new concepts or skills. In Table 15.2, you'll see an example of this session. We're providing you with the template so that you can duplicate it and the example so that you have some concrete ideas—or so that you can use that exact PD plan yourself!

Practice with Feedback

In Table 15.3 you'll see a template of an hour-long PD session for a session in which you are *practicing with feedback*. In Tables 15.4 and 15.5, you'll see an example of this session. We're providing you with the template so that you can duplicate it, and the example so that you have some concrete ideas—or so that you can use that exact PD plan yourself!

Reflection and Meaning-Making

In Table 15.6 you'll see a template of an hour-long PD session for a session in which you are *engaging with new concepts or skills*. In Table 15.7, you'll see an example of this session. We're providing you with the template so that you can duplicate it, and the example so that you have some concrete ideas—or so that you can use that exact PD plan yourself!

Table 15.1: Hour-Long PD Session Template: Exposure to New Concepts or Skills

Objective: Explore a New Concept or Skill		
What	**Time**	**Description**
Opening	5–8 min.	Invitation to share one word to describe the energy each person brings to the group. Review group norms and the session's objective and agenda. Learners set a personal intention for the session.
Introduction to the topic	5–10 min.	Elicit the wisdom of the group. What do people know about the topic already? What have they already tried in their coaching practice? What questions do they have? How will learning more about the topic enhance their practice?
New content	10–20 min.	Bring new ideas into the group, such as a short text, a video, a presentation, or a graphic.
Meaning or application	20–27 min.	Write independently or discuss the new content in pairs or trios. How does this new content help address our questions and needs? If possible, apply or practice in some way (e.g., a short role-play, an exercise from this workbook, scripting, planning).
Closing	5 min.	Each person captures their key takeaways and next steps in writing, and then shares a sentence or a word with the group that captures their biggest learning.

Table 15.2: Example of Hour-Long PD Session for Exposure to New Concepts or Skills

Objective: Coaches will develop a more nuanced understanding of the confrontational stance and its uses.		
What	**Time**	**Description**
Prework	15–20 min.	Read *The Art of Coaching* pp. 195–203
Opening	5–8 min.	Invitation to share one word to describe the energy each person brings to the group. Review group norms and the session's objective and agenda. Learners set a personal intention for the session.
Introduction to the topic	10 min.	• Independent writing (2 min.): When am I likely experience confrontation as positive? When am likely to experience it as negative? • Pair share (4 min.): Exchange responses. • Whole group (4 min.): How have we experimented with the confrontational stance in our coaching? When has it worked? What questions or concerns do we have about using it?

Table 15.2: (Continued)

Objective: Coaches will develop a more nuanced understanding of the confrontational stance and its uses.		
What	**Time**	**Description**
New content	15 min.	Read the transcript of a coaching conversation in Chapter 4. Reflect on the coach's use of the confrontational stance. What forms does it take? What is the impact of using it?
Pair share	5 min.	What did you notice about the coach's use of the confrontational stance?
Application	10–15 min.	On a notecard, each person writes a belief they've heard or could anticipate hearing that might be worth unpacking with a coach. For example, "I'm just not sure these students can read grade-level texts." Pass cards to the person on your left. Using the confrontational coaching stems, write a question or phrase the coach could use if responding from the confrontational stance. Repeat twice for a total of three responses on each card. Pass the cards once more. Each person reads the statements on their card and the proposed responses.
Whole group discussion	5–10 min.	How can the reading, the transcript, and the exercise we just did help us address the questions and concerns we have about using the confrontational stance? What can we commit to trying?
Closing	5 min.	Each person captures their key takeaways and next steps in writing, then shares a sentence or a word with the group that captures their biggest learning.

Table 15.3: Hour-Long PD Session Template: Practice with Feedback

Objective: Practice with Feedback		
What	**Time**	**Description**
Opening	5–8 min.	Invitation to share one word to describe the energy each person brings to the group. Review group norms and the session's objective and agenda. Learners set a personal intention for the session.
Set up the practice	5 min.	Discuss the purpose of the practice and the specific skills that it will develop. Review the process you will follow (e.g., steps and timing of a protocol, grouping, roles).

(Continued)

Table 15.3: (Continued)

Objective: Practice with Feedback		
What	**Time**	**Description**
Run the practice	35 min.	If needed, split into groups of two to four people. During practice, we recommend protocols like the role-play protocol, the consultancy protocol, the artifact analysis protocol, and the discussion protocol (all of which are in this chapter).
Feedback and reflection	10 min.	** Steps 3 and 4 could be combined so that each person receives feedback and reflects on their learning after their turn practicing. In this case, we also recommend holding 5 minutes for small or whole group reflection at the end.
Closing	5 min.	Each person captures their key takeaways and next steps in writing, then shares a sentence or a word with the group that captures their biggest learning.

Table 15.4: Example of Hour-Long PD Session: Practice with Feedback

Objective: Coaches will build skill using the mind the gap framework to identify a client's learning needs.		
What	**Time**	**Description**
Prework	20–30 min.	Read the mind the gap article and graphic organizer available on the Bright Morning website. Select one person in the group to share an authentic dilemma from their coaching practice.
Opening	5 min.	Invitation to share one word to describe the energy each person brings to the group. Review group norms and the session's objective and agenda. Learners set a personal intention for the session.
Set up the practice	5 min.	Review the consultancy protocol (found in this chapter).
Run the practice	45 min.	Use the 45-minute timing for the protocol.
Closing	5 mins.	Each person captures their key takeaways and next steps in writing, then shares a sentence or a word with the group that captures their biggest learning.

Table 15.5: Example of Hour-Long PD Session: Practice with Feedback

Objective: Coaches will build our self-awareness as listeners and skill in quiet listening.		
What	**Time**	**Description**
Opening	5 min.	Invitation to share one word to describe the energy each person brings to the group. Review group norms and the session's objective and agenda. Learners set a personal intention for the session.
Practice round 1	15 min.	Who am I as a listener? (15 min.) • Complete the activity on p. 227 in this workbook. • Pair share: Exchange one to two observations from your responses to the activity.
Practice round 2	15 min.	Listening to your listening • Review the table on p. 244 of this workbook. Complete the reflection questions. • Select one person in the group to talk for 4 minutes or play a short video. Each person tallies the mental journeys they take while listening. • Pair share: What insights are you having into who you are as a listener?
Practice round 3	15 min.	Dyads • Divide into pairs. Each person speaks for 4 minutes while the other listens quietly. (See the Bright Morning website for additional guidance on running dyads.) • After each person has spoken, debrief in pairs: What did it feel like to listen in this way? What did it feel like to be listened to in this way? What insights are you having about yourself as a listener?
Closing	10 min.	• Each person captures their key takeaways and next steps in writing. • Whole group: Exchange takeaways and next steps. • Last word: Each person shares one or two words that reflect a commitment they want to make to continue growing as a listener.

Table 15.6: Hour-Long PD Session Template: Reflection and Meaning-Making

Objective: Reflection and Meaning-Making		
What	**Time**	**Description**
Opening	5–8 min.	Invitation to share one word to describe the energy each person brings to the group. Review group norms and the session's objective and agenda. Learners set a personal intention for the session.
Introduction to the topic	5–10 min.	What beliefs and understanding about the topic do I bring into this conversation? How is this topic present in my coaching practice? What questions do I have? How will learning more about the topic enhance my practice?
Reflection protocol	30–40 min.	Use one or more exercises from this book or pull from another source.
Group debrief (optional)	10 min.	If not included in the protocol, ensure time for the group to synthesize key themes in the reflection and to identify questions that need further learning or reflection.
Closing	5 min.	Each person captures their key takeaways and next steps in writing, then shares a sentence or a word with the group that captures their biggest learning.

Table 15.7: Example of Hour-Long PD Session: Reflection and Meaning-Making

Objective: Coaches will write a vision for coaching that reflect our unique gifts and aligns to our school's definition of coaching.		
What	**Time**	**Description**
Opening	5–8 min.	Invitation to share one word to describe the energy each person brings to the group. Review group norms and the session's objective and agenda. Learners set a personal intention for the session.
Introduction to the topic	10 min.	• Read the example vision and mission statements on p. 39 of this workbook • Trios: What do we notice about these statements? What inspires us? What questions do they raise?

Table 15.7: (Continued)

What	Time	Description
Reflection protocol	30 min.	• Pair share: Take turns responding orally to the five reflective prompts in "Toward a Coaching Mission and Vision." As you listen to your partner, identify themes in their responses, moments when their energy increases, or anything else that stands out to you. • Each partner reflects what they heard using the prompt, "It sounds to me like, as a coach, what matters deeply to you is _____." • Independent writing time. Craft a first draft of a mission or vision statement on a large sheet of paper (11x17). This is a messy first draft. That's okay.
Gallery walk	10 min.	Post the drafts around the room or spread around a large table. Circulate to as many drafts as you can. Use post-it notes to identify: • Star: I find _____ inspiring. • Question mark: This makes me wonder _____.
Closing	5 min.	Read the comments on your first draft and identify a time in the next three days to revise your statement. Share the time with your partner along with one word to describe how you are feeling coming out of this exercise.

Objective: Coaches will write a vision for coaching that reflect our unique gifts and aligns to our school's definition of coaching.

Sample Multihour Professional Development Sessions

If you have a half-day of learning together, it is ideal to include exposure to new concepts and skills, practice with feedback, and ample time for meaning-making and reflection. It is also ideal that these half days occur regularly to build the knowledge, skills, and self-awareness needed to become a Transformational Coach.

Examples of Exposure to New Concepts or Skills

- education equity
- instructional expertise (e.g., pedagogical content knowledge, best practices)
- working with adult learners
- social-emotional intelligence
- understanding individual and organizational change
- systems thinking
- intercultural communication
- adult development theory

Examples of Practice with Feedback

- quiet listening
- reflective listening
- identifying learning gaps
- using the ladder of inference to unpack beliefs
- strengths-based coaching
- identifying spheres of control and influence
- using a variety of question stems
- varying usage of coaching stances
- conversation planning
- developing work plans with clients
- collecting and using observational data

Examples of Meaning-Making and Reflection

- identifying and working with core values
- personality types and communication preferences
- identity development
- educational philosophy

- creating a coaching vision, mission, or manifesto
- diversity, equity, and inclusion work

These lists are not exhaustive. They serve only to illustrate that the field of coaching, like the fields of teaching and leadership, is rich and complex. Having been an effective teacher or administrator is not a guarantee that one will be an effective coach, though it certainly helps. It is important that we hold realistic expectations regarding coaches' learning curve and ensure they have the time and resources needed to master their new craft.

If you have three hours or more for professional development, you will likely have several learning objectives. Your workshop should include opportunities for new content, practice, and reflection. As a starting point, in Table 15.8, we offer a generic template for a plan that can be adapted to your specific learning objectives. Following the template, you'll find a couple of sample plans for specific topics.

Table 15.8: Template for a 3-Hour PD Session

What	Time	Description
Opening	20–30 min.	<ul><li>Welcome and grounding—inspire and provide focus</li><li>Being present protocols (see p. 487)</li><li>Orient to one another—connect with others in the group, review and set group norms or agreements</li><li>Orient to learning—review the agenda, set an intention for the day</li></ul>
Learning block 1	60 min.	See "Sample 1-Hour PD Sessions" for ideas. Aim to have a coherent thread through the learning blocks and to gradually increase the challenge or remove learning supports as you progress through them.
Break	10–15 min.	
Learning block 2	60 min.	
Learning block 3 (optional)	45–60 min.	
Closing	15 min.	Each person captures their key takeaways and next steps in writing and then orally shares a sentence or a word with the group that captures their biggest learning.

Note: If running a full-day session, the afternoon will have a flow similar to the morning.

Table 15.9: Example of a 3-Hour PD Session

Objective: Coaches will strengthen their ability to build and maintain trusting relationships with clients. Coaches will develop a plan to better understand their school community.		
What	**Time**	**Description**
Opening	20–30 min.	• Poem: "Clearing" by Martha Postlewaite • 3-minute exercise to connect with the breath • Whip-around: One word to describe the energy you are bringing in today • Review community agreements. • Review the agenda and identify one moment you're particularly excited for. Share with a partner. • Set an intention for the day. Option to share with a partner.

Learning block 1	70 min.	Trust in coaching
		• (5 min.) Whole group discussion: Why is trust foundational to a coaching relationship?
		• (2 min.) Individually read the questions in the activity "Reflecting on Trust (see p. 135).
		• (20 min.) With a partner, take turns responding to the questions.
		• (3 min.) At the end, each partner reflects back two to three observations about how the other person relates to trust.
		• (20 min.) Whole group: Review the ways of being that build trust (see p. 126). As a group, complete this graphic organizer on a white board or poster:
		
		<table><tr><td>**Intentional**
		A coach might say:
		A coach might do:</td><td>**Open-Minded**
		A coach might say:
		A coach might do:</td></tr><tr><td>**Sincere**
		A coach might say:
		A coach might do:</td><td>**Transparent**
		A coach might say:
		A coach might do:</td></tr></table>
		• (10 min.) Individually reflect:
		  • When am I most likely to show up in these four ways?
		  • When is it challenging for me to show up this way?
		  • What might be the unintended consequences of not showing up this way during coaching?
		  • In the past, what has helped bring me back when I've noticed myself showing up in ways that are less intentional, open-minded, sincere, or transparent?
		• (10 min.) With partner, share final reflections on the role of trust in coaching.

Objective: Coaches will strengthen their ability to build and maintain trusting relationships with clients. Coaches will develop a plan to better understand their school community.

What	Time	Description
Break	15 min.	

Learning block 2	60 min.	Exploring our clients' context
		• (1 min.) Transition: Another way we build trust with clients is by demonstrating our commitment to understand unique assets and challenges of their context. There are a number of ways we can do this.
		• (9 min.) Individually skim these three activities in Chapter 6 (The Exploration Project Plan, Knowing Your Community: Shadowing a Student for a Day, Knowing Your Community: Understanding School Culture). Select one activity you'd like to try in the next two weeks.
		• (40 min.) Divide into groups according to the activity you chose. Read through the activity carefully. Work together to create a plan. Prepare as much as possible. For example:
		  • If completing the exploration checklist, identify the specific data you wish to collect and how you will gather it. Who will you talk to and when? When might you observe your client? If using a survey, begin to draft the questions.
		  • If shadowing a student, identify the student if possible. Plan for how you will ask the student's permission to shadow them for a day. Draft the e-mail explaining your intention to your client.
		  • If conducting interviews, identify who you might interview. Plan for how you will ask their permission, and perhaps even send the email now. Draft your interview questions.
		• (10 min.) Regroup a partner who will be using a different method. Share your plans and offer each other affirmations and suggestions.

Closing	15 min.	• (5 min.) Independent reflection: What's left to be done to prepare for the activity you began planning today. What are your next steps? • (9 min.) Whole group: What is your biggest takeaway about building trust with clients from today's learning experience? (manage talk time according to the group size) • (1 min.) As you leave, thank someone who contributed to your learning today.

Table 15.10: Sample Plan for a Daylong PD Session

Objective: Coaches will expand their definition of coaching. Coaches will identify the three phases of a Transformational Coaching conversation and practice with at least one strategy for each phase. Coaches will explore the impact of using Transformational Coaching strategies.

What	Time	Description
Opening	30 min.	• Poem: "To Be of Use" by Marge Piercy • 5-minute body scan • Whip-around: What animal represents the energy you are bringing in today? • Review community agreements • Review the agenda and identify one moment you're particularly excited for. Share with a partner. • Set an intention for the day. Option to share with a partner.
Learning block 1	60 min.	Defining Transformational Coaching • (15 min.) In pairs, discuss the activity "Analogies for Coaching" in Chapter 2. Complete the graphic organizer on p. 28 first, and then read and discuss the additional thoughts that follow. • (25 min.) Individually read the activity "What Is Transformational Coaching?" in Chapter 2 and complete the self-assessment on p. 33–34. In pairs, discuss the reflection questions. • (20 min.) Whole group discussion using a chalk talk using the question, How is coaching described by different stakeholders in our context?
Break	15 min.	
Learning block 2	60 min.	Talking about Transformational Coaching with others • (5 min.) Transition: Reread what surfaced during the chalk talk. During this next segment, we'll clarify how we want to talk about coaches with administrators, teachers, and other stakeholders. • (15 min.) Individually read *The Art of Coaching* pages 18-29. As you do, underline words or phrases that reflect how you would like to talk about Transformational Coaching with others. • (10 min.) Draft an elevator pitch for coaching. (See the activity "Toward a Definition of Coaching" in Chapter 2 for guidance.) • (15 min.) In pairs, practice giving your pitch. Offer each other affirmations and suggestions. Revise your pitch as needed. • (5 min.) Two to three people volunteer to share their pitch with the whole group

Objective: Coaches will expand their definition of coaching. Coaches will identify the three phases of a Transformational Coaching conversation and practice with at least one strategy for each phase. Coaches will explore the impact of using Transformational Coaching strategies.

What	Time	Description
Break	5 min.	
Learning block 3	55 min.	Listening • (1 min.) Transition: While it's helpful to be able to talk about Transformational Coaching, it's even more important that our coaching actually *be* transformational! We'll spend the rest of today digging into the three buckets of Transformational Coaching and practicing these skills. • (10 min.) Read "The Three Buckets of Transformational Coaching," (in the Introduction). • (1 min.) Transition: We'll begin where all coaching begins, with listening. • (12 min.) In pairs, use the questions in the activity "Who Am I as a Listener?" in Chapter 8 to reflect together. • (20 min.) Individually read the introduction to the activity "Reflective Listening" in Chapter 8. In pairs, take turns reading the scenarios aloud while the other person listens as a coach. Practice using reflective listening to respond. Each person will read and respond to all four scenarios. Time permitting, read and discuss the imagined responses offered at the end of the activity. • (12 min.) In the same pairs, try some authentic practice. One partner sets a timer and speaks for 3 minutes. The other then uses reflective listening to respond. Switch roles. Use the remaining time to discuss: What did it feel like to listen in this way? What did it feel like to be listened to in this way?
Morning reflection	15 min.	• (8 min.) Independent writing and reflection: What are my key takeaways from this morning? What insights am I getting into my personal inquiry question? How have I been living into my intention? • (7 min.) Pair share
Lunch	60 min.	

(Continued)

Objective: Coaches will expand their definition of coaching. Coaches will identify the three phases of a Transformational Coaching conversation and practice with at least one strategy for each phase. Coaches will explore the impact of using Transformational Coaching strategies.

What	Time	Description
Afternoon opening		• Individually review your intention and personal inquiry question. Are any adjustments needed for this afternoon? • Review the agenda for the afternoon • Do a quick energizer like a rock, paper, scissors tournament.
Learning block 4		Thinking • (15 min.) Individually read the mind the gap blog post from the Bright Morning website. Have printed copies of the graphic available for each person. • (35 min.) Divide into trios and distribute the role-play scenarios available on the Bright Morning website. For each scenario, discuss which gaps might be present for the client. What do you wonder? What might you ask to explore whether a certain gap is present? • (10 min.) Whole group discussion: How do thinking tools like mind the gap contribute to our effectiveness as coaches? How do we envision using it?
Break	15 min.	
Learning block 5	60 min.	Responding • (1 min.) Transition: For this last part of the day, we'll focus on the third phase of coaching, Responding. Once we've listened carefully and reflected on what we've heard, how do we respond in a way that grows our client's awareness and supports them to take productive action? • (10 min.) Individually read the introduction to the activity "Coaching Stances: An Overview" in Chapter 8. Reflect on which stances feel most natural and which are most challenging. • (20 min.) In pairs, discuss and complete the practice exercise in the activity using Appendix B in *The Art of Coaching*. • (20 min.) With the same or a new partner, discuss and complete "Common Mistakes Coaches Make in Conversation" in Chapter 8, then read "So What Do I Do Instead?" • (10 min.) Whole group, discuss: What are our key takeaways about responding to clients in ways that affirm and empower?

Table 15.10: (Continued)

Objective: Coaches will expand their definition of coaching. Coaches will identify the three phases of a Transformational Coaching conversation and practice with at least one strategy for each phase. Coaches will explore the impact of using Transformational Coaching strategies.		
What	**Time**	**Description**
Closing	30 min.	• (10 min.) Independent writing time: What are my key takeaways from today? What are my next steps? What insights have I gotten into my personal inquiry questions? In what ways did I honor my intention today? • (8 min.) Pair share reflections • (10 min.) Whole group: each person shares one thing they're taking away and one appreciation for someone who contributed to their learning today. • (2 min.) Poem: "Invitation" by Ann Betz

Concluding and Celebrating

We are beyond thrilled that you've made journey through this workbook! Imagine that you're at an Art of Coaching workshop and you're showing Elena your workbook and it's got sticky notes all over it and it's full of your handwriting and scribbles and the pages have sprinkles of coffee drops and maybe dark chocolate smudges. She would be dancing. Jumping up and down. Cheering. Seriously. Just meet her and see. And she'd be doing this because she'd know that you are now far more prepared to make every conversation count toward creating a more just and equitable world.

We want you to celebrate your learning because we are confident that you've made tremendous growth as a Transformational Coach in the process of working through this book. First, list your top five takeaways of any kind from your learning journey:

1.

2.

3.

4.

5.

Now, how has your way of being as a coach shifted? Describe this shift, or represent it with images or symbols if you prefer.

Write yourself an appreciation note, being specific about all the learning you did and acknowledging your hard work.

From *The Art of Coaching Workbook: Tools to Make Every Conversation Count* by Elena Aguilar. Copyright © 2021 by Elena Aguilar. Reproduced by permission.

Finally, draw a picture of yourself now, as a Transformational Coach, having learned all that you've learned. You might depict new tools you're holding, add thought bubbles to show your beliefs, and include captions. This picture deserves color and decoration, so grab some markers, gel pens, star stickers, or whatever you'd like and have fun. And if you share your drawing with Elena, she'll be super happy and she'll write you back! (You can find her on social media or at elena@brightmorningteam.com.)

ACKNOWLEDGMENTS

Elena would like to thank Caitlin Schwarzman for invaluable feedback and editing on this workbook; Lori Cohen and Laurelin Whitfield for contributing their expertise, experiences, and insights; Lindsey Dixon for being an 11th-hour sounding board and editor; Rebecca Blackmer for being an 11th-hour proofreader; and Amy Fandrei at Jossey-Bass for her enthusiasm for any project I propose. And to the thousands and thousands of educators who have attended my workshops since 2013 and who have shared their feedback, thank you—this book is for you.

ABOUT THE AUTHOR

Elena Aguilar is the author of *The Art of Coaching, The Art of Coaching Teams, Onward: Cultivating Emotional Resilience in Educators, The Onward Workbook, and Coaching for Equity*. She was a longtime contributor to *Edutopia* and *EdWeek* and frequently publishes articles in *Educational Leadership*. Elena is the founder and president of Bright Morning Consulting, an educational consulting group that works to transform education. Bright Morning offers in-person and virtual workshops and online courses based on Elena's books. Elena is also a highly sought-after keynote speaker and hosts a podcast called the Bright Morning Podcast. You can learn more about Bright Morning at http://brightmorningteam.com.

Elena lives in Oakland, California, with her husband and son. She also writes fiction, essays, and memoirs, which you can read at http://elenaaguilar.com. When she's not writing, coaching, or teaching, she enjoys being in nature, reading fiction, making art, and traveling abroad.

APPENDIX A

Transformational Coaching Rubric (TCR) 2.0

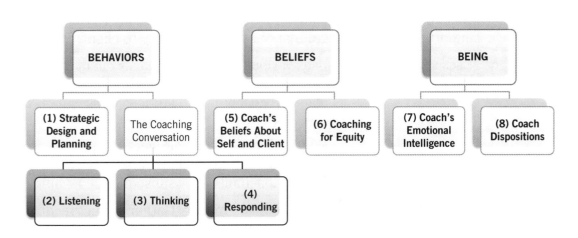

* *The Art of Coaching* (Aguilar, 2013) includes a rubric called the Transformational Coaching Rubric. Therefore, this rubric is called the TCR 2.0.

Domain 1: Strategic Design and Planning

Indicator	Foundational	Intermediate	Advanced
a. Conversation planning	May occasionally plan for a coaching conversation	Writes up plans for coaching conversations	Plans for coaching conversations using multiple planning tools
b. Work plans	May create work plans for some clients but does not engage in a rigorous goal-setting process	Creates work plans based on SMARTE goals	Plans conversations in support of work plans Work plans align to school or district vision and larger context
c. Zone of proximal development (ZPD) and gradual release	Understands the concept of a ZPD as it relates to coaching and its importance	Attempts to work within client's ZPD but cannot yet articulate a plan for gradual release	Intentionally scaffolds learning for clients and can articulate decision-making to gradually release responsibility to client
d. Use of data	Uses some data to inform coaching	Uses various forms of data to inform work plan and coaching sessions Engages client in gathering data to inform coaching	Engages client in analyzing and responding to data (e.g., student work, surveys, test scores) Reflects on all conversations and uses reflection to inform subsequent coaching
e. Feedback on coaching	Invites feedback from client and welcomes survey and anonymous feedback	Uses feedback from client to adjust coaching practice Practices in advance of coaching sessions with prompting	Gathers direct feedback and feels able to gather indirect feedback in a number of ways; uses feedback as a learning opportunity Practices some coaching sessions in advance and can identify those that must be practiced
f. Sense of impact	Is unsure of the impact of coaching on client; questions whether coaching is doing anything	Points to some evidence of the impact of coaching, but impact may feel haphazard and unpredictable	Knows how to gather evidence to indicate the impact of coaching and can present a variety of data to prove positive impact

Domain 2: Listening

Indicator	Foundational	Intermediate	Advanced
a. Active listening	Occasionally uses active listening; feels somewhat comfortable using it	Uses active listening during the first 10 minutes of the conversation	Uses active listening throughout to identify high-leverage access points to deepen the conversation
b. Use of silence		Allows for pauses in the conversation Speaks for less than a third of the conversation	Holds silence comfortably
c. Listening to own listening	In the moment, may be unaware that their listening is wavering; may be aware afterward	Often notices when their listening wavers and is able to redirect self In reflection, aware of how they listen, their mental journeys	Listens deeply for extended periods In refection, aware of how they listen, their mental journeys, and the impact their listening has on the client and conversation
d. Client's nonverbals	Pays attention to client's nonverbal cues as evidenced by reflection after the conversation	Pays attention to client's nonverbal cues as evidenced by decisions during the conversation	
e. Coach's nonverbals	Is aware of own nonverbal cues as well as tone of voice, pitch, pace, and volume	Regulates own nonverbal cues and tone, pitch, pace, and volume	Uses own nonverbal cues and tone, pitch, pace, and volume to deepen trust, facilitate learning, and strengthen the coaching process

Domain 3: Thinking

Foundational	Intermediate	Advanced
← *Frameworks evident in planning but less obvious in the conversation itself* →		*Frameworks clearly evident in the conversation and used spontaneously and adaptively*
Mind the gap. Approaches problems of change as problems of learning Is grounded in a developmental approach	**Ladder of inference.** Used during the planning process	**Ladder of inference.** Used spontaneously during coaching
Spheres of influence	**Coaching lenses** • Adult learning (*awareness*) • Inquiry • Compassion • Emotional intelligence (*awareness*)	**Coaching lenses** • Adult learning (*strategic use*) • Emotional intelligence (*strategic use*): Seeks to cultivate client's emotional intelligence. • Change management • Systems thinking • Systemic oppression
Strengths-based coaching. Recognizes client's strengths and cultivates client's awareness of those	**Strengths-based coaching.** Uses client's strengths as a way to explore areas for growth **Personality types** (*awareness*)	**Personality types** (*strategic use*)

Coach develops skill in a range of frameworks to analyze the client's practice and plan a strategic approach to meet the client's explicit goals and implicit learning needs.

Domain 4: Responding

Indicator	Foundational	Intermediate	Advanced
a. Coach's role vis-à-vis client	May believe their role is to facilitate learning at some points and direct it at others	Believes they have the greatest impact when they facilitate, rather than direct, learning	Maintains a facilitative approach as much as possible and strategically directs client to maximize learning
b. Varied approaches	Uses a variety of coaching stems	Moves between the different coaching stances	Moves intentionally between the different coaching stances
c. Coaching stances	Comfortably uses supportive and cathartic stances	Uses the cathartic, supportive, and catalytic stances	Is comfortable and confident using the confrontational stance Is intentional and selective about when and why to use prescriptive and informative stances
d. Fluency in coaching	May experience conversations as unpredictable and sometimes uncomfortable	Articulates their thinking and rationale during a conversation that leads them in a particular coaching direction	Identifies every decision in a coaching conversation and explains their reasoning for making that decision

(Continued)

Indicator	Foundational	Intermediate	Advanced
e. Facilitative activities	Supports client to identify needs and then access resources and build relationships to address needs	Uses a range of facilitative activities: • Role-playing • Videotaping • Surveys • Metaphorical thinking • Visualization and guided imagery • Writing and storytelling • Positive self-talk • Visual and artistic activities	Uses a diverse repertoire of facilitative and directive coaching activities strategically and spontaneously, even when not planned in advance
f. Directive activities	Plans for a limited range of coaching activities but may not successfully integrate them into the coaching conversation or does so in a very directive manner (e.g., leading the co-planning process)	Uses a range of directive activities: • Observation tools • Giving feedback • Modeling • Elbow teaching • Co-planning • Real-time coaching • Field trips • Shared reading • Looking at data	

From *The Art of Coaching Workbook: Tools to Make Every Conversation Count* by Elena Aguilar. Copyright © 2021 by Elena Aguilar. Reproduced by permission.

Domain 5: Coach's Beliefs About Self and Client

Indicator	Foundational	Intermediate	Advanced
a. Coaching from vision	Names core values and how they impact coaching work and relationships	Has a coaching mission or vision statement that may guide their work	Points to evidence in every conversation of being anchored in their coaching manifesto, vision, or mission statement.
b. Power of conversation	Believes that every conversation counts	Believes that listening is the core practice of a Transformational Coach.	Empowered in every conversation and able to do something new or different
c. Own role in the impact of coaching	Believes that who they are and how they show up in a conversation matters	Believes that their presence and way of being is the essential element in a coaching conversation	Uses their way of being to positively impact the conversation
d. Client's core values	Is aware of client's core values	Uses awareness of client's core values to enroll client in the work and in a conversation	
e. Fixed versus growth mindset	Knows the distinction between fixed and growth mindset	Identifies a client's fixed mindsets and has some tools for addressing them	Is aware of client's mindsets—fixed or growth—and can facilitate the development of a growth mindset
f. Adult learning principles	Believes that all adults can learn given the right conditions	Identifies the presence or absence of conditions that foster adult learning Believes that learning is sometimes messy, unpredictable, and inconsistent	Creates the conditions that foster adult learning
g. School transformation	Believes that transformational change in schools is necessary	Believes that transformational change in schools is possible	Consistently conveys hope and possibility

Domain 6: Coaching for Equity

Indicator	Foundational	Intermediate	Advanced
a. Identifying and shifting limiting beliefs	Notices when a client is expressing a biased belief	Takes action to explore and shift a client's biased beliefs; some strategies are effective while others are not	Quickly recognizes when a client is harboring a biased belief and can make decisions about when and how to do so Persistently and effectively unpacks biased beliefs across the course of a coaching relationship using a range of strategies
b. Coach's sociopolitical consciousness	Is aware of historical and contemporary systems of oppression Is aware of own identity development, privilege, internalized oppression, and conscious and unconscious bias Recognizes power dynamics at play	Is aware of how historical systems of oppression (including white supremacy, patriarchy, and capitalism) manifest in schools, classrooms, and the behaviors of educators Has some strategies to maneuver through power dynamics Believes that to interrupt inequities, they must continuously engage in their own learning about systems of oppression	Conversations and coaching actions that lead to the disruption of inequitable practices and systems Recognizes high-leverage entry points to interrupt inequities Is aware that even with a heightened sociopolitical consciousness, may still have biases; recognizes that coaching for equity is an opportunity for continued learning

Indicator	Foundational	Intermediate	Advanced
c. Fostering others' socio-political consciousness		Guides client to increased awareness about systemic oppression, including about white supremacy, patriarchy, and capitalism Has some strategies to help client become aware of their identity development, privilege, internalized oppression, and conscious and unconscious bias Guides client to recognize power dynamics at play in a classroom and school	Guides client to increased awareness about how historical systems of oppression manifest in schools, classrooms, and educators' behaviors Guides client to interrupt the power dynamics in a classroom and school that uphold systemic oppression Inspires clients to continuously reflect on their biases Understands the role that empathy plays in interrupting inequities and cultivates empathy in clients
d. Cultural competence	May struggle with coaching clients across lines of difference	Effectively coach some clients across lines of difference	Perceives and adapts coaching to communication styles that differ across identity markers including culture and age Demonstrates the ability to effectively coach across differences including race, ethnicity, gender, class, sexual orientation, age, and language

(Continued)

From *The Art of Coaching Workbook: Tools to Make Every Conversation Count* by Elena Aguilar. Copyright © 2021 by Elena Aguilar. Reproduced by permission.

Indicator	Foundational	Intermediate	Advanced
e. Coaching for systems change	Believes their role is to interrupt systemic oppression in schools Recognizes the power dynamics at play in an institution that upholds systems of oppression	Has some strategies to address systems and structures that perpetuate oppression Maintains commitment to interrupting inequities and oppressive systems and to creating schools that serve every child every day Recognizes the power dynamics at play in a system and has some strategies to navigate those	Builds trusting relationships with a wide variety of educators within a system to collaborate on interrupting inequities Uses coaching strategies to engage in productive conversations with colleagues and supervisors across the system Navigates power dynamics in a system Identifies high-leverage entry points for change in systems, structures, and institutions
f. Coach's emotional intelligence (when addressing inequities)	May be triggered by a client's beliefs May or may not be aware of the role that systemic oppression has played in their emotional experiences as an educator	Has some strategies to respond to the ways that inequities affect their emotions	Effectively uses a variety of strategies to respond to own emotions while coaching for equity; use of these strategies allows coach to effectively interrupt inequities Has conversations about equity without judging the client and with compassion for the client while also communicating an expectation that the client can change

Domain 7: Coach's Emotional Intelligence

Indicator	Foundational	Intermediate	Advanced
a. Self-awareness	Notices some emotions, particularly upon reflection May be triggered occasionally May feel defensive about some feedback received May take things personally	Is aware of a range of emotions in the moment Is aware of triggers, understands their origins, and manages them Generally accepting of feedback but may not know what to do with it	Notices emotions in the moment and, upon reflection, has insight into them Is rarely triggered Is grateful for any and all feedback from clients; doesn't need feedback to feel affirmed
b. Self-management	Has some strategies to manage their own emotions when coaching is challenging Sets intentions before coaching sessions	Manages their own emotions Apologizes and takes responsibility for how they show up with a client	Often appears calm and grounded Sets intentions before coaching and reflects on them afterward Feels confident and able to coach anyone; finds great joy and satisfaction in coaching
c. Social awareness	Is aware of how their emotions impact clients	Accesses positive emotions in themselves to positively impact clients	Identifies coaching moves that create a safe learning environment for clients Has empathy for clients

(Continued)

Indicator	Foundational	Intermediate	Advanced
d. Relationship management	Has some strategies for building trust, but doesn't consistently build trust Trust building is not intentional and is contingent on relationship dynamics, personalities, and conditions	Intentionally builds trust with most clients Rebuilds trust when it is broken or weak	Readily and easily builds trust with almost any client Feels confident and able to coach anyone; finds great joy and satisfaction in coaching Recognizes when client needs to release emotions to fully engage and has strategies to confidently facilitate that release
e. Cultivating emotional resilience	Understands what emotional resilience is and why it's important to intentionally cultivate it in educators	Has strategies to cultivate emotional resilience in others; uses these strategies when a client is struggling	Finds opportunities in every conversation to cultivate resilience

From *The Art of Coaching Workbook: Tools to Make Every Conversation Count* by Elena Aguilar. Copyright © 2021 by Elena Aguilar. Reproduced by permission.

Domain 8: Coach's Dispositions

Indicator	Foundational	Intermediate	Advanced
a. Compassion	Has compassion for those they find easy to relate to	Has compassion for all within their immediate circle	Demonstrates unwavering compassion and positive regard for all
b. Curiosity	Is genuinely curious	Is firmly grounded in an inquiry stance and is constantly curious	Is insatiably curious about others, what is possible, and one's self; hopeful about what is possible
c. Trust in the coaching process	Often feels impatient; questions whether coaching can actually have an impact on someone	Manages impatience Recognizes the many factors that play a role in transformation	Remembers that there may be times when we don't see evidence of change in a conversation, but that doesn't mean that change won't happen Is open to possibility and refrains from acting on urgency in an unproductive way Understands that we might lay seeds of transformation that sprout in another season
d. Humility and mutuality	May feel they can be effective only with certain people	Feels moderately effective with most people and may have preferences	Is aware of and appreciates the reciprocal nature of learning and the potential for their own improvement through the process

(Continued)

Indicator	Foundational	Intermediate	Advanced
e. Learner orientation	Continues to build knowledge of the disciplines in which they work (e.g., literacy, math, leadership, classroom culture, management, school transformation) Seeks out professional learning opportunities and consultations; stays informed about current research on best practices	Solicits both formal and informal feedback and takes action based on feedback Collaborates effectively with colleagues to support their professional growth	Consistently reflects on their own learning and development and actively seeks out ways to develop and augment skill, knowledge, or capacity Identifies professional areas of strength and growth; feels inspired and energized to continue developing
f. Courage	Finds moments when they can speak and act with courage	Feels more often able to speak and act with courage; navigates some of the fear related to accessing courage	Feels consistently anchored in their own courage and connected to the courage of others; frequently takes risks in what they say and do

From *The Art of Coaching Workbook: Tools to Make Every Conversation Count* by Elena Aguilar. Copyright © 2021 by Elena Aguilar. Reproduced by permission.

APPENDIX B

The Phases of Transformational Coaching

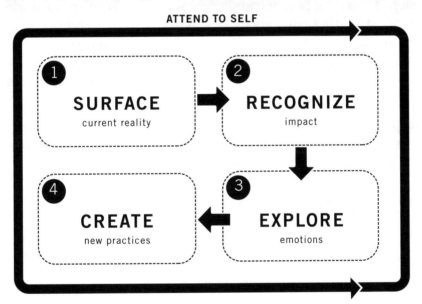

SURFACE: SURFACE CURRENT REALITY	
Purpose: To see the lay of the land—the client's teaching or leadership practice, their beliefs, their way of being, and the context in which they work; to build a trusting relationship with client.	

Actions	**Resources, tools, and strategies**
Attend to (coach) self • What am I feeling? • What do these feelings want to tell me? • How can I anchor in Transformational Coach ways of being? • How do I anticipate the role that my own identity will play in my ability to coach? • Who can support me in this process? Who can I talk to? Who can listen to me? Who can give me feedback?	• Transformational Coaching rubric 2.0 • The core emotions
Observe and understand • Observe client's behaviors (e.g., teaching, leadership). • Understand client's teaching practice and organizational context (e.g., gather data, speak to stakeholders, do community walks). • Seek to understand the client's mental models. • Notice client's ways of being. • Look and listen for inequities.	• Mind the gap • Coaching stances • Listening strategies • Teacher-to-student interaction tracker • Surveys • The equity rubric (published in *Coaching for Equity*)
Build relationship with client • Use reflective listening. • Pay attention to nonverbal communication. • Actively build trust. • Take the supportive and cathartic stances.	• Celebrating strengths • How to build trust (in *The Art of Coaching*)

From *The Art of Coaching Workbook: Tools to Make Every Conversation Count* by Elena Aguilar. Copyright © 2021 by Elena Aguilar. Reproduced by permission.

RECOGNIZE: RECOGNIZE IMPACT

Purpose: To help the client see the impact they are having on their students and how their behaviors, beliefs, and ways of being either dismantle or perpetuate systemic oppression.

Actions	Resources, tools, and strategies
Attend to (coach) self • What am I feeling? • What do these feelings want to tell me? • How can I anchor in Transformational Coach ways of being? • What do I need to successfully be able to coach my client? • How can I continue to expand my knowledge about systems of oppression? • What new insights am I gaining about my own practices? • Who am I reaching out to for support? Am I getting what I need and want from them? If not, how might I let them know what I need? Who else could I reach out to?	• Transformational Coaching rubric 2.0 • The core emotions
Connect and reflect • Gather and organize data to explore the impact of the client's behavior and beliefs on students, community and self. • Explore and reflect on the unintended consequences of client's behaviors and underlying mental models. • Understand and address the detrimental impact of white supremacy and patriarchy on everyone, including the client.	• Video • Student data • Surveys • Classroom observation tool • Teacher-to-student interactions • The coaching lenses • Informative texts • Confrontational, cathartic, and catalytic approaches • Listening strategies
Build relationship with client • Practice a range of listening strategies. • Actively build trust. • Ask for feedback on your coaching.	• Feedback on surveys • All coaching strategies

From *The Art of Coaching Workbook: Tools to Make Every Conversation Count* by Elena Aguilar. Copyright © 2021 by Elena Aguilar. Reproduced by permission.

EXPLORE: EXPLORE EMOTIONS

Purpose: To guide the client to surface, acknowledge, accept, explore, understand, process, and release emotions.

Actions	Resources, tools, and strategies
Attend to (coach) self • Who am I being? • What am I feeling? • What do these feelings want to tell me? • How can I anchor in the Transformational Coach ways of being? • Who am I reaching out to for support? Am I getting what I need and want from them? If not, how might I let them know what I need?	• Transformational Coaching rubric 2.0 • The core emotions
Explore emotions • Hold space for emotions, including anger and grief, and instigate emotional breakthrough. • Coach client to take responsibility for behaviors, beliefs and ways of being. • Solidify commitment to change.	• Cathartic, catalytic, and confrontational approach • Core values activity • Legacy and purpose questioning • Sphere of influence
Build relationship with client • Stay humble and compassionate. • Remain calm and grounded when strong emotions are expressed. • Use many listening strategies.	• All coaching strategies

CREATE: CREATE NEW PRACTICES	
Purpose: Create new behaviors, beliefs, and ways of being.	
Actions	**Resources, tools and strategies**
Attend to (coach) self • What am I feeling? • What do these feelings want to tell me? • Which of the Transformational Coach ways of being is most relevant now? • What do I need to know now to successfully coach my client? • How have I grown and changed through working with this client? • Which of my coaching skill sets has most expanded? • Who has helped me in my coaching journey? How have they helped me? How can I acknowledge and appreciate their contributions?	• Transformational Coaching rubric 2.0 • The core emotions
Build new practices • Develop and refine new behaviors. • Construct new beliefs. • Create new identities and ways of being. • Augment knowledge. • Deepen will and commitment to healing and transformation.	• Co-planning • Modeling • Observations with the client • Data gathering and analysis • Real-time feedback • Ladder of inference • Legacy questions and creation vision • All coaching strategies • Scaffold learning • Release from responsibility
Build relationship with client • Celebrate client's growth and positive impact on students. • Communicate appreciation for client. • Invite feedback on coaching.	• Supportive and instructive stances • All coaching strategies • Feedback surveys

NOTES